THE WORLD ENCOMPASSED

Sir Francis Drake

THE WORLD ENCOMPASSED

Drake's Great Voyage 1577–1580

BY

DEREK WILSON

HAMISH HAMILTON

LONDON

First published in Great Britain 1977
by Hamish Hamilton Ltd
90 Great Russell Street London WC1B 3PT

SBN 241 89624 X

Typesetting and origination by
Thomson Litho Ltd, East Kilbride
Printed in Great Britain by
Ebenezer Baylis & Son Ltd,
The Trinity Press, Worcester, and London

CONTENTS

ILLUSTRATIONS

Maps drawn by Patrick Leeson

CHAPTER ONE

'That none should know of our enterprise'

AUTUMN 1577

On 20 September 1577, Antonio de Guaras, a Spanish agent, sat in his London lodging house writing a report to his master, Philip II. The intelligence which he laboriously translated into code concerned an Englishman in whom the King of Spain always showed a special interest. 'Drake the pirate is to go to Scotland...for the purpose of getting possession of the prince of Scotland for a large sum of money.'[1] Guaras was wrong.

The following day Captain John Wynter sailed the Queen's ship, *Elizabeth,* into Plymouth Sound in the belief that he was taking up the position of vice-admiral on an expedition to explore *Terra Australis,* the unknown antarctic continent, and to seek new trade routes to the Orient. He was wrong.

During the ensuing two weeks a hundred and fifty mariners enlisted with Drake and Wynter, thinking that the captains were bound for Alexandria to take on a cargo of currants. They were wrong.

So much secrecy and so many deliberately circulated rumours attended the mustering of ships and men during that wet summer, that only one assertion could be made with confidence: the famous (or, if you were Spanish, the notorious) Francis Drake was getting together a small but extraordinarily well equipped fleet in Plymouth harbour.

The local mariners and merchants who watched, with expert eyes, the bustling activity on board the five vessels did not believe the official story about a Levantine venture. Nor were they surprised that Francis Drake was fitting out a new expedition. The only fact which did surprise them was that it had taken four years for Drake to follow up his last triumph, the memory of which was vivid in the minds of Plymouth people. They had been at divine service in the parish church on that August Sunday in 1573 when, suddenly, the doors had burst open and the cry had gone up, 'Drake's come back!' Excitedly they had rushed out, leaving the minister in his pulpit, to see the captured Spanish frigate and to gaze spellbound at the bars of bullion, the chests of coins and jewels that were unloaded on to the quay. From the captain and his men they heard all about the audacious raid on the treasure house, at Nombre de Dios, the march across the Isthmus of Panama, the capture of a mule train laden with bar silver, the narrow escape with booty loaded on to rafts. That expedition had made Francis Drake a wealthy man and one who could afford to fit out another fleet to go pillaging on the Spanish Main. The men of Plymouth believed that that fleet was now being assembled. They, too, were wrong.

The only man in England who knew the truth spoke not one word of it—not to his wife, nor the friends who came to visit the elegant house in Looe Street, nor the chandlers with whom he bargained for supplies, nor even the fine gentlemen of the court who had come down from London with him at the beginning of August. Francis Drake did not even think very much about the perilous enterprise on which he and his companions would soon be launched. He was a man who warmly took to heart the text 'Sufficient unto the day is the evil thereof'. If the present held little real 'evil' for him it certainly held worries enough.

The greatest worry of all was that the whole venture might be called off. The scheme was largely formed in his mind before he stepped ashore after the Nombre de Dios voyage. Yet all his early attempts to further it came to nothing. His name was revered among the common people and his exploits peddled around the shires in the form of pamphlets and songs. But while England waited for Drake to be launched upon fresh exploits the Queen ignored him; the great captain's ships were exployed upon nothing more exciting than running men and supplies into Ireland where the Earl of Essex was on campaign.

Drake did not abandon his dream. He gathered whatever information he could from charts, books and fellow travellers. He cultivated men with influence at court who might be useful in the furtherance of his plans. At last, he obtained the backing of some of the great men of the Council and even of the Queen. But that did not mean that his troubles were over. Elizabeth was only with difficulty persuaded to support him, and her mind was as variable as the winds off the Scillies. She had demonstrated this quite clearly in 1574. She granted Richard Grenville, Drake's neighbour and rival, a charter for a voyage to *Terra Australis*. Grenville equipped his fleet in this very harbour. Then, when everything was almost ready, a messenger arrived with a royal command that the ships were not to sail. Her Majesty had decided that the appearance of English vessels off the coast of South America might upset relations with Spain.

It was, therefore, with considerable anxiety that Drake chivied chandlers, carpenters and crewmen, urging them to do their work properly but with haste. There was always a great deal of work to be done at the beginning of a long voyage and Drake knew that any lack of attention to detail could prove disastrous. If the suppliers were not watched they would sell him green timber, meat not freshly salted, beer that had lain too long in cask. If the hulls were not properly caulked they would be leaking badly before they had been a month at sea. If sufficient canvas were not stowed to replace several sails a ship could find herself stranded and powerless after a succession of bad storms. Therefore, Drake and his captains spent most of late September and early October personally supervising the preparations.

One by one the casks of biscuit, beans, peas, lentils, salt pork, flour, onions, beer and vinegar, the cheeses and the jars of honey were stowed below. The hens and pigs were penned. The gunpowder and cannon balls were safely locked into the magazines. The spare canvas and spars, the timber, pitch, blocks, nails, leather and the tools essential for repair work were carried aboard. Four small ships, or pinnaces, were lashed to the decks in sections, ready to be assembled and launched in smooth water. There were the harpoons, nets and fishhooks which for weeks on end would be the mariners' only means of supplementing their diet with fresh food. There were the fireboxes where that food would be cooked. Everything was loaded aboard except the water, and that was deliberately left until the last moment so that it would stay fresh for as long as possible.

As the men stumbled and cursed under their loads it was not only their superiors who watched them. Many citizens of Plymouth were intrigued to know what Francis Drake was carrying with him on his journey. They might well have been surprised to see the items going into the great cabin on the fleet's flagship the *Pelican*. Anyone who had visited Drake in his Plymouth home would have noted his love of luxury amounting to ostentation. Yet it came as something of a surprise to discover that he was intending to live in the same style on shipboard. Into Drake's cabin and the great cabin beneath the *Pelican*'s poop deck went the

An ivory cross-staff used for measuring the declination of the sun and pole star

3

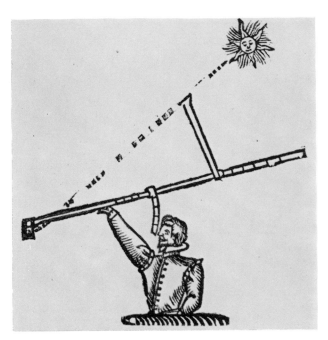

John Davis's backstaff. With this instrument observations of the sun could be made without the observer being dazzled

admiral's massive sea chest and his painted drum (already becoming a legend), his charts and books of navigation, including (what must have been interesting to anyone able to understand its significance) a copy of *Magellan's Voyages,* his terrestrial and celestial globes, his cross-staff, astrolabe and quadrant. There was nothing unusual about any of that. What were unusual were the carved chairs and tables, the cushions of silk and turkey work, the oriental rugs to cover the tables and the large service of silver table-ware. Even some of the cooking utensils were of silver, and Drake was furnished besides with 'divers shows of all sorts of curious workmanship'.[2] Moreover, into the hold along with the seamen's ale, went kegs of expensive wine, packages of crystallized fruits and other delicacies. These, together with the fine clothes, the servants and the musicians, were the accoutrements of an ambassador, not a sea captain.

There were other pieces of equipment to excite comment; the armament, for instance. The flagship alone carried eighteen demi-culverin, and the smaller vessels were all well provided with cannon. In addition they were loaded with more than enough hand weapons—bows, arquebuses and calivers—for the 164-man complement, to say nothing of the part armour and the forge, bar steel and blacksmith's tools ready to carry out running repairs and manufacture new weapons.

4

It was not only curious bystanders the sailors had to contend with as they tried to do their work. There were also the ten 'gentlemen adventurers' Drake had brought from London to join the expedition. Fastidiously they picked their way among the pitch barrels and spilled fish guts, to supervise the safe stowing of chests full of clothes, books and plate and to commandeer ship's quarters commensurate with their rank. They were young men of landed families, men with court connections whose fathers or uncles had bought into the venture. They had no knowledge of the sea but they did have what qualified them just as well to bear authority over seasoned mariners—social status. No one seriously doubted that class and rank—those God-given badges of difference—applied as much in the middle of the ocean as they did on the rural English manor.

Plymouth, from a map of 1643

The sailors grumblingly endured the brusqueries and insults of these ignorant popinjays. They looked with more indulgent amusement upon the other members of the admiral's entourage. There was the chaplain, Francis Fletcher, a doctor and an apothecary, Drake's young trumpeter and a band of musicians who would not let any of the rough seamen touch their precious pipes, viols and tabors.

At last all the preparations were complete. It was the end of October and no delaying message had come from London. All that was wanting now was a favourable wind, but would they have one at this season? As the seamen lounged in the taverns of Plymouth's narrow streets, they grumbled about the stupidity of starting a major voyage so late in the year. Drake, too, watched the sullen clouds boiling up interminably in the west and his anxiety grew.

Then, on 15 November, the wind veered round to the north. The crews were mustered, local men bade farewell to their families, promising to return with untold riches to wives who would be thankful if they returned at all. The water casks were filled and brought aboard. The gentlemen left their comfortable lodgings ashore and took up residence in their

Taking compass bearings and recording bearing and distance travelled on a traverse board

6

cramped shipboard quarters. A large crowd on the quayside watched the five vessels stand out into Sutton Pool to await the ebb. There they stood until dusk. Then, the watchers could just make out figures swarming up the rigging to release the great sheets of canvas. But they heard clearly the familiar sounds of the windlass crews chanting in unison as they drew up the anchors, the sails cracking as they were pulled taut and the timbers creaking as the ships slowly made way towards the Cattewater and the open sea. Wherever Drake and his companions were bound, everyone aboard and ashore knew that not all the ships and men would return safely from what was obviously going to be a long voyage.

Taking a quadrant reading

Three days later the five ships lay battered and storm-scarred in Falmouth harbour, a mere forty-five miles to the south-west. Trouble had come with the first dawn. All night the ships had run well before the offshore wind. With the exception of such gentlemen as found the creaking motion of the vessels distinctly unsettling, the off-duty crews spent a comfortable night. The boatswain in charge of the second watch (from midnight to 8 a.m.) had little to do except keep an eye on his compass bearing and take regular soundings, making sure he kept about thirty-five fathoms of water beneath him in order to be well clear of treacherous rocks such as Dodman Point and the Manacles. The duty boy had turned the half-hour glass beside the compass for the last time when the sun rose astern and lit up the craggy outline of Black Head and Lizard Point, the last corner of home.

It was as they rounded the Lizard that the ships ran into a steadily freshening sou'wester. The masters took in sail and relied on their lateen mizzens to manoeuvre away from the land. It was a losing battle. No ship of that period could make headway against a clean contrary wind, especially one which was intensifying all the time as this one was. Drake and his officers knew the weather of their own western coasts and knew there was only one course of action to take. Led by the *Pelican* the ships turned about and ran under half sail for Falmouth. Probably the masters knew the harbour and its approaches well but they may have consulted their dog-eared rutters, just to be on the safe side.

> To enter Falmouth ye shall find a rock in the middle of the entering, leave it on the larbord side and go toward east by those and when ye be past it go straight in for the bay is . . .large, anchor where ye will at 5 or 6 fathoms amid the bay and if ye will go at the turning of the full sea . . . there is a bank to pass which ye shall find at low water at two fathoms and a half.[3]

The fleet reached Falmouth safely but their troubles were not over. The storm steadily increased in ferocity. The gentlemen, who had hastened to acquire lodgings in the town, watched the water in the harbour itself lashed into a frenzy and saw their ships gyrating wildly and tugging at their anchor cables like maddened bulls determined to be free. They had no difficulty in believing the locals who told them there had never been a storm like it in living memory.

On board the tossing vessels the mariners had no time to reflect on the severity of the gale. They staggered about the slippery decks lashing down all loose equipment, re-pegging the masts at main deck level as they worked loose, pumping excess water from the holds and battening all hatches afresh. The storm reached its peak about noon on 17 November. Attempts to keep the vessels head on to the wind had to be abandoned. Caught amidships by the savage gusts, the ships heeled over at an alarming angle. The master of the *Pelican* at last gave the order to cut the mainmast by the board. Then the *Marigold* broke away from her moorings. She, too, sacrificed her mainmast but this did not prevent her being driven ashore.

Slowly the tempest abated. The stark outline of Pendennis Castle emerged from the haze of mist and rain. There was time for tired sailors to sleep and for masters and captains to survey the damage. Apart from the two mainmasts and their rigging there was a considerable amount of superficial damage in need of urgent attention. Under the direction of the boatswains, carpenters and crews buckled down to the repair work. During their spells off duty they enjoyed their unexpected bonus of Cornish ale and women and ate their way through the expedition's carefully garnered provisions.

Drake was not a patient man. He fumed and fretted at the continuing bad weather and at the slow progress of refurbishing and refitting. When it became obvious that they would have to turn back to Plymouth for some essential parts he must have fell to wondering whether his great venture was doomed. He wanted desperately to be quit of England's coast; out of reach of royal messengers: it would take little, he well knew, for the Queen to change her mind. The persuasive Burghley with his talk of peace and his concern not to give offence to Spain might win the day as he had done many times before. Then horsemen would quickly be on the Great West Road with orders for Drake to 'delay departure pending her Majesty's pleasure'. The foul weather did bring one crumb of comfort: if it could turn a safe anchorage into a maelstrom it must also be rendering the Queen's highways virtually impassable.

On 27 November Drake was able to take his fleet out of Falmouth. The next day he and his 164 men were back where they had started, in Plymouth Harbour.

CHAPTER TWO

'What Privilege,
God hath endued this Iland with'

THE YEARS BEFORE

'These are the signs preceding the end of the world,' wrote an English Puritan to a foreign friend in January 1578. 'Satan is roaring like a lion, the world is going mad, Antichrist is resorting to every extreme, that he may with wolf-like ferocity devour the sheep of Christ.'[1] His concern was shared by more exalted and politically experienced observers: 'God only now must defend her and us all,' opined Leicester; Walsingham resigned himself to prayer, 'for other help I see none'.[2] Fate had marked out Spain and England as rivals who must, sooner or later, come to blows. They were opposed in everything they stood for: the champion of the old religion faced the upholder of the new; the defender of an old empire confronted the thrusting new imperialism of a young and eager rival; the monolithic power of a reactionary state supported by the Holy Inquisition opposed a tiny nation which was already acquiring a reputation as a crusader for freedom.

Nor was the situation a simple one of Anglo-Spanish rivalry. French politics was the battle ground of dynastic and religious factions. English diplomats were kept on their toes attempting to prevent the complete ascendancy of the Guise Catholic interest while trying to satisfy the Huguenot party's demands for succour with fair words rather than hard cash. The Pope made sporadic efforts to muster the support of the Church's champions against the schismatic Queen of England. The Netherlands, the focal point of English foreign policy, was a constant source of concern. Long-standing and vital mercantile ties as well as a shared Protestantism drew the two nations together. Thus, when, in 1568, the Netherlands revolted against their overlord, Philip II, Elizabeth could not feign lack of interest. The conflict in the Low Countries flowed back and forth, largely to the disadvantage of the rebels, and the bolder spirits in Spain saw the reconquest of the Netherlands as only a first step towards the invasion of England.

That such an invasion would find some support in England there was little doubt. Since 1568 Mary Queen of Scots had been a prisoner south of the border and the focal point of Catholic hopes. Seminary priests were infiltrated into England to begin the work of reconversion. Catholic nobles, egged on by the Spanish ambassador, had staged a number of more or less hare-brained plots. The only long-standing result of this treasonable activity was the expulsion of Philip II's ambassador in 1572.

In the face of all these difficulties and provocations most of Elizabeth's Council repeatedly urged her to take firm and decisive action. She should marry and thus put an end to speculation over the succession. She should execute the Queen of Scots and thus remove this persistent threat to her security. She should aid the Dutch leader, William of Orange, with men and money and thus exclude Spain from the Netherlands once and for all. Her interventions on behalf of the French Huguenots should be more decisive. But it seemed as though the only person in England who could not see the inevitability of an armed confrontation with Spain was the Queen herself. She would never take decisive action if it was possible to await the outcome of events. She would never say 'yes' or 'no' if it was possible to say 'perhaps'. She refused to commit herself until no other course was possible. One thing she understood very clearly was the cost of government. For most of her reign the Treasury was bankrupt or on the verge of bankruptcy, a fact which made her evaluate in cash terms every policy decision she ever made. Mercenary armies and succour to foreign rebels cost money and held out little prospect of even long-term return. Normally she was supported in her cautious attitude towards foreign commitments by her chief minister, Lord Burghley. Burghley knew well enough the state of England's unpreparedness for a struggle with the wealthy and powerful Habsburg Empire. But Burghley found little support among his colleagues for his policy of appeasement. Walsingham, Leicester and Hatton were the leaders of a party which demanded that Elizabeth face up to reality and take a decisive initiative. The comparison with Anglo-German relations in the period before the Second World War is not altogether far-fetched. Most of western Europe outside France was either ruled directly by Philip II (and Portugal was added to his empire in 1580) or dominated by his allies. The two countries were ideologically opposed. Spain was responsible, through the Inquisition, for a cruel and far-reaching persecution of minorities. Whatever Philip's avowed intentions towards England there could be no doubt that he was very concerned to bring that erring island, of which he had once been king, back within the Catholic fold if not back under Spanish control.

Nor was there any doubt about the feelings of most Englishmen. Since the time of Mary Tudor and her ill-conceived marriage with Philip Habsburg there had been widespread mistrust and hatred of Catholic Spain. Among the mercantile community, which came into close contact with foreigners this feeling amounted almost to paranoia. And not without cause: hundreds of English merchants and seamen suffered at the hands of the Inquisition which was, at times, little more than the agency of Spanish national vendetta against commercial and political rivals. Among scores of the Queen's subjects who suffered in 1572 was a young Welshman who felt that he had Francis Drake to blame for his predicament. Six years previously this good Catholic had been on a voyage to the West Indies. One of his shipmates was a zealous Protestant named Francis Drake and as a result of his colleague's proselytizing zeal the Welsh lad, Morgan Gilbert, became a convert to the 'Reformed' faith. This conversion must have made life easier for him on board ships of Protestant Elizabeth's fleet—until 1572. In that year Gilbert was captured by Spaniards and, inevitably, handed over to the Inquisition for examination. His religion cost him two hundred lashes and twenty years in the galleys. Whether Morgan Gilbert survived this ordeal we do not know. The fate of another sufferer is not so obscure. Thomas Percy, a cloth merchant who had considerable business interests in Spanish territory, was also arrested by the Inquisition. He complained of his treatment to his own government. The Inquisitor, he reported,

> commanded the Alcalde to have me into the prison of torment where all things were prepared for me and I was stripped of my clothes as naked as ever I was born. And then the porter brought me a pair of linen breeches. And then came in the judge and his scribe and he sat down in a chair within the prison, having a cushion of tapestry work under his feet. And then I kneeled down upon my knees, holding up my hands to him, desiring him to be good unto me and to do me justice. He said unto me, 'Confess the truth and we ask no more.' I answered and said, 'I have confessed the truth and you will not believe me.' Thereupon the porter and another took me by the arms and caused me to sit upon the side of a barrico* and brought one of my arms over the other and cast a rope five times about them and so drew the rope with all their might.
>
> I, thinking they would have plucked the flesh from the bones, cried upon the judge to show me mercy, saying to him 'You say this is a house of mercy but it is more like a house of murder than of mercy.' Whereupon he commanded me to be laid upon the barrico. At the end thereof there was an earthen pan and in it a strip of fine cotton, three yards long or more. From this I should have received slow drops of water into my mouth while I was bound over the barrico, which is a grievous pain. When I saw so little mercy in him I asked him what he would that I should do. He said, 'I would you should tell the truth.' I replied, 'I have said the truth and you will not believe me. I must say as you say or else you are disposed to murder me.' He said, 'No, not murder; justice.' And so I confessed what he wanted me to say that I had said and thought. He caused it to be written down and so went his way. And I was unloosed again.

*A barrel set upon its side. Prisoners had their feet fastened and were then stretched backwards over the barrico.

Percy lost everything, suffered public humiliation and had his health broken by further imprisonment before he was set at liberty.

Such harassments had already gone on for over three decades before Drake set out on his epic voyage. The mercantile community did not suffer them without retaliation. Elizabeth might shrink from open conflict with Spain but her seamen had long since declared war. Piracy was as old as maritime commerce itself and the ruffians who from time immemorial had operated out of the havens of Ireland, Wales and the West Country were a quite unromantic set of desperadoes. But piracy took on a new face in 1545 when Robert Reneger of Southampton captured the Spanish treasure ship *San Salvador* and lifted 124 chests of sugar, 140 hides and a large, but undisclosed, quantity of gold. At the time England and Spain were firm friends but this amity was not reflected in the King's attitude towards Reneger. After an official reprimand Reneger was warmly welcomed at court, given a command in the royal fleet and allowed to keep a large proportion of his loot. In 1577 he was still living in Southampton the comfortable life of a man of substance.

What may have comforted him almost as much as his fortune was the knowledge that his exploit had inspired a whole new generation of English maritime adventurers who rapidly took over from the French as the most outrageous band of sea rovers afloat. The seizure of the *San Salvador* had provoked Spanish reprisals against perfectly innocent English merchants. This accelerated the growing hostility between Spain and England, and outrages multiplied on both sides. It was this hostile rivalry which sparked off England's explosion into the world of overseas exploration, colonisation and enterprise.

In the mid-sixteenth century Europe was poised on the brink of discovering the unknown ninety per cent of the world. More than sixty years had passed since the great pioneering voyages of Columbus, da Gama and Magellan. Since then exploration and exploitation of new lands had been almost entirely in the hands of the Spanish and Portuguese, a state of affairs which apparently received divine blessing in 1494 when, in the Treaty of Tordesillas, the Pope had solemnly drawn a line around the globe dividing all *Terra Incognita* between Spain and Portugal.

For some years the Iberian *conquistadores* had energetically exploited their monopoly. The Spaniards had been rewarded by the discovery of precious metals in Peru and Mexico. The Portuguese had fastened on the lucrative, though more diffuse, orient trade—gold and ivory from Africa, spices from the Moluccas, gems from India. Once they had acquired their seaborne empires the governments in Madrid and Lisbon were more intent on preserving their mastery and commercial profit than in maintaining the momentum of exploration. The challenge of uncharted seas and unknown shores was taken up by the French, the Dutch and paramountly by the English who came late into the colonial race.

Spanish and Portuguese Rule in South and Central America

New Spain

Audiencia of Santo Domingo

Havana

San Juan de Ulua

Veracruz

Acapulco

Audiencia of Guatemala

VICEROYALTY OF NEW SPAIN

Santo Domingo

Nombre de Dios

Santa Marta

Panama

Cartagena

Audiencia of Santa Fé de Bogotá

VICEROYALTY OF PERU

ATLANTIC OCEAN

Equator

Amazon

BRAZIL

Callao • Lima

Cuzco

PERU

Arica

Potosí

PACIFIC OCEAN

DOLDRUMS

Río de la Plata

Buenos Aires

St. Julian's Bay (Port St. Julian)

Land claimed by Spain

Land claimed by Portugal

Prevailing wind

Current

N.B. The fact that land was claimed does not necessarily mean that it was effectively controlled by the colonising power. Madrid and Lisbon both had difficulty forcing their rule on native populations and maintaining the allegiance of settlers, nor were frontiers automatically recognised by other nations.

An Italian boxed compass c. 1570

The foundations of England's mercantile and royal marines were laid by Henry VIII. It was his Lord Admiral, John Dudley, who (during the reign of Edward VI) lured to England the greatest navigator of the age. From his own exploits, his wide reading and his intimate knowledge of other mariners, Sebastian Cabot, Pilot-Major of Spain, had accumulated a greater store of maritime expertise than any contemporary. In 1547, Dudley bribed him to come to England and unlock his secrets for the benefit of English mariners. For the ten years remaining to him Cabot was active instructing eager young navigators at his Bristol academy and leading special training voyages. His labours soon bore fruit. In 1553 maritime and mercantile interests combined to form the 'Merchant Adventurers of England for the discovery of lands, territories, isles, dominions and signories unknown'. The following year saw the foundation of the Muscovy Company and by the end of the decade English ships were sailing to all points of the compass—Newfoundland, the Baltic, the Guinea Coast and the Americas.

The new skills were also invaluable to privateers and pirates who now ventured far across the Atlantic to seek out the wallowing merchantmen homing from Africa or the Main, laden with valuable cargo. No hard and fast line can be drawn between pirates, privateers and merchants. Established traders sometimes received letters of marque to apprehend enemy shipping (this did not include Spanish or Portuguese shipping before 1585). Some captains lived by piracy but made occasional legitimate trading ventures. Others lived a commercial life of impeccable propriety— until fate placed a Spanish merchantman at their mercy. Yet it remains true that as the years passed more and more English and French leeches profitably bled Spain's New World trade. Ambassadors complained, the High Court of Admiralty made the occasional show of severity against pirates, but little effective action was, or indeed could be, taken to stop robbery on the high seas.

One very good reason why piracy went unchecked was that the profits of piracy were finding their way into some very exalted pockets. Whatever their political and religious commitments, members of the Council and the court were only too ready to back mariners of proven worth who could be relied upon to give them a handsome return on their investment in a trading venture, however widely that word 'trading' was interpreted. Ship-owners and captains, therefore, vied with each other for the patronage of the great. The most successful of the enterprising captains of the 1560s was John Hawkins of Plymouth. It was he who pioneered the triangular trade between Europe, West Africa and the West Indies, the principal objective of which was to supply slaves to the plantation owners of the New World. These ventures involved not only the creation of important new markets but also the exploration of new trans-Atlantic routes and, when opportunity occurred, the plundering of Spanish ships and settlements. Shareholders in these highly lucrative voyages included Leicester, Burghley, Lord Admiral Clinton and the Queen.

Hawkins who came from an established family of well-to-do Plymouth merchants, was now a man of substance and influence. He received a grant of arms from the Queen, was welcomed at court and could number several of the leading men of the court among his personal friends. John Hawkins did not lack for poor relatives anxious to cash in on his good fortune. One of them was Francis Drake.

It was while sailing under 'Cousin' Hawkins' flag in 1568 that Drake became involved in one of those rare incidents that changes the fate of men and nations. In February of that year Hawkins' fleet of six ships, including two of the Queen's own vessels, was forced to drop anchor off the tiny island of San Juan de Ulua on the Spanish Main. Shortage of food and damage sustained by a storm at the tail end of the hurricane season made it impossible for him to attempt the homeward voyage without first refitting and revictualling. He would have preferred a far less conspicuous anchorage, for San Juan de Ulua, just offshore from Veracruz, was the principal haven of the well-armed fleets plying between Old Spain and New Spain. Hawkins had established cordial business relations with the governors of the small coastal settlements where he sold slaves but the officials in the Escorial and their Caribbean viceroys bitterly resented the Englishman's persistent and successful activities in 'their' waters.

Hawkins set about the necessary caulking, lashing, splicing and patching with all possible speed. But time was not on his side; forty-eight hours after his arrival a Spanish fleet of twelve sail was observed picking its way carefully between the reefs and sandbanks towards San Juan de Ulua. It was the force of galleons sent to guard the annual treasure convoy and see it safe across the Atlantic. It also carried aboard its flagship no less a person

16

John Hawkins, a portrait made in 1581

then Don Martín Enríquez, the incoming Viceroy of New Spain. Hawkins had the position and the power to forbid Enríquez access to his own harbour but, rather than provoke an international incident, he offered the Spaniard an exchange of hostages, and terms which would allow both fleets to use the haven. The Viceroy accepted the treaty with every intention of breaking it, and beginning his reign with the remarkable coup of ridding the Main of England's most notorious pirate.

Once safely anchored, Enríquez secretly built up his strength with soldiers shipped from the mainland at night. His sailors were encouraged to fraternise with their English counterparts on the island. Hawkins was wary but when a trumpet blared out from the Spanish flagship he was taken almost completely by surprise. His men ashore were massacred immediately and his ships raked with gunfire from the enemy. The English vessels were not slow to reply and battle raged from 10 a.m. until nightfall. With the dark the remnants of Hawkins' expedition escaped the fury of the Spanish cannon and fireships, only to discover a fierce gale raging outside the anchorage. Two crowded ships reached the open sea—the royal galleon, *Minion*, commanded by the admiral and Drake's fifty ton *Judith*. They were soon separated and each vessel made a nightmare journey home. Hawkins was forced to set a hundred men ashore on a Caribbean island because he could not feed them. A further seventy-five died hideously of disease and starvation when the supply of dogs, cats and rats ran out. Four hundred men sailed with Hawkins. Seventy returned.

The massacre of San Juan de Ulua marked a stage in the disintegration of Anglo-Spanish relations as decisive as the Reneger incident. As news of the Spaniards' treachery spread, English resentment built up to a new level. Feelings ran particularly high in the South-West where there was scarcely a family which had not suffered some loss on the ill-fated voyage. But the man who reacted most strongly and permanently was Francis Drake, whose life from 1568 onwards was nothing more then a personal crusade against the subjects of King Philip.

The continuance of piracy in which the leaders of English society connived was a steady poison in the body of Anglo-Spanish diplomacy. Yet the patient showed a remarkable resistance and Elizabeth seemed to have some justification for hoping that he might be kept alive. For, if the Queen of England could not afford war neither could the King of Spain. Elizabeth used her influence to secure peace in the Netherlands and a settlement which would guarantee religious liberty for the Dutch. Patiently enduring several setbacks, Elizabeth saw her policy come to fruition in February 1577. The Perpetual Edict was agreed between the States General and Don John of Austria, Spanish Regent in the Netherlands. For the first time in years the Low Countries was united under the sovereignty of Spain. France was too preoccupied with her internal conflicts to intervene. Scotland was quiet. Mary Stuart was safely immured at Sheffield Castle and was reported to be in poor health. As spring broke it seemed that Elizabeth's 'wait and see' attitude had triumphed. She had bought peace and security—and she had bought them cheaply.

The majority of her councillors were more wary. Don John, they asserted, saw himself as a Catholic champion who would not be bound by the Perpetual Edict. He was just buying time. English spies were convinced that the Regent had a personal ambition to lead the long-threatened invasion, marry Mary Stuart and rule a new united kingdom of England and Scotland. His first task, having allayed English suspicions, would be to defeat the forces of William of Orange. Leicester, Hatton (captain of the guard) and Walsingham urged that this was a time for greater solidarity with England's Protestant brethren, not less. Moreover, the Queen should seek every opportunity to harass and embarrass Spain; to show that, both in Europe and overseas, her arm was long and strong. It was important to demonstrate her determination to stand by her Netherlands' allies. It was equally important to demonstrate her determination to support her seamen's right to free navigation in all waters.

The progressive party in the Council had been annoyed when Grenville's expedition to *Terra Australis* had been cancelled in deference to King Philip's feelings. Now they were planning another foray into Spanish imperial waters and they were determined that it should not, like its predecessor, suffer as a result of diplomatic cold feet. Sir Christopher Hatton's secretary, Thomas Doughty, had recently introduced them to a fiery Protestant captain who had proved his worth on several expeditions to the Main and was as determined an enemy of Spain as they were. The fellow had also been recommended to Walsingham by the Earl of Essex under whom he had served in Ireland. For all his lack of breeding and his pathetic *nouveau riche* pretensions Francis Drake was just the man to carry out the enterprise they had in mind.

The members of Elizabeth's Council, particularly the younger and more vigorous ones, were far from being mere politicians and courtiers. Hatton (at thirty-seven the youngest councillor, and Elizabeth's latest charmer), Leicester (forty-four, the same age as the Queen) and Walsingham (forty-seven)[3] were widely and deeply educated men, patrons of scholars, playwrights, Puritan ministers, explorers and mercantile adventurers. Of their circle was the great astronomer, alchemist and mathematician, Dr John Dee. He was navigational adviser to the Muscovy Company, a personal friend of Gerard Mercator, the author of five major works on astronomical direction-finding (one of which, *The British Complement of the Perfect Art of Navigation*, was published in this very year, with a dedication to Sir Christopher Hatton), and a pioneer of the techniques of mathematical navigation (as opposed to navigation by observation of terrestrial and astronomical phenomena).

Dee was not only an academic theorist; he was an enthusiast, an

Dr. John Dee, the great Elizabethan magus

evangelist of exploration and maritime enterprise. He was sure, he wrote in 1570, that English captains would be more adventurous if they realised

> What Privilege, God had endued this island with, by reason of situation, most commodious for *Navigation*, to places most famous & rich. And though (of late) a young gentleman, a courageous captain, was in great readiness, with good hope, and great cause of persuasion, to have ventured, for a discovery, (either *Westerly*, by *Cape de Paramantia*: or *Esterly*, aboue *Noua Zemla*, and the *Cyremisses*) and was at the very near time of attempting, called and employed otherwise . . . Yet, I say . . . Some one, or other, should listen to the matter: and by good advice, and discreet circumspection, by little and little, win to the sufficient knowledge of that trade and voyage: which, now, I would be sorry, (through carelessness, want of skill, and courage,) should remain unknown and unheard of. Seeing, also, we are herein, half challenged, by the learned, by half request, published. Thereof, verily, might grow commodity, to this land chiefly, and to the rest of the christian Commonwealth, far passing all riches and worldly Treasure.[4]

In his house at Mortlake, crammed with books, herbs, alchemical apparatus, navigational instruments and even strange mechanical birds whose clockwork interiors produced imitation songs, the earnest scientist with the long, unkempt beard enthralled his distinguished patrons with his theories and 'proofs'. Gold, he asserted, was generated by heat and therefore every endeavour should be made to open up the unexplored and undiscovered lands of the tropic zone. The lands certainly existed; their surface areas could be calculated accurately. Since the earth could only maintain its orbit if the two hemispheres exactly balanced, it followed that the unknown land areas south of the equator must be of vast extent. And the time was right for English endeavours in the southern seas. English men, ships and skills were already outclassing those of their maritime rivals—the Spanish, Portuguese, French and Dutch. William Frobisher was at that very time seeking a north-west passage to Asia, claiming for the Queen large tracts of the Eskimos' icy land, and loading his ships with what he believed to be gold ore.

The time was right for Dee, Hatton, Leicester, Walsingham and other enthusiasts but was it right for the Queen? Against the possibly exciting results of a voyage to South America and beyond, she had to balance the more tangible needs of national security. After years of threatening unrest and turmoil in the Netherlands she had just brought off a tentative peace and she was determined not to lose the benefits of this singular diplomatic *coup*. Sometime in the spring of 1577 her progressive councillors laid before her their scheme for an expedition to be led by Francis Drake. Elizabeth graciously received it; she showed genuine interest in it; she discussed it with all her advisers, even with Lord Burghley whose opposition to the scheme was unrelenting; and she did—nothing. The royal favourites, Leicester and Hatton, urged the project as much as they dared. Equally enthusiastically Burghley countered their appeals. Drake hung around the court, not daring to leave lest the Queen should summon him to discuss the voyage, wasting his substance on lodgings, expensive hospitality and bribes to court officials. The weather turned warmer; it was the season of the sweating sickness and other epidemics in cramped, insanitary London, and the royal household left for its annual progress. Fretting at the expense—which might well bear no fruit—Drake joined the entourage which made its way into Hertfordshire to be lavishly entertained at Sir Nicholas Bacon's* new Gorhambury mansion. The court made its leisurely way through the home counties and ended up at Greenwich early in July.

It was then that the tide of fortune turned. Leicester, Hatton and Drake were not the only men suffering frustration and impatience that summer. Don John of Austria was a man of action. In 1571 it was he who, at the battle of Lepanto, had stopped the seemingly inexorable advance of the Turks into Christendom. As a peacemaker in the Netherlands, required

*It was on this occasion that the elderly Bacon showed that young courtiers did not have a monopoly of gallantry. The door used for the Queen's ceremonial entrance was nailed up afterwards so that no other foot should ever profane the threshold.

Robert Dudley, Earl of Leicester

Edward Fiennes de Clinton,
Earl of Lincoln, Lord Admiral

Backers of the expedition

Sir Francis Walsingham

Sir Christopher Hatton

Queen Elizabeth

to observe diplomatic niceties with the Habsburgs' rebellious subjects, he was seriously miscast. In the middle of July he recalled Alexander Farnese and the recently-departed Spanish army. He seized the fortress of Namur and planned the complete conquest of the Netherlands.

When the news reached her Elizabeth was furious. She scarcely needed Leicester to point out to her the error of trusting perfidious Spain. She immediately sent money to William of Orange, and opened negotiations aimed at sending to his aid Duke Casimir of the Palatinate at the head of a mercenary army. Burghley's peace policy was in ruins and he retired from court to take his 'old crazed body' to Buxton for the waters.[5] And at Greenwich the Queen graciously consented to receive Francis Drake.

According to Drake the interview was almost clandestine in its secrecy. No one was present who was not acquainted with the main purpose of the voyage—the purpose which never appeared in the official charter drawn up and signed by the backers;[6] the purpose which Elizabeth demanded should be kept secret from all men, especially Lord Treasurer Burghley; the purpose intimated in her own words, 'I would gladly be revenged on the King of Spain for divers injuries that I have received.'[7] They discussed at some length how this might best be achieved and Drake persuaded Her Majesty that Philip would feel most acutely a blow at the source of his New World treasure supplies. Drake was as anxious as Elizabeth that the main objective of the voyage should not be committed to writing, knowing

...that her Majesty was mortal, and that if it should please God to take her Majesty away, it might be that some prince might reign that might be in league with the King of Spain, and then will mine own hand be a witness against myself.[8]

A charter was drawn up which defined the aims of the expedition in terms of the discovery of *Terra Australis* and the establishment of English colonies on the coasts of South America not claimed by any other Christian prince.[9]

The list of shareholders who now subscribed to the venture included the Lord Admiral, Leicester, Hatton, Walsingham, John Hawkins, Sir William Wynter, surveyor and master of the ordnance to the navy (the uncle of John Wynter who accompanied Drake as captain of the *Elizabeth*), and Drake himself. It did not include the name of the major investor, Elizabeth of England.

The Queen played with relish her part in covering up for her mariners. When Spanish spies reported to Madrid their suspicions about the so secret venture, Elizabeth wrote personally to Philip to counteract their suggestions.

We beg very affectionately that all suspicions may be banished from between us, if any such have been raised by the acts of wicked men with the object of destroying the close friendship which we enjoyed in our earliest years.[10]

The Spaniards were not the only masters of duplicity. Nor was Elizabeth. Burghley soon learned of the Queen's secret meeting with a notorious pirate and Spaniard-hater. He was determined to discover the real objectives of the voyage and tried to find someone privy to the scheme who could be bribed. Useless to try any of his Council rivals, but what of Hatton's new secretary and Drake's friend, Thomas Doughty? The young man was no match for William Cecil, the seasoned intriguer. Vain and ambitious, he was easily flattered into believing that the post of paid informer to the lord treasurer was an important step on the ladder of a promising political career. He had not been present at the secret conference and knew nothing of Drake's unwritten commission as a freebooter, but he knew that the voyage was bound for the South Sea which King Philip regarded as his private lake. So much he told his new master. Before ever the little fleet made its abortive sortie from Plymouth, Lord Burghley knew almost as much about its proposed itinerary as did Drake himself.

Neither Drake's backers nor his opponents had much thought to spare for what was happening in Plymouth during the autumn of 1577. Affairs on the Continent were decidedly *mouvementé*, and they were not favourable to England. The Protestant leaders in the Netherlands were united in only one thing—their ability to squander Elizabeth's gold to no avail. Don John's power grew by the day. What was worse, the end of the latest

French civil war freed the Guise faction to resume its intrigues with Mary Stuart's supporters. All Elizabeth's enemies were ranged against her. Her Council resumed its usual squabbles—more action! less action! war! peace! The situation certainly seemed desperate when the unknown Puritan wrote, 'these are the signs preceding the end of the world'. Elizabeth wrestled with her doubts. Had she been too precipitate in giving offence to Philip of Spain? Had she committed herself to enterprises whose outcome she would regret? If she entertained any idea of revoking Drake's charter, she was too late. The *Pelican* and her companion vessels had, at last, made good their escape from England.

CHAPTER THREE

'This Englishman'

28 NOVEMBER—13 DECEMBER 1577

The man who fretted and fumed on the quayside at Plymouth over the delay of his expedition was a man who found inactivity intolerable in himself and inexcusable in his subordinates. His energy was compulsive, his ceaseless industry an ingrained habit. He had few genuine friends, for it is not easy to love a man as self-contained and sensitive as Francis Drake certainly was. He was one of those people who realise their human potential to the full and who are, therefore, impatient of lesser mortals whose lives, for one reason or another, lack purpose. He was restless—a man possessed by demons. No success could slake his thirst. New lands for discovery and conquest were always appearing on his personal horizon, and death would overtake him at the last while he was still travelling towards that horizon under full sail.[1] The demons which prodded and goaded Francis Drake into relentless endeavour were ambition, religious zeal and hatred of Spain.

Fortunately, we have no need to rely on conjecture as to his appearance. Nuño da Silva, the Portuguese pilot recruited by Drake during the voyage, has left us a vivid account of the English captain who impressed him so greatly:

> This Englishman calls himself Francis Drake and is a man aged 38. He may be two years more or less.[2] He is low in stature, thick set and very robust. He has a fine countenance, is ruddy of complexion and has a fair beard . . . In one leg he has the ball of an arquebuse that was shot at him in the Indies [i.e. at Nombre de Dios]. He is a great mariner, the son and relative of seamen, and particularly of John Hawkins in whose company he was for a long time . . . Francis Drake took with him from England, all told, 270 men,* amongst whom there were some of whom he made more account and had seated at his table, namely, the captain, pilot and doctor. He also read the psalms and preached . . . He also carried with him, from his country, a negro, named Diego, who spoke Spanish and English, and whom he had taken prisoner from a frigate in the North Sea [i.e. the Atlantic], near Nombre de Dios, about seven or eight years previously.[3]

* This is a transcription error and should probably read '170 men'.

The admiral who now travelled the seas attended by his negro slave, his page, his drummer, his trumpeter and his band of musicians had come a long way from a childhood of embarrassing poverty and difficulty. He was born, the eldest of twelve children, into a tenant farming community on the southern slopes of Dartmoor. When he was seven a violent pro-Catholic rising rent the West Country. Known Protestants, among whom the Drakes were numbered, had to leave their property and livelihood and flee for their safety. Francis' family found temporary sojourn on the island in Plymouth Sound, which is still known as Drake's Island. From there they travelled to Kent where, through the charity of relatives and friends, a home of sorts was found in a creaking hulk on the Medway not far from Chatham dockyard. The head of the family found employment as a preacher aboard ships of the royal navy and later as Vicar of Upchurch.

It was natural that Francis and many of his brothers should be apprenticed to the sea. When Francis had scarcely reached double figures he entered the service of the master of a sluggish coasting vessel. The barque wallowed through the eastern inshore waters with cargoes of coal and timber and an expedition to Zeeland or France was a rare adventure for the high-spirited lad. Drake's maritime apprenticeship was, thus, essentially a practical one. What he learned on his first ship was the art of pilotage as opposed to that of oceanic navigation. He learned to steer a ship by landmarks and the stars. His equipment included nothing more sophisticated than the lead and line, the simple compass and a rutter (a mariner's handbook of ancient lore concerning tides, compass bearings and soundings). Yet he cannot have been ignorant of the arts and speculations of those

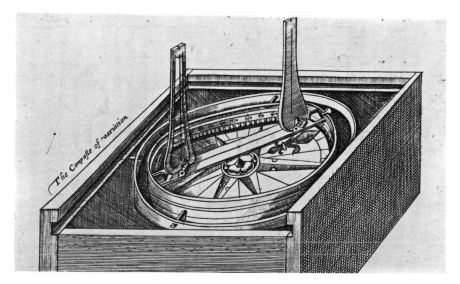

The compass of variation

pioneering the new science of navigation. He must have seen inside the great cabins of his father's friends among the captains of the Queen's fleet. He must have been shown charts, astrolabes and tide calculators. He probably began to explore for himself the mathematical systems of the computation of latitude, longitude and distance without landmarks.

A nocturnal and tide computer

His enthusiasm, industry and natural feel for the sea impressed his master and brought early reward. When the old man died he left his ship to his apprentice, so young Drake found himself an owner-captain before he had even come of age. For some years he continued to ply the coastal trade but now that he was his own man he could not rest content with this restricted sphere of activities. He was envious of the pioneers forging new commercial links with Muscovy and the Levant, edging ever nearer to fabled Cathay. His own Devonian kinsmen, the Hawkinses, were challenging the Portuguese and Spanish New World monopolists by running slaves from West Africa to the Indies and bringing home cargoes of hides and gold.

In 1563 the young owner-captain sold his barque and prevailed upon his cousin John Hawkins to take him onto the firm's pay roll. For four years Drake plied the deep ocean routes to the Guinea coast and the West

Indies. He took his part in the slave traffic with as few twinges of conscience as troubled his fellow captains. He experienced the horrors of the foetid, fever–ridden swamps of negro-land, known even then as the 'white man's graveyard'. Above all, he studied to make himself a master of deep sea navigation.

There was a great deal to learn but he applied himself with such dedication that he soon mastered all the essentials of this new art—at least to his own satisfaction. 'Francis Drake is so boastful of himself as a mariner and a man of learning that he told them that there was no one in the whole world who understood the art (of navigation) better than he.'[4] It is significant that Drake should have claimed to be a 'man of learning' as well as a mariner for the time had passed when navigational skills could be acquired by experience alone. That might serve very well for sailing in coastal waters but he would have been a foolhardy captain who took a shipload of men across uncharted oceans without some knowledge of geography, astronomy, mathematics and their application to the new science of navigation.

In the very years that the young Drake was serving his deep sea apprenticeship English printing presses were pouring forth the earliest verna-

An astrolabe (Reproduced by kind permission of St. Andrews University)

cular navigation manuals. In 1566 the first English translation of the works of Euclid appeared with a preface in which Dr Dee made clear the application of mathematics to navigation and hydrography. In the following year William Bourne, port reeve of Gravesend, published *An Almanacke and Prognostication for iii yeres, with serten Rules of Navigation.* This provided a scientific calculation of the declination of the sun on various days over a three-year period. A few years later Bourne wrote *A Regiment for the Sea*, the first real navigation manual in English. What was particularly noteworthy about Bourne's work was that it was designed 'for the simplest sorte of seafairing man'. The author explained in easily comprehended terms the movements of the sun and moon, the various ways of calculating tides, distances and latitude, the best ways of using compass, cross-staff and astrolabe, how to allow for variations of the pole star, and gave advice towards the calculation of longtitude. Other books also appeared and Sir Humphrey Gilbert urged the setting up of a school for mariners to teach the principles of oceanic navigation, a scheme taken up by Sir Thomas Gresham who made provision in his will for such a school.

Taking an astrolabe reading

Drake, thus, had ample opportunity to augment his practical experience with a study of navigational theory and he took full advantage of it. Like every good captain he also made his own rutters. Throughout every voyage he kept notes on tides, currents, distances and bearings, accompanied by drawings of unknown stretches of coastline. He spent four years in John Hawkins' service—four years which ended disastrously with the slaughter at San Juan de Ulua.

Using a card to obtain a more accurate astrolabe reading

Whether or not Don Martín Enríquez was justified in using duplicity and severity in dealing with men he considered little more than pirates is a matter of debate. What is certain is that Drake regarded the Viceroy's action as inhumanly treacherous. It confirmed his deepest prejudices about the agents of antichrist. More than that, the failure of this expedition represented a severe financial setback for Drake. Up to that point he had been on the winning side in his contest with fate. Now she had dealt him an abysmal hand but only, he was convinced, by producing cards from the bottom of the pack. He was determined to regain the initiative. First of all, he made representations to the Council, demanding an enquiry and restitution by the Spanish government. All he obtained from this was a lesson in practical politics. Once again, all he had to rely on were his own resources. If Spain were to be forced to recompense him for his losses and for the lives of crewmen and friends, he himself would have to do the forcing.

Thus did Francis Drake dedicate himself to a career of piracy and plunder against the goods and subjects of His Sacred Catholic Royal Majesty. He made two reconnaissance trips to the West Indies, then, in May 1572, he set out on a fifteen month rampage of looting and violence along the length of the Main. He attacked Nombre de Dios, the shanty town which served Spain as the principal storehouse of Peruvian gold brought across the Isthmus of Panama, and would have emptied its treasure house had he not been severely wounded and forced to call off the raid. Over several hundred miles of coastline the Englishmen ranged relieving Spanish settlements and ships of anything which was of value to them, scuttling their own vessels in favour of captured prizes, watching their comrades die of disease and battle wounds, enduring storms, long periods without adequate food, perilous nights within hastily-constructed stockades in enemy territory—and all in the hope of landing the great prize, a cache of Spanish treasure. Throughout these dangerous and difficult months they were spurred on by greed and their general's frequent assurances that they might 'depend upon God's almighty providence which never fails them that trust in Him.' [5]

Drake now pinned all his hopes on a joint expedition with the Cimarrons across the Isthmus. These hill bandits were a mixed people whose root stock were slaves escaped from the Spaniards and their one aim in life was to be as much nuisance as possible to their arrogant ex-masters. They agreed to lead the Englishmen to a hidden horde of gold and silver stolen from the Spaniards and to help them raid the baggage trains. In February 1573 Drake and a party of picked men followed their Cimarron guides into the jungle, swamps and high passes of the Cordilleras. Emerging after some days of gruelling march at the top of an impressive ridge, the Cimarrons pointed out a tall tree at whose summit they had constructed a platform. Drake and his 'ship's cook', John Oxenham, climbed to this vantage point and were rewarded by a thrilling sight. In the northern distance the horizon was that of the familiar Atlantic. The glistening waters to the south were the Pacific, the ocean which England only knew of from the accounts of bold foreign adventurers. No wonder he prayed aloud that God would spare him to sail just once in an English ship upon that sea. His ambition now had a new horizon.

There was much more to Drake's exciting new vision than the wish to be the first Englishman to sail the Pacific. Access to that ocean would, he knew, open up for his countrymen half the world, a half that included the fabled lands of Cathay, Cypangu and the Spice Islands. These regions had been barred to two generations of English adventurers by the Portuguese in the east and the Spaniards in the west. Now Drake realized that only a narrow strip of land divided the Atlantic coast of Central America, which he had effectively terrorized with two ships and a handful of men, from this ocean of promise and opportunity. More than that; a permanent foothold on the isthmus and an easily-established naval supremacy on the sea beyond would make his queen undisputed mistress of the treasures of Mexico and Peru, the loss of which would totally destroy Spain.

King Philip's officers were certainly well aware of the new threat as the treasurer of Nombre de Dios pointed out when reporting on the outcome of Drake's trek across the isthmus:

The attack occurred near the Venta de Chagre [Venta Crucis], which is six leagues from Panama. They burned that post, and there killed a friar of the Order of Saint Dominic, and three soldiers and passengers, and wounded others...

And if they do this while the fleet is here, it is presumed that when it shall have gone they will inflict much damage on all this land, since they are in league with the said *cimarrones,* who have guided them close to Panama. They can enter the Pacific to commit piracies on the ships coming down from Peru, from which will result grave damage.[6]

After the attackers had successfully intercepted one of the bullion-laden mule trains, another official prophesied that, 'encouraged by the very valuable booty they have secured, these corsairs will return to this realm in very much greater strength, and by means of their federation with the negroes so situate themselves as to succeed in any venture they may undertake.' [7] Doubtless the worried and overworked colonial agents deliberately exaggerated, in their concern to spur Madrid to action, but no one knew better than they just how vulnerable were the undermanned garrisons and isolated Spanish settlements surrounded by hostile natives, who were ever on the brink of rebellion.

No one, that is, except Francis Drake and his companions. As the forty or so Englishmen made their way home with a cargo of 100,000 gold pesos,* the leader carried in his head a far greater prize—the germ of an idea that would win the precious metal of the New World for England, without the need for costly pirate voyages.

Furthermore, he now had the means to play a prominent part in developing and executing that idea. The Nombre de Dios voyage, as it came to be called, made him a wealthy man able to buy a substantial house in Plymouth and three fine ships. As well as fortune he enjoyed considerable fame. The recent expedition, as well as being so audacious as to capture the imagination of all who were not firm friends of Spain, had also been the most successful raid on the Main in terms of booty and had very clearly exposed the weakness of Spanish control along her extended lines of communication. Francis Drake was henceforth a marked man; to the Spaniards he was 'the Corsair Draco'; to Englishmen and all Europeans who admired courage and daring he was a hero.

But, for all that Drake was now rich and famous, he lacked one thing vital to the accomplishment of his great design—he lacked royal favour. Friends at court he certainly had and such influence as he could muster he used to gain employment in the Queen's service. But Elizabeth had no job for him

* Drake had apparently lost almost half of the original complement of seventy-four men. Two of the fatalities were his own brothers, John and Joseph. The exact size of the haul is uncertain. Drake is unlikely to have made a true declaration for customs purposes and he had to share his booty with some French allies who had joined in the raid on the mule train. cf. G. M. Thomson, *Sir Francis Drake,* p. 93.

more exciting or rewarding than ferrying troops to Ireland for the Earl of Essex's campaign. European affairs were in one of their 'knife-edge' phases and Captain Drake was far too tumultuous a man to be accepted at court or even openly recognized by the Queen. Before Drake's return from the Main all European Protestants had been shocked by the Massacre of St Bartholomew in France which signalled the dominance of the Catholic party there. This was followed by the accession of Henry III, no friend of England. It was certainly not a time for revivifying old enmities; rather were Elizabeth's envoys in Paris and Madrid employed in cobbling together treaties of spurious amity.

So no major expedition in the direction of the Spanish Americas was sanctioned. Grenville's projected voyage to *Terra Australis* was cancelled in 1574. On the Main the expected escalation of piracy failed to materialize and Philip's governors breathed again. They had taken such precautions as they could; strengthening defences and posting more sentries but the hoped for help was not forthcoming from the bankrupt government in Madrid.[8]

Indeed, the safety of the treasure fleets suffered a serious setback in 1574 with the death of Pedro Menéndez de Avilés, *adelantado* of Florida. Menéndez had perfected the convoy system and also built up a powerful fleet to patrol the Main and protect the treasure fleets. As so often happened in the Spanish colonial service, which was a collection of less or more gifted individuals united by only the vaguest concepts of common policy, Menéndez's work died with him. English and French raids continued but the Spanish authorities, aroused by Drake to a new vigilance, defended their territories with vigour.

> The galleons having left Nombre de Dios, in the direction of Veragua there appeared one morning an English corsair calling himself John Noble, who had been in that vicinity when the last fleet was here. He pillaged certain barks and frigates on the coastwise trade and began to disturb this realm. God granted that by means of the measures taken both at Nombre de Dios and also at Veragua he should be captured with all his men, twenty-eight in all. They were all killed, excepting two boys who were condemned to the galleys for life and are now serving in your majesty's galleons. The captain and two of them were hanged at Nombre de Dios, which has occasioned great joy and animated all, and the realm is entirely quiet.[9]

Drake followed with interest but also with anxiety the news of such doings in the Indies. He was frantically concerned that no one else should beat him to his grand design and also worried lest the inept blunderings of such as John Noble should put the Spaniards too much on their guard. One of his own colleagues came into this category. John Oxenham, who had stood beside him on that Panamanian tree top and shared the magical

34

moment of the first sighting of the Pacific, was as much possessed as Drake by the vision of sailing an English ship on that sea. Drake had promised him a place on his hoped-for expedition but as the months slipped by with no prospect of Drake's plans coming to fruition Oxenham had sought other patrons. He joined Grenville's crew for the projected *Terra Australis* venture. When that, also, failed to materialise it became obvious to him that the Queen was not going to allow any major expedition to follow up the important discoveries of the 1572–3 journey so Oxenham made his own arrangements. He fitted out a ship of 140 tons, got together a crew of seventy men and sailed for the Main late in 1575.

John Oxenham shared his ex-captain's vision and, like Drake, he had enthusiasm, ambition and determination. But he was not the man to lead others into hardship and danger. The comparison between the two captains is instructive. Both were rough Devonians who chose to make their fortunes through maritime enterprise. Both had skills of seamanship and many of the personal qualities necessary for success. Both could be firm and ruthless with their followers when occasion demanded. But Oxenham quarrelled with his own men, antagonised the Cimarron allies upon whom he was dependent and so mismanaged the crossing of the isthmus that the most inept of Spanish pursuers could have tracked down the invaders. Oxenham was a brave man but he lacked two gifts essential in a leader. One was the energy to drive himself as hard as and harder than his followers. Men will follow the most brutal taskmaster if they are confident that he is bearing his own greater burdens with fortitude and that all his demands are made with their safety and the success of their enterprise in mind. The other gift he lacked was sensitivity—that intuition which tells a commander when to harangue and when to cajole, when to be generous and when unyielding, when to extract the last ounce of strength from his men and when to accept defeat gracefully, when to extend the olive branch and when the naked steel. Drake possessed these gifts and they go a long way towards explaining his astonishing success and undying fame.

Oxenham's party blundered and squabbled its way across the isthmus and, in the South Sea, succeeded in capturing two treasure vessels. Their retreat with their booty back across Panama was so badly handled and so hampered by disputes among the Englishmen and between the Englishmen and their native guides that they were easily tracked down, some even being handed over by the Cimarrons to their enemies. Most of Oxenham's men were summarily executed but he and two others were taken to Lima for examination by the civil authorities and the Inquisition.

How soon news of Oxenham's failure reached England we cannot know. Did Drake hear of his old comrade's capture while he was trying to interest influential backers in an altogether more ambitious voyage to the Americas? It was impossible for him to infer anything with certainty from Oxenham's long absence; it might suggest the collapse of the project or success of

35

such proportions as to discourage the Englishmen from a hasty return home. Neither explanation would give Drake much pleasure.

If he had known Oxenham's real fate he would have been genuinely alarmed. The captain's successful crossing of the isthmus; his construction of a twelve-oared boat from local cedar; his trip across to the Pearl Islands; his removal of gold, silver and pearls from the Spanish residents there; his freeing of seventy slaves; and his destruction and pillaging of shipping, had set the colonial community by the ears. That was not all.

> What is felt most deeply, being cause for tears, is the little veneration they show the saints and the worship of God. They broke up images and crucifixes, they overturned the altar, knocking it to pieces. They used albs and vestments as kitchen aprons. They beat and buffeted a Franciscan friar who happed to be there, ridiculing the pope, confession and absolution. They committed many other insults and insolencies, for which God give us due vengeance, in defending His honour by your majesty's unconquerable arms...
>
> The English captain . . . is very happy to have opened a way from the Atlantic to the Pacific. He expects to be greatly rewarded by his queen for so doing and promises that next year he will enter there to settle with 2000 men and make himself master of all this realm, the strength of which is very little to resist such an onslaught as he announces, unless greatly reinforced by your majesty, whom we entreat to have compassion on us, your majesty's vassals, and to send succour sufficient to withstand such force.[10]

Racked and thumbscrewed in the city prison at Lima, Oxenham had a great deal more to say, though in a less boastful vein. He told his inquisitors that there was much interest among English mariners in venturing into the South Sea and founding colonies on the unoccupied coasts of South America. Such a voyage might only be undertaken with the Queen's commission. Richard Grenville had received such a commission but it had been revoked because the Queen did not wish to upset her brother King Philip. Then Oxenham's captors asked him specifically about Francis Drake.

'If Captain Drake received the Queen's commission would he try to enter the South Sea through the Straits of Magellan?'

'Yes. He is a very good mariner and pilot. There is no man in England better equipped to achieve this.'

'Will the Queen grant Drake a licence?'

'I don't think so but Drake has told me that after her majesty's death he will certainly bring men and ships to the South Sea and found colonies.'

'So it is only your Queen who prevents Drake coming back to raid our settlements?'

'Yes.'[11]

By the time that the examination of Oxenham and his colleagues took place Drake's voyage was well under way but the tenor of the questions shows that the Spanish colonial authorities were alive long before to what he had in mind. The possibilities were as clear to them as they were to him. There were two: an onslaught on the Isthmus of Panama in sufficient strength to give England a stranglehold on the scrawny neck of Central America; an expedition into the Pacific via the Straits of Magellan. The first would be a costly and overt act of war which Elizabeth would never sanction. The second, even if the Queen could be induced to approve it, would be dangerous in the extreme but, if successful, would enable the English to establish bases on the uncolonised coast of Chile and attack at will the source of Spanish wealth.

A horizontal plane sphere

It was over half a century since Ferdinand Magellan, a Portuguese sailor in the pay of Spain, had threaded his way through the 320 miles of narrow channel between the Cape of Virgins and Cape Desire. During those fifty years the implications of his momentous discovery had remained largely unrealised. This was not due to a lack of enterprise or bravery on the part of Portuguese or Spanish sailors. There had been several attempts—some successful—to navigate the straits and exploit the commercial prospects of the westward route to Asia. There were three main difficulties: the passage of the straits was, even in good weather, a difficult feat—and the weather was seldom good. The crossing of the vast and empty Pacific was for sailors a nightmare through which stalked the terrifying figures of hunger, thirst and

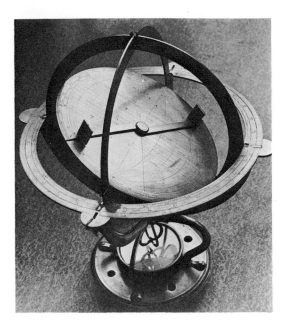

An armillary instrument (Reproduced by kind permission of St. Andrews University)

scurvy. Thirdly, there was no going back. Until 1565, when Andrés de Urdaneta pioneered a more northerly route, ship after ship had come to grief trying to beat eastwards against the relentless Pacific trade winds. The return journey through the straits was generally believed to be more difficult than the outward one; a belief deliberately encouraged by the Spaniards. Any captain leaving Europe for a passage through the Straits of Magellan was virtually committing himself to a repetition of Magellan's circumnavigation—a voyage which had cost the lives of 245 men, including the leader (out of an original complement of 280). The Spaniards had little cause to make use of the long, hazardous haul around South America; for most purposes the overland route across the isthmus was perfectly satisfactory. But the straits were there, a narrow postern gate in the defences of the Spanish empire. Realistic officials in the colonies and Madrid knew that it was only a matter of time before someone tried to enter by that gate. Those who had encountered the self-confident and outrageous Draco the Corsair knew that he was just the sort of man to make the attempt.

The corsair himself earnestly and frequently repeated his prayer to God that it might be so. He obtained his own copy of Pigafetta's *Le Voyage et Navigation faict par les Espanolz èc isles de Mollucques,* the earliest account of Magellan's voyage.[12] He already owned *The Decades of the newe worlde or west India . . . Wrytten in the Latine tounge by Peter Martyr of Angleria and translated into Englysshe by Rycharde Eden,* the standard English reference work on westward navigation. He had an insatiable acquisitiveness for charts and rutters, particularly those produced in Portugal and Spain. He had recently acquired a handwritten Portuguese manual of navigation which, as well as containing details of all the better known oceanic routes, contained two rutters relating to navigation in South American waters. One dealt with the coast of Brazil; the other gave instructions for sailing southwards to the straits and the north past the crag- and island-strewn shores of Chile and Peru.[13] He owned or had studied Abraham Ortelius' map of 1570 which confidently delineated *Terra Australis Incognita,* of which Tierra del Fuego was thought to be a part.

Drake studied and planned during those years of enforced confinement to home waters. It was probably as well that he was confined. Reflection on the political possibilities and close scrutiny of all the known facts about voyaging to the straits and beyond matured his ideas, turning ambitious schemes into considered plans. What he proposed to attempt, and what he talked about excitedly to any he could trust who might help him realise his dreams, was a well equipped expedition to penetrate the South Sea via the Straits of Magellan in order to show Spain that her mastery of the seas was at an end and to plunder at source the rich river flowing from the Potosí mines. Later, when he wished to lend his plans more respectability, he spoke of finding sites for colonies, of exploring the unknown south continent and of seeking the Straits of Anian. This latter was a supposed passage linking the Pacific and Atlantic oceans to the north of America. English geographers persisted in their belief in a navigable north-west passage long after Spanish and Portuguese explorers had abandoned the exploration of the west coast of North America, convinced that it linked up directly with the coast of Asia.

The enormity of the proposed undertaking was breathtaking. No English mariner had attempted the passage of the straits since 1526 when Henry Latimer and Roger Barlow had joined Sebastian Cabot's expedition to the Moluccas, an expedition which had got no farther than the Plate estuary. It was an expedition to the unknown and, inevitably, the unknown was peopled in the popular imagination with all manner of horrors. As well as the usual hurricanes, whirlpools, sirens and monsters of the deep said to bedevil uncharted seas, legends spoke of cannibals, headless men, warlike savages and hybrid man/fish, man/bird, man/lion creatures. For experienced mariners who could take a more balanced view the possibilities were scarcely less daunting. They knew from reports by Portuguese and Spanish sailors just how difficult it was to negotiate the winds and currents around the coasts of South America and beyond. As to the inhabitants of the unknown lands *en route,* they had either been colonised by agents of Spain or Portugal who would certainly be unfriendly or were still 'untamed', the preserve of natives whose reaction to strangers could not be predicted.

In the back of Drake's mind there must always have been the fear of meeting Magellan's fate, hacked to pieces on some distant beach.

However, in the years between 1573 and 1577, such dangers were distant and problematical. Drake's immediate problem was to obtain influential backers for his project, backers who would commend him to the Queen. Walter Devereux, Earl of Essex, was sorely in need of reliable captains and men. In 1573 he became one of that long line of politician-generals whose careers have been ruined by the attempt to pacify Ireland. Drake offered his services and for a couple of years was involved in the massacres and the vacillation between ferocity and negotiation which passed for English policy in that wretched island. But Essex was sufficiently impressed with his equally adventurous contemporary[14] to provide Drake with letters of intro-duction to Secretary Walsingham.

It was also in Ireland that Drake met Thomas Doughty—a fateful encounter indeed. Doughty was a young, professional courtier with a legal training and probably some experience of foreign travel. At least one man who met him was impressed by Doughty's talents and personal qualities.

> He feared God, he loved his word, and was always desirous to edify others and confirm himself in the faith of Christ. For his qualities, in a man of his time they were rare, and his gift very excellent for his age, a sweet orator, a pregnant philosopher, a good gift for the Greek tongue, and a reasonable taste of Hebrew; a sufficient secretary to a noble personage of great place, and in Ireland an approved soldier, and not behind many in the study of the law for his time; and that which is a sufficient argument to prove a good Christian, and of all other things a most manifest witness of a child of God to men, that he was delighted in the study, hearing and practice of the word of God, daily exercising himself herein by reading, meditating to himself, conferring with others, instructing of the ignorant, as if he had been a minister of Christ.[15]

At the time of their first meeting Thomas Doughty was both a captain and a messenger, flying back and forth between Ireland and the court with confidential despatches for Essex. Drake found much to admire and envy in this poised, well-educated young man. By birth and training, if not by wealth and status, the young courtier was well equipped to move with confidence and ease among England's leading men of affairs. He talked freely of Burghley and Leicester, Walsingham and Hatton as though he had a long and intimate acquaintance with them. He discoursed wisely on matters of home and foreign policy. With silver-tongued eloquence he voiced opinions on the theory of statesmanship, lacing his discourse with quotations from the Bible and the classical philosophers. Doughty was the cultured and sophisticated man of the world. He was in one sense all that Drake wished to be and could never be. He was also the key which might unlock for Drake the door to the royal court.

There was much more to Thomas Doughty, however, than just the ambitious courtier. He was a scholar in an age when scholarship embraced a variety of disciplines and recognised few barriers. Physic, philosophy, theology, astrology, mathematics, cosmography, navigation—all were rivulets flowing from the same eternal source and those seeking knowledge drank deeply and indiscriminately. To the ignorant and the superstitious (and all men in the sixteenth century were superstitious) all knowledge was secret, mysterious, awe-inspiring. It conveyed power to its possessors. Those who could read the stars and cast horoscopes, were they not in league with forces outside the terrestrial sphere? Who knew what dark things were written in the scholars' heavy books with their strange language and mysterious symbols? Within a few years Englishmen would be avidly reading a new translation out of the German entitled *The Historie of the damnable life, and deserued death of Doctor Iohn Faustus* and in 1591 Christopher Marlowe would turn this long-popular legend into a powerful play.

Doughty was a friend and disciple of England's greatest scholar, Dr John Dee, and shared the latter's fascination with the new art of navigation. That was not all that Doughty shared with the great magus. In 1583 an angry mob broke into Dee's house at Mortlake and destroyed all the 'sorcerer's' supposedly magical books and instruments—his chemical apparatus, his quadrant, his zodiacal tables for casting horoscopes, his maps and charts. There were also those who suspected Doughty of necromancy.

Doughty admired Drake, the man of action and dynamic vision. He was thrilled by the blunt Devonian's stories of past adventures and his plans for future glory. Mutual regard and a shared Bible-based religious zeal brought Doughty and Drake together in close friendship. The mariner confided all his secret ambitions for a journey to the South Sea and the courtier promised to use his influence to help Drake achieve those ambitions.

But men are not always what they seem. There were other more sinister aspects of Doughty's many-faceted character. The man was a student of intrigue, adept at obtaining confidential information and using it to advantage. He revelled in the power which came from being a party to important secrets and it was his chief ambition to be a manipulator of men and great events. The Earl of Essex certainly came to regret reposing trust in one who 'had before that time spoken as much as any other of his devotions to me and my cause'. What had happened was that in the politically exciting atmosphere of the court Doughty had allowed himself to be flattered and bribed into plots against his master by those who opposed Essex's handling of Irish affairs. As a result of his 'compliance' the young courtier was soon able to change patrons. He became secretary to Christopher Hatton. Doughty was installed at court by the middle of 1576. He lost no time in using his new position to advance Drake's cause. Drake had other court connections; Essex had commended him to Walsingham and he was known personally to the Lord Admiral, Edward Fiennes Clinton, Earl of Lincoln. Yet, as an active advocate in high circles, Doughty was of considerable, perhaps vital, importance to Drake.

When at last Drake was summoned to Westminister to discuss with the Queen and members of her Council the possibilities of a voyage to the South Sea, he spent many hours with his courtier friend, discussing political tactics and practical plans for the expedition. Doughty was unable to take a large financial stake in the venture but both he and Drake knew that he had already done more than enough to warrant a place on the flagship, if not a command of one of the other vessels. Had Drake not been so dazzled by his colleague's man-of-the-world air, he might have realised that the gifts which equipped a man for antechambers and audience rooms were not necessarily those which would stand him in good stead during a long and dangerous sea voyage. For the moment, however, the two men were close friends and joint planners of an expedition which they hoped would make their fortunes. As he walked the streets of Plymouth Doughty was as anxious as Drake to be underway.

Most of the other men who tied their destiny to that of the hero of Nombre de Dios are now mere names, remembered only because of the part they played in the circumnavigation voyage.[16]

Of the ninety-six names which have been preserved there are a few to which we can give some substance. The expedition's élite were the gentlemen adventurers, whose acknowledged leader was Thomas Doughty. They included Gregory Cary (or Carey) a relative of Lord Hunsdon, the Queen's cousin, and John Chester whose father was one of the most important men in the city of London and an ex-lord mayor. There was William Hawkins, a young nephew of the great Sir John Hawkins, under whom Drake had served. Leonard Vicarye was probably a kinsman of the late Thomas Vicary, royal surgeon (perhaps he was the expedition's doctor) while George Ffortescu's father was keeper of the royal wardrobe. Thomas Doughty had brought with him his younger brother, John. The admiral had two close relatives aboard. John Drake was a young cousin whose major asset was, apparently, his artistic talent. Nuño da Silva described the lad as 'a great painter' and recounted how he and the admiral spent hours together in the great cabin drawing coastlines, trees, birds and other natural phenomena into the rutter which was compiled of the voyage.[17] Also present was Francis' youngest brother, Thomas. The Portuguese pilot described him as 'twenty-two years of age with a fair complexion and a scanty beard, which is fair. He is low of stature but is broad-shouldered and sturdy.* He is a good seaman.'[18] Thomas's relationship to the admiral might well have assured him of a privileged place on shipboard but da Silva thought it worthy of special mention that he 'served as a sailor, like any one of the crew.'[19]

* The Drakes were apparently a family of stocky, well-set men and women, a strain still easily recognisable to anyone familiar with the farming-fishing communities of Devon.

Francis Fletcher, the expedition's puritanical preacher, is a man of whose antecedents and subsequent career one would love to know more. The notes kept by Fletcher constitute our main source of information about the earlier part of the voyage and it would be valuable to have some external information about their author so that we might know how much confidence to repose in his account. It is clear that during the course of the circumnavigation Fletcher changed from a loyal supporter of Drake into one of his sternest critics. Greater knowledge of the man would help us to decide how to apportion blame for the rift. Things, however, are rarely simple for the historian and it seems that Fletcher's life, apart from the vital three years during which he accompanied Drake, will remain ever veiled in obscurity. By his own admission the parson was a much-travelled man, having been in Spain, Russia, the Mediterranean area and the Levant. He had been on earlier voyages of exploration but whether as preacher or sailor is not clear. He was a man of extreme enthusiasm, whether setting down in his journal the details of exotic plants and animals (proofs of the varied bounty of Almighty God) or destroying the images and crucifixes set up by detestable 'papists'. Unfortunately his zeal often led him into excesses; his travellers tales of tropical volcanoes six miles high and African savages who urinate, defecate and copulate as acts of public worship must be dismissed as pure invention.

About John Wynter, who commanded the *Elizabeth*, we know more. He came of an ancient Bristol sea-faring family. His father, Sir William Wynter, after an active career in home and foreign waters had become one of the most influential members of the navy board, combining the offices of surveyor of the Queen's ships and master of the ordnance of the navy. John, though only in his late twenties, had seen a great deal of service under some of England's leading captains and was well qualified for the position of vice-admiral and the command of the Queen's own ship.

During the course of the voyage positions of importance changed hands as men or ships died and as captains forfeited the trust of their admiral. The captain of each vessel was usually a gentleman who might or might not have maritime experience. He enjoyed overall command but left the routine running of the ship to the master. At the outset of the voyage command of Hatton's *Marigold* was vested in his chosen representative, John Thomas. John Chester had the *Swan* and the little Christopher was under the command of Thomas Moon, a trusted Devonian who had sailed with Drake to Nombre de Dios in the capacity of ship's carpenter.

Among the expedition's complement there must have been many other men who had sailed with Drake before. The admiral chose with care the seamen who were to man his own ships, the *Pelican, Swan* and *Christopher*. Time spent on careful recruiting and selection was time well spent, for no other profession was attracting riff-raff as rapidly as the maritime profession. Unemployment and social distress coupled with the fabled profits made from piracy were filling the seamen's ranks with large numbers of amateurs. The risks of injury and the enormous loss of life at sea were no deterrents to desperate men, especially when the lure of quick riches added a delicious incentive to enlistment. Most men failed to return from long ocean voyages but some of those who did were set up for life and could afford to buy land, a tavern, a few horses or the stock to begin some other business. Most amateur sailors preferred the hit-and-run piracy of the narrow seas but there were many avaricious thugs who were prepared to try their fortunes with Francis Drake whose crew had shared such magnificent booty at the end of the Nombre de Dios voyage. Many of the men who signed on for the expedition probably believed what they were told, that Drake was bound on a trading voyage to Alexandria, but their incentive was not the meagre mariner's wages such a trip would produce but the hope that the great Corsair would lead them in the capture of rich prizes. As the voyage lengthened and it became obvious that they were destined for uncharted seas, resentment would grow below decks, but by then it would be too late.

It was not only among the lower orders that there would be misunderstanding and resentment. The journey began with no clear definition of authority among its leaders. That Drake was Admiral or, as he was frequently called, General, was perfectly clear. No one disputed his command over the men, but what was his position vis-à-vis the gentlemen? Most of them were Drake's social superiors, scions of wealthy and ancient families. Some could claim considerable authority based on their connections. Wynter had not only a father but also an uncle on the navy board; both had heavy investment in the enterprise. Thomas Doughty regarded himself as a joint planner of the voyage and also Christopher Hatton's personal representative. There was probably some agreement which gave him command of the military aspects of the expedition. Doubtless there were other gentlemen who believed themselves to have, by virtue of their financial investment or their family contacts, an important voice in all decisions. Since the other leaders were only privy to the official charter and thought that the voyage was primarily a voyage of exploration it was clear that there were conflicts ahead, conflicts which would be decided in favour of whoever had the strongest will.

So much for Drake's men. He took five ships when he set out from Plymouth in the autumn of 1577. Their names were *Pelican, Elizabeth, Marigold, Swan* and *Christopher*. Even by the standards of the day Drake's ships were small for such a venture as he proposed. The *Henry Grace à Dieu*, completed in 1514, had been over 1,000 tons. Howard's fleet which beat off the Armada included fifteen capital ships of over 500 tons. The merchantmen operated by the established houses of Bristol, London, Hamburg and Antwerp were of substantial build. Yet Drake's flagship weighed just over 100 tons. Her overall length was about 100 feet and her beam was 20 feet.[20] She was to a casual observer a typical, small armed merchant

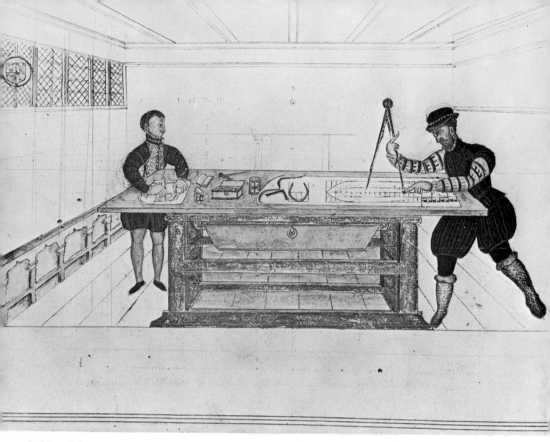

A shipwright at work, from a book by Matthew Baker, England's leading exponent of the craft

ship of the period, sturdy and well built, though whether she was laid down in an English yard or taken as prize of war we do not know. Nuño da Silva wrote in respectful, but not glowing, terms of the *Pelican*:

[She] is in a great measure stout and strong. She has two sheathings, one as perfectly finished as the other. She is fit for warfare and is a ship of the French pattern, well fitted out and finished with very good masts, tackle and double sails. She is a good sailer and the rudder governs her well. She is not new, nor is she coppered nor ballasted. She has seven armed port-holes on each side, and inside she carries eighteen pieces of artillery, thirteen being of bronze and the rest of cast iron . . . This vessel is water-fast when she is navigated with the wind astern and this is not violent, but when the sea is high, as she has to labour, she leaks not a little whether sailing before the wind or with the bowlines hauled out. Taking it all in all, she is a ship which is in a fit condition to make a couple of voyages from Portugal to Brazil.[21]

45

A modern replica of the Golden Hind, *built at Appledore in 1973–4*

The *Pelican's* three masts carried a total spread of more than 4,000 square feet of sail and, when necessary, she was quite capable of outstripping vessels many times her size.

It is when we consider in detail some of the *Pelican's* equipment that we realise she was no ordinary vessel. She carried topgallant sails for the fore and mainmasts which gave her a considerable extra turn of speed. Her armament would certainly not have disgraced a ship twice her size. From her fourteen ports poked a battery of slim, deadly, long-range demi-culverin. Their nine-pound balls would not sink a ship but they would create havoc with the sails, spars, timberwork and bodies of any potential aggressor long before that aggressor could come close enough to inflict retaliatory damage. In addition there were small swivel-mounted falconets for sweeping enemy decks with shot. The hand weapons were no less impressive and Drake took every opportunity to acquaint Spanish officials with the quantities of arque-buses, calivers, pistols, pikes, fire-pikes, fire-bombs, bows, arrows and swords that he was carrying. Small the *Pelican* may have been but there were few more belligerent and efficient ships afloat than she.

Seventy or eighty men ate, slept, worked, sang, gambled, recovered from or succumbed to wounds on the two principal decks of this floating arsenal. Under such conditions discipline and order were vital to survival. Every-thing necessary for the voyage was stowed and fastened securely in its proper place. In the hold were the timber and iron needed for repairs, spare weapons, kegs of gunpowder (well sealed with pitch), gunshot, barrels of salted meat and fish and drinking water. The lower deck housed small arms in racks (ready for instant distribution but useless to would-be mutineers without the powder and shot under lock and key below), lanterns, cooking utensils and the portable fire-box which was brought on deck twice a day when there were meals to be cooked. Each sailor marked out his own sleeping place between the guns or, in hot weather, in some corner of the upper deck where he would not be in the way of the men working the ship. Here he lashed his small sea chest.

Quarters for the gentlemen, the captain, the master and the admiral were of a different order. Two cabins were situated below the poop or after deck set out with carven tables of oak overlaid with turkeywork carpets and stout chairs with velvet cushions. Drake's cabin also contained a substantial bed and was decorated with rugs and fine hangings fixed to the sloping walls. Here he would hold state to receive native dignitaries. Here he would dine Spanish prisoners off silver plate while he emptied their ships of bullion. The adjoining great cabin was where Drake ate and conversed with the gentlemen, captains and pilots. Here he studied his charts and made his day-to-day plans with those he chose to consult. Here, too, most of the gentlemen settled for the night on their truckle beds. On the poop deck was a small 'round house' whither Drake and the senior members of the company might resort in hot weather. It was here that the admiral and his

Drake's cabin aboard the Golden Hind *replica*

young cousin spent hours together making careful paintings and drawings of anything worthy of permanent record.

Modest as the *Pelican* was, she outclassed all the remaining members of the flotilla. Drake's other ships were the *Swan,* a canter or supply ship of 50 tons, and the 15 ton bark *Christopher* (sometimes referred to as the *Benedict*). Drake knew that the twin curses of a long voyage were scurvy and dysentery and that one way to minimise their impact was to ensure a plentiful supply of fresh food. This was where the *Swan* was so valuable. She was slow and ponderous. She often held up the progress of the convoy. She sometimes got lost. But her presence with the fleet did mean that wholesome victuals could be taken on and stored whenever opportunity arose. The bark was the errand boy of the fleet. Its role was vital in keeping the larger ships together, locating vessels scattered by storms, carrying instructions from the admiral to other captains, fetching the doctor to sick crewmen and generally carrying men and messages wherever they were wanted.

Of the ships which Drake did not own little needs to be said at this stage. The *Elizabeth* had a burthen of 80 tons. She was a well equipped little ship of the royal navy which stood up well to the buffetings of the Atlantic and which might well have completed the circumnavigation had the hearts of her men been as stout as her own. Hatton's little *Marigold* of 30 tons, though representing a not inconsiderable investment in the enterprise, was patently too small a vessel for the journey Drake had in mind.

Drake, his men and his ships waited in Plymouth from 28 November until 12 December. The repairs had long since been completed. Only the weather had yet to mend. On the 13th, a Wednesday, the sun rose into a clear sky. The wind had veered to a fresh offshore breeze. The western horizon was a clear, bold line. Immediately, the admiral ordered embarkation. With pennants fluttering and streamers dipping their tips in the water the little fleet moved out with the ebb.

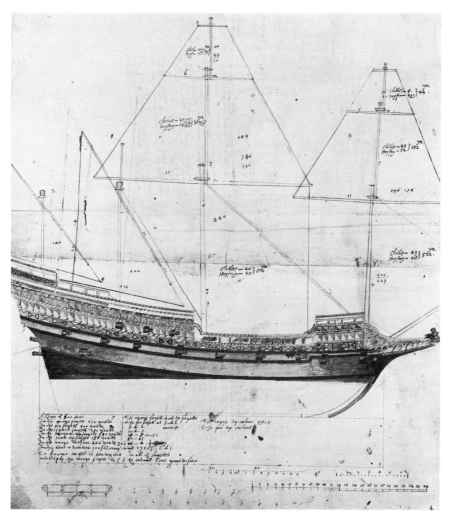

Design for a ship by Matthew Baker

CHAPTER FOUR

'Along the land of Barbaria'

14 DECEMBER 1577—31 JANUARY 1578

Drake was immediately faced with a problem: sooner or later—and probably sooner—he would have to put an end to speculation about the voyage's real objectives. The captains and, to a lesser extent, the crews would have to be won over to the idea of venturing into the unknown waters towards the nether pole and into the great South Sea where glittering prizes would be theirs for the picking. The risks were considerable and many of them were obvious; the rewards might also be immense but they were far from obvious to Drake's men. It was vitally important that the expedition should get off to a good start. There were those who were muttering that the month's delay already suffered was an ill omen and that the voyage would be 'unlucky'. Drake thought less in terms of luck and more in terms of divine favour but he knew that he needed speedily some dramatic signs of that favour—signs that would assure him of his men's complete confidence. Those signs were soon forthcoming.

As soon as the coast of Cornwall disappeared below the skyline Drake had to set the course for all the ships in the convoy. He instructed the captains to sail for the coast of Barbary and fixed Mogador (31°.30′ N, 9°.47′ W) as the rendezvous point for any ships which became separated from the fleet. This was well to the south of the Straits of Gibraltar so it was soon apparent to all that the 'Alexandria' story was a fabrication. But beyond this information the admiral revealed nothing. The moment for revelations was not yet.

The route was a familiar one to any sailors who had been on the African slave run. It was the route pioneered by Vasco da Gama in 1497 and followed ever since by Portuguese captains headed for the eastern empire and by those trading slaves and ivory along the Guinea coast. It hugged the African strand as far as the Cape Verde Islands. From that point the ways of those engaged in the African trade and those bent on the longer voyage diverged, the latter striking far out into the southern Atlantic and not making a landfall until the Cape of Good Hope was reached. Drake's instructions, therefore, did little to narrow the field of speculation about his true intentions. If anything they must have heightened the apprehensions of the crew. Might it not be that they were all headed for the white man's graveyard, the sickly, humid waters off the West

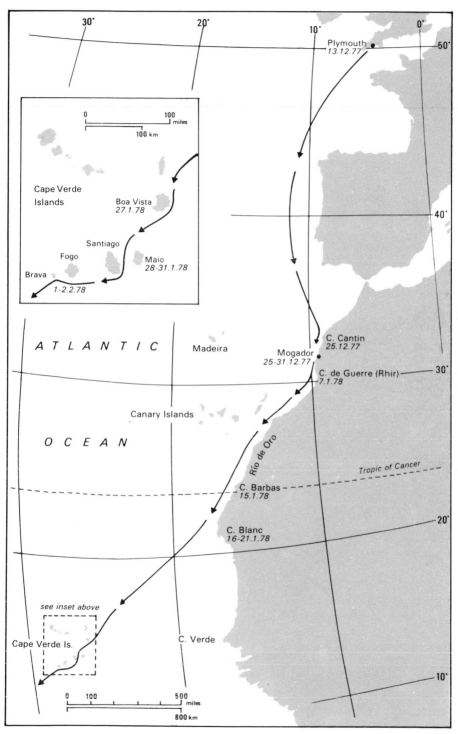

30°　　　　　20°　　　　　10°　　　　　0°

Plymouth
13.12.77　　　　50°

**Cape Verde
Islands**

0　　　　100 miles
100 km

Boa Vista
27.1.78

Santiago

Fogo

Maio
28-31.1.78

Brava

1-2.2.78

A T L A N T I C

Madeira

C. Cantin
25.12.77

Mogador
25-31.12.77

C. de Guerre (Rhir)
-7.1.78　　　　30°

Canary Islands

O C E A N

Río de Oro

Tropic of Cancer

C. Barbas
15.1.78

C. Blanc
16-21.1.78　　　　20°

see inset above

Cape Verde Is.

C. Verde

0　　　100　　　500 miles
800 km

10°

African coast, alive with evil vapours which carried fever? But there was yet another possibility, for it was from the Cape Verde Islands that Portuguese voyages bound for Brazil set out across the Atlantic.

The expedition's second beginning was very different from its first. The winds were fair and favourable and the five ships dipped steadily southwards through the long grey swell. There was time for the gentlemen to find their sea legs, for the crews to accustom themselves to shipboard routine and get the measure of their captains and masters.

Drake knew that a hundred and sixty-four pairs of eyes and ears were upon him so he took every opportunity of impressing his followers. At meal times in the great cabin he showed the gentlemen adventurers that, whatever blood or education they might boast, none was his equal in opulence and refinement. His table was laid with a service of silver edged in gold. Preserved fruits and other delicacies graced the board and ewers of perfumed water stood ready to cleanse sticky or greasy fingers. While musicians played, the diners assembled, none presuming to sit until Drake had entered and taken his place. As the meal progressed, Drake being tended by his page and his negro servant, the admiral played the gracious host, encouraging the flow of elegant conversation which ranged over every topic of interest to civilized Englishmen. While viols lilted softly in the background, he invited comments on matters connected with the voyage and the running of the ship, for Drake respected, even envied, intellectual sophistication, the gift that smooth-tongued courtiers like Thomas Doughty had of playing with words and ideas. Drake listened and considered but his ultimate decisions were his own.

The crew of the *Pelican* were regularly given the benefit of their leader's wisdom. Morning and evening they were gathered together for worship. The services were led by Francis Fletcher but often Drake preached his firm, clear-cut, Bible-based, Puritan theology. He was careful to relate divine truth to the day-to-day events on board ship. Drake was the sort of commander who exercised his authority openly, even ostentatiously. He was given to sudden storms of temper, whether genuine or feigned for effect we do not know. He was harsh in punishing offenders but did not otherwise keep the crew on a tight leash. He paid wages regularly and was always ready to listen to complaints. The men of the *Pelican* soon felt that they understood their admiral. And they did—to a far more marked degree than the gentlemen. For all Drake's sophisticated airs he was much closer in spirit to the simple mariners under his command than he would ever be to the amateur sailors of the upper deck.

The expedition made good time and on the morning of Christmas Day the golden sands and hazy mountains of 'Barbaria' were sighted. This region of Morocco was ruled from the twin capitals of Fez and Marrakech by sultans of the Sa'dian dynasty who derived their wealth from the extremely lucrative trans-Saharan trade between the Mediterranean coast

Navigating by astrolabe and cross-staff, c. *1557*

and the negro kingdoms of the western Sudan. Early in their colonising heyday the Portuguese had established forts along this shore but the tall, turbaned Muslims had long since ousted the infidels. This does not mean that the Sa'dian attitude towards Christian Europe was one of unbribled hatred; the politico-economic situation in the Maghrib was far too complex for that to be the case. The sultans relied heavily on the co-operation of their Portuguese, Spanish and Venetian trading partners. Sometimes they needed European help in fending off the attacks of the mighty Ottoman Turks, now firmly established in Algeria. However, at the time of Drake's brief visit, the Moroccans were absorbed by another problem; they were having one of their frequent civil wars. With Turkish aid 'Abdul-Malik had usurped the throne of Muhammad al-Muttawakil. The deposed sultan had appealed for help to the King of Portugal and ships from Lisbon were daily expected on the western coast. This was the situation when Drake's five vessels sailed past Cape Cantin and the port of Safi and dropped anchor in the evening off Mogador.[1]

Few English merchants and travellers had direct dealings with the Muslim kingdoms of North Africa and the Levant so Drake and his men had no idea what to expect from the inhabitants of this barren coast. Legend and phantasy made up the deficiency of knowledge. Francis Fletcher affected to believe a story of divine judgement visited upon the evil Muslims of these parts.

> ... the inhabitants being proud and exceeding all other in wickednesses, the Lord sent an army of Lions upon them, who sparing neither man, woman, nor child, but consuming all from the face of the earth, took the city in possession to themselves and their posterity to this day, whereof it is named *Civitas Leonum*.

The tale was given some support when, looking towards the shore, the ships' companies saw a group of lions come, roaring, down to the water's edge at nightfall.[2]

Having sent a boat in to take soundings Drake ordered the whole fleet to enter the wide anchorage on the morning of 27 December. There for three days the crews rested. Now there was time for a belated Christmas feast augmented by the local fish 'very wholesome but very uglie'[3] and doves and the long-winged Barbary hawks in which the scrubland abounded. Drake also ordered that one of the pinnaces which had been stowed in sections should now be assembled.

On the morning after their arrival the Englishmen saw a group of long-robed Berber tribesmen waving to them from the shore. By signs they made it clear that they wished to send a deputation aboard so Drake despatched a boat across the harbour to bring off two of their number, leaving one of his own men ashore as a pledge of good faith. It was the admiral's first opportunity to show hospitality to foreign potentates and he made them a 'dainty banquet'. The chaplain could not refrain from observing, 'It is a law amongst them to drink no wine, notwithstanding by stealth it pleaseth them well to have it abundantly.'[4] The Moroccans ate and drank their fill. They were shown over the flagship. By signs they expressed a desire to trade with the white men and they arranged a further meeting for the following day when they would bring to the shore some of the goods of their own country. But the language barrier prevented the chieftains gaining the information for which they had come aboard. These men were of 'Abdul-Malik's following and they wanted to know whether the strangers were Muhammad's Portuguese allies or whether they bore messages from King Sebastian. They smiled, they bowed, their eyes shone with welcome but all the time they were calculating the numbers of men aboard Drake's ships and assessing how well armed they were. At length, with many 'salaams' they climbed over the *Pelican*'s side, were rowed back to the beach, mounted their horses and galloped off to confer with their colleagues.

Drake, of course, was ignorant of the political implications of the visit. He congratulated himself on having established friendly relations and was pleased at the prospect of being able to buy fruit and other food from the natives. The following morning he set off early along the coast, perhaps to test the seaworthiness of the pinnace. The trade with the Moroccans he confidently left to subordinates. When, shortly afterwards, a string of some thirty well-laden camels was seen making its way down to the waterline there was no lack of volunteers for the shore party. With eager strokes the boat moved across the bay and ran onto the beach. No sooner had it done so than the air was rent with wild cries. The bewildered Englishmen saw a score or more of armed men leap from hiding places among the rocks and rush towards them. The first sailor ashore was John Fry. Before he could scramble back into the boat he was grabbed from behind and dragged, shouting and struggling, across the sand. His more fortunate colleagues managed to push the boat out into deep water. They grabbed the oars and prepared to fend off their attackers but the Moroccans made no attempt to pursue them. As the sailors watched helplessly they saw their comrade, John Fry, set upon a horse and led away among the undergrowth. The rest of the party—men, horses, camels—also turned inland. With little noise and no commotion they followed their captive and his guards. Within a couple of minutes the clouds of dust were settling upon a deserted beach.

When Drake returned he was furious at the 'perfidy' of the Muslims and not a little hurt that he had been taken in by them, but he seems to have made no attempt to follow the kidnappers.[5] To have done so would, indeed, have been futile. Mounted as they were, both captive and captors would already be miles away in a hostile and completely unknown country. For Drake to have organised a search for Fry would have been to endanger the lives of his men unnecessarily. Fry's friends and shipmates probably did

Weighing anchor

55

not see things quite the same way but they could only murmur behind the admiral's back as he gave the order to weigh anchor.*

As the ships made their way south-westwards along the coast, the men marvelled at the distant prospect of snowy peaks in the High Atlas. The offshore breezes which carried the fleet on its way were dry, hot and dusty and beyond Cape Bojador there was nothing to be seen to larboard but barren dunes.

Rounding Cape Rhir on 7 January the Englishmen caught their first sight of European shipping—three small Spanish fishing vessels, probably based in the Canaries. As soon as he had established their nationality Drake sent Wynter off in the pinnace to capture the *canteras*. The astonished fishermen surrendered without a struggle and submitted to having their vessels searched and anything of interest to the English admiral removed. Drake's men were put aboard the captured ships and for two weeks the Spaniards were forced to accompany their captors some nine hundred miles out of their way. What was the purpose of this piratical bullying? We can find several reasons, though no excuse, for Drake's action. Fresh food was always useful and the fish laboriously gathered by the Spaniards went to augment the expedition's larder. In this respect, however, the prizes were disappointing for as Captain Wynter recorded, 'these fishers did us small pleasure'.[6] At this stage of the voyage Drake probably felt that he could not afford to ignore any Spanish or Portuguese vessel he came across: their

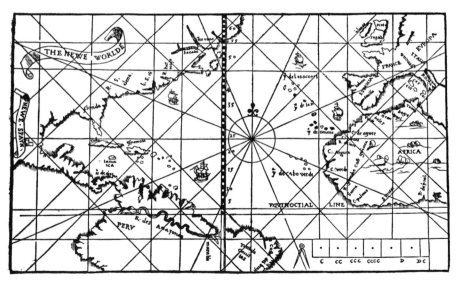

A chart of the Atlantic, 1561

*Any worry about Fry proved premature. He was treated with every courtesy and, after interrogation, conducted to the Mediterranean coast and set aboard an English ship.

captains might possess charts or rutters dealing with the trans-Atlantic and South American coastal routes which would be invaluable to him. But probably his chief motive was a desire to impress and win the confidence of his men. Let them know that he would be merciless towards the enemies and potential enemies of England; let them vent their hatred of Spain at every opportunity; let them pillage even the humblest representatives of King Philip and they would be satisfied.

It is doubtful whether all the gentlemen were impressed by the seizure of a few fishing boats. They were not squeamish; they were counting on a share of the voyage's profits and knew that most of those profits were likely to come from plunder. Yet Thomas Doughty, John Wynter and some of the others were inspired by loftier motives and were beginning to have qualms about a voyage which seemed to be degenerating into a piratical orgy or a vehicle for the expression of their admiral's obsessive Hispanophobia.

With fair winds and weather, 'as if Neptune had ben present',[7] the expedition made good time and on 16 January they sailed along the promontory of Cape Blanc and dropped anchor in its shelter. This was an important harbour for Portuguese ships plying between Europe, Guinea and the Cape Verde Islands. It was well protected from the Atlantic storms. Its waters teemed with fish. And the nomadic peoples of its barren hinterland had gold, slaves, musk and ambergris to sell cheaply. The commodity these people most lacked was fresh water and their need for it was so great that they were prepared to strike bargains which were exceedingly favourable to their trading partners. Several Portuguese ships were in harbour when Drake's expedition arrived.

What did the Portuguese make of the strange convoy—the five well-armed merchantmen, the little pinnace going before taking soundings of the entrance channel and the fishing boats bobbing in the fleet's wake like so many ducklings? They must have assumed at first that the newcomers were their countrymen or, perhaps, Spaniards. Then, when they learned the truth alarm must have spread from ship to ship. It was too late. Drake deployed his vessels strategically within the anchorage and then paid visits to each of the Portuguese ships in turn. Only one was carrying cargo of any use to him. From her hold he removed several barrels of fish and four hundredweight of biscuit.[8]

Drake needed every scrap of food he could lay hands on. Within days he would be asking his men to venture out into the unknown southern Atlantic. They would be several weeks out of sight of land—probably longer than any of the mariners had ever spent on the open sea. There would be trouble unless he could show them that they were in no danger of running out of victuals. Accordingly he gave orders that every member of the crew not engaged in other duties was to catch fish. Soon the men were leaning over the rails or sitting in the boats with their lines and nets hauling in the strange fish, gutting them, and packing them into barrels with salt. The ever-curious Chaplain Fletcher, though no draughtsman, made drawings of these strange creatures of the tropical deep.

He also had time and leisure to observe the habits and way of life of the people. He was not favourably impressed with what he saw: 'There is not to be found in all those parts of the world a more beastlike people.'[9] They worshipped the sun, they practised ritual sacrifice and, totally lacking in human decency, they carried out in public those actions about which civilised men were more reticent. This was the sort of tall story the people at home expected to hear from travellers to strange lands. Pastor Fletcher of his charity would not disappoint them. Nor did he fail to draw a moral or two from the lives of these 'savages'. They were object lessons on the wrath of God, for why else should He have made the land parched and waterless. And yet, says Fletcher, 'I prefer them before the Papist in their Religion', for the Africans made a god of the sun which, since they knew no better, was reasonable, but the Roman Catholics though they knew of God preferred to worship images.

In the midst of all this activity Drake called a meeting of the captains and the gentlemen to tell them his plans for the next stage of the voyage. It was a meeting that had to be handled with great care. John Wynter and Thomas Doughty, the only others privy to Drake's official commission, knew that their objective lay beyond the Straits of Magellan and that officially the admiral only had authority to seek out in *Terra Australis*, South America and the Moluccas uncolonised lands suitable for trade and possible settlement. Drake needed their support in overcoming the natural reluctance of the men, who were already apprehensive as they gazed at night on such unfamiliar constellations as the Southern Cross and realized that they were being taken far into the unknown. If the crews were to be persuaded to brave the open Atlantic and the notorious straits it would only be by the promise of fabulous rewards awaiting them in the lands beyond— of Spanish galleons laden with treasure which would fall into their hands as easily as unarmed Spanish fishing boats. But Wynter and Doughty were strongly opposed to unprovoked acts of piracy and had probably already intimated as much. Drake knew he could overawe his subordinates for the time being but he always had to bear in mind the future. What trouble might discontented colleagues not make for him in the royal court at journey's end? What if pro-Spanish policies were prevailing at that time? What if the Queen were dead and succeeded by a sovereign intent on *rapprochement* with Spain? There was little doubt that *sauve qui peut* would then be the order of the day; the Wynters and Doughtys of the expedition would claim that in defiance of his orders Drake had turned the voyage into a freebooting trip by making lavish promises of plunder to the men.

Secrecy and misunderstanding were partners in this voyage from the start and were to take a terrible toll before its conclusion. The wonder is they did not wreck it altogether. What did Drake tell his colleagues as they sat on the poop deck of the *Pelican*, their conversation punctuated with triumphant shouts of the fishermen? Probably no more than they needed to know—that the fleet was bound for the South Sea via Magellan's Straits. What might happen thereafter he perhaps left deliberately vague, permitting his captains to embroider on the bare facts as best they could to ensure the continued loyalty of their crews.

On 21 January, having divested themselves of the captured Spanish vessels, the fleet stood out from Cape Blanc and steered a south-westerly course for the Cape Verde Islands, the north-east trade winds obligingly filling its sails. The Portuguese caravel was forced to accompany the fleet to show the way, for its captain was bound for Santiago, the principal island of the group, and he had aboard a pilot who knew these waters well. The cluster of nine principal and several smaller isles had been in Portuguese hands for a century. By exploiting slave labour obtained from raids on the mainland, the colonists cultivated cotton, orchilla and indigo. They dug for salt on the island of Sal, raised some livestock, hunted wild cattle and goats largely for their hides and manufactured a very passable dyed cotton cloth. Some six days sailing from Cape Blanc, the islands were a very important staging post on the Portuguese slave route to Brazil, and the principal settlements were the centres of a vigorous slave market. Island-based merchants traded their merchandise with the mainland in return for captives taken in war by the Guinea coast chiefs. These were then sold to outward- or homeward-bound captains.

Coasting the dangerous rocks and shoals of Boa Vista, the travellers came to the green and friendly-looking island of Maio and sailed into the main harbour, named to this day Pôrto Inglês. Their main need now was fresh water for they had found none along the burning desert coast of Africa and, after six weeks, the water in the ships' casks was deteriorating.

A depressing spectacle met the eyes of the shore party. The few houses round the small anchorage were desolate and open to the sky. The church of St. James was the haunt only of goats and wild fowl which caused Fletcher to record, not without obvious satisfaction, that 'the best sacrifices offered ... was the dung of one and the excrements of the other'. Some of the sailors spent the night in the church before going on to explore further inland. The next day they ranged freely over the island of Maio and found it to be extremely green and pleasant. The Englishmen came serendipitously on such exotic delights as coconuts, bananas and wild grapes. Fleet-footed goats studied them suspiciously from the safety of rocky ridges and skipped away when any attempt was made to approach them. The human inhabitants of the island were just as elusive. They lived only in the remoter regions and were so frightened of their visitors that neither Drake nor his men were able to establish any contact at all with them.

The reason for all this desolation and terror was piracy. The Guinea coast was infested with sea raiders who preyed on the rich merchantmen on the African and Brazilian routes. These routes converged at Santiago, the principal Portuguese settlement in the Cape Verde Islands. The pirates found the neighbouring isle of Maio extremely convenient as a base from which to launch their attacks. It was the ferocious rapacity of these brigands that had forced the inhabitants to take to the hills.

Amongst the luxuriant tropical vegetation the explorers found the water they were searching for. According to Fletcher it was 'most sweet water bearing the taste of milk: which I conceived to be qualified from the roots of the muscadine vines.' Alas, like Tantalus, the sailors could look at the water but derive little benefit from it. The springs were in the rockiest, most inaccessible parts of the island. They made several vain attempts to carry their casks to the sources, before sweating and angry, they had to forsake their endeavour. Maio was not a tropical paradise but it had much to commend it—pleasant climate, abundant vegetation, agricultural potential. In the verdict of the expedition's chaplain we hear the voice of a nascent jingoistic colonialism:

> ...it is a thing to be lamented that so sweet fruitful and profitable a land should either be possessed by so ungrateful ungratious a people as are the Portugals: or be so subject to such caterpillars of every kingdom & nation as are pirates and thieves of the sea, but that it should be... inhabited by a people fearing the Lord to praise him for his benefits which he plentifully hath bestowed upon it...

But it was of no use to the Englishmen and Drake gave the order to weigh anchor the next morning. It must have been with heavy hearts that some of his sailors bent their backs to the windlasses.

A day's sailing brought the company to Santiago, a very different prospect to Maio, with its soaring mountains and obvious signs of Christian civilization. Prominently displayed on every cape and headland were large crucifixes. Such objects of 'papistical superstition' angered Drake and he allowed his chaplain to go ashore with a boatload of men to break one of these crosses down. This senseless iconoclasm, though cheered by many of the crew, offended others, among whom we may probably include the cultured Thomas Doughty. Soon the southerly tip of the island came in view and with it the main harbour (also known then as Santiago, though now called Praia). As suddenly came a cry from the mast head, 'Sail ho!'

Less than four miles away two westward-bound merchantmen were standing out from the harbour, Immediately Drake himself took the pinnace and went in pursuit. The lighter, faster ship made first for the farther of the two vessels and soon overhauled her. This, as events turned out, was a tactical error. The Portuguese captain offered little resistance and soon found himself a prisoner under guard in his own cabin while some of the Englishmen took over the ship and brought her round into the wind. Drake and the pinnace were quickly away in pursuit of their second quarry,

Ships attacking a Portuguese carrack

which had turned back towards the harbour. The race was furious. From the other deck-lined ships the English watched as the pinnace closed on the 100-ton caravel and as both vessels drew nearer to the harbour. The pinnace was within hailing distance of its prey when an explosion shuddered out across the water. It came from the direction of the harbour fort and a cloud of smoke drifting upwards showed that the garrison had opened fire on the pirates. The shot fell well short and for several minutes more Drake continued the pursuit. Then it became obvious that he could not secure the second prize without running too great a risk. He hove away to rejoin the fleet and gave orders to sail to the south-west.

When they were well out of sight of land Drake and some of the gentlemen went aboard the prize. They found that they had every cause to congratulate themselves on their good fortune. The *Santa Maria* of Lisbon (thereafter known as the *Mary*) was a well-found merchant ship of some 100 tons outward bound on a voyage to the colonies in Brazil and loaded to the gunwales with trade goods: '. . . singular wines: sacks & Canaries with woollens and linen clothes, silks and velvets, & many other good comodities . . .' We can, fortunately, be more specific about the *Mary*'s cargo. She had left Lisbon in November with linen, canvas, rapiers, corks, hats, skins, combs, fish-hooks, nails, billhooks, knives, scissors, olive oil, broadcloth, kersey and thread. At Las Palmas she had taken on 150 casks of

Canary wine.[10] In fact she was carrying just that sort of mixed cargo we would expect to be going to settler communities in the New World which were in constant need of manufactured goods. It was also the sort of cargo which was a godsend to mariners embarked on a long voyage—nails, cloth for extra warm clothing, canvas for repairing sails, a variety of tools and implements, a variety of foodstuffs as well as the wine. For once Fletcher was not exaggerating when he recorded that all these goods from the *Mary*, '...stood us in that stead that she was the life of our voyage the neck whereof otherwise had been broken for the shortness of our provisions'.

But the *Mary* was carrying a far more precious cargo. His name was Nuño da Silva of Oporto. He was of middle years, born and bred to the sea and one of the most experienced pilots regularly employed on the Brazil route. He was exactly the man Drake had been hoping against hope to find, for he knew full well that the next stage of his voyage—venturing into the empty unknown of the South Atlantic would be full of hazards. Drake's knowledge of the prevailing winds was scanty, his knowledge of currents negligible. Below the line celestial navigation took on an altogether different complexion; the familiar stellar signposts were replaced by others more difficult to read. Drake knew that he could probably overcome these problems and establish his latitude with reasonable accuracy but longitude was another matter altogether; it could not be accurately measured and therefore the effects of currents on a ship's progress could not be gauged. Only a few years later an expedition by Sir Richard Hawkins almost came to grief in those very South Atlantic waters.

> ...we came within five degrees of the equinoctial line, where the wind took us contrary by the south-west...and to advantage ourselves what we might, we stood to the eastwards...The next day about nine of the clock, my company being gathered together to serve God, which we were accustomed to do every morning and evening, it seemed unto me that the colour of the sea was different to that of the days past...the captain and master of my ship...made answer, that all the lines in our ships could not fetch ground: for we could not be less than three-score and ten leagues off the coast, which all that kept reckoning in ship agreed upon, and my self was of the same opinion. And so we applied ourselves to serve God, but all the time that the service endured, my heart could not be at rest...Our prayers ended, I commanded a lead and line to be brought, and heaving the lead in fourteen fathoms, we had ground, which put us all into a maze, and sending men into the top, presently discovered the land of Guinea some five leagues from us... Here is to be noted, that the error which we fell into in our accounts, was such as all men fall into where are currents that set east or west, and are not known, for that there is no certain rule yet practised for

trial of the longitude...God Almighty dealt...mercifully with us in showing us our error in the day; and in time that we might remedy it...[11]

So the little Portuguese pilot was a priceless asset to Drake. He was scarcely less of an asset to historians, for in his log and his statements later to the Inquisition he recorded details of day to day events on that incredible journey, and recorded them with the trustworthy detachment of a foreign observer. Drake treated Nuño da Silva with every courtesy and told him he could have whatever he wanted—except his freedom. The Portuguese dined at the admiral's table and had his quarters with the gentlemen. Drake spent long hours with him poring over charts and together they translated into English the pilot's charts of the Atlantic and the coast of Brazil. Very soon the two men had established a working relationship with a considerable regard for each other and long before the expedition reached Peru da Silva was fluent in English.

Drake now released his first Portuguese prize and, when this had sailed away, he set the *Mary*'s crew in the pinnace and allowed them to depart also. He redistributed his own men and gave the command of the *Mary* to Thomas Doughty, which was no more than Doughty's due as senior gentleman. Now that he was provisioned and had the help of da Silva Drake was anxious to get under way as soon as possible. But still there was the problem of water. This would have to be found somewhere in the Cape Verde Islands. The six ships sailed past Fogo whose ever-smouldering volcano rose some 10,000 feet into the sky (not the six miles that Fletcher in his journal attributed to what he called 'one of the Rare wonders of the world'). And so they came to Brava, the last island and one of the smallest in the group.

Going close in shore the travellers saw a very welcome sight—spindly rivulets of water 'falling down to the sea banks like silver streams'. The fleet dropped anchor and boats were immediately lowered with casks to be filled with the precious liquid. This done, Drake spent one more day at anchor so that all the captains could check that their ships were ready for the long crossing ahead. On 2 February,[12] after commending themselves to God, the sailors hoisted sail and steered their vessels into the unknown or, as Fletcher put it anticipating the language of early film travelogues:

> & so we take our farewell from the ancient known parts of the world or earth to travel into the new discovered parts of the world by the gracious providence of our God the God of all the world who hitherto in his singular mercy & grace had preserved us alive...

CHAPTER FIVE

'The land of demons'

1 FEBRUARY—20 JUNE 1578

On the last day of January 1578 the crews watched the wooded slopes of La Brava grow fainter until, at last, the island dipped below the clear horizon. They turned to gaze into the empty ocean ahead, and the older mariners crossed themselves, cursed their ill luck and vowed to be more devout in their prayers. For the fleet was heading south-west by south into the Torrid Zone, the Doldrums, the Devil's Sea. Drake aimed to cross the South Atlantic by the most direct route, hoping to make landfall on the coast of Brazil with as little delay as possible. But he was sailing now into a region totally unknown to him and probably unknown to all his men. He could only rely completely on the morose Nuño da Silva and trust in God that his tiny ships could struggle through the humid, airless Doldrums before all the meat was rotten and the water foul.

*The sea monster, one of the terrors of the deep in which
sixteenth-century mariners believed*

Drake's six ships wallowed across the Equator making painfully slow progress; tacking to find the faintest breath of wind; sometimes motionless for days together. Rations were cut in order to make the food and water last. Every exertion under that hot and copper sky drew out rivulets of sweat.

Yet inaction was almost as bad: the men crawling into whatever shade they could find—bored, fearful, resentful, their tongues working hard to create saliva in their parched mouths. And to the physical discomforts of the crossing were added spiritual fears. Not one of the hundred-and-sixty or so men and boys doubted that these southern seas were the haunts of demons and monsters, ghost ships and the tormented souls of mariners who had perished in the leaden waters. As they lay about the decks the older men told gruesome tales of ships lured to their fate, destroyed by sudden storms or doomed to sail an enchanted, eternal voyage across the empty pitiless sea. In such an atmosphere disagreements could quickly flare into a brawl; discontent could grow into mutiny. Slowly, imperceptibly at first, the cords of conflict tightened.

The first incident occurred before the ships left the haven of La Brava. The inevitable rift between the gentlemen and the seamen had begun. While the mariners bent their backs heaving cables and risked their necks unfurling sails from the swaying yards, the favoured gentlemen lolled on the afterdeck and even played cards with the Portuguese prisoners. Some, it was said, had taken gifts or bribes, from the captives. Rumour spread, and grew as it did so. Soon the story was going round that Master Doughty, captain of the *Mary*, the most hated of all the gentlemen, had pilfered articles from the cargo. Since a share of the loot was the only incentive the seamen had for enduring the rigours of the voyage they were enraged at the thought that one of the 'peacocks' was getting more than his entitlement. They muttered angrily among themselves and told each other that something must be done about it.

At last, John Brewer, who, as Drake's trumpeter, had some personal contact with the admiral, was egged on to report the men's suspicions. He rowed across to the *Pelican* as the ships lay at anchor at La Brava. Drake flew into one of his characteristic rages. The fact of theft was serious in itself, but in the midst of a tiny community of men under great stress, it would, as he knew, have catastrophic results. Immediately, he had himself rowed across to the *Mary* to confront Doughty with his accusers.

The elegant captain's calm was unruffled. Pilfering from the Portuguese cargo? Certainly not. In the main cabin, he laid on the table a few pairs of gloves, a ring of no great value and a handful of Portuguese coins. Was this what all the trouble was about? These trinkets were presents from one of the captives for whom he had been able to perform some small service. Should he have refused them? And, anyway, were these insignificant articles worthy of the admiral's personal attention?

Drake felt foolish. He turned on the crestfallen Brewer and castigated him for listening to gossip and bearing false accusations. When the trumpeter had been dismissed Drake apologised to Doughty and took a goblet of wine with him. Now it was the gentleman's turn to make accusations. If the admiral had come to enquire about thefts of cargo, he suggested

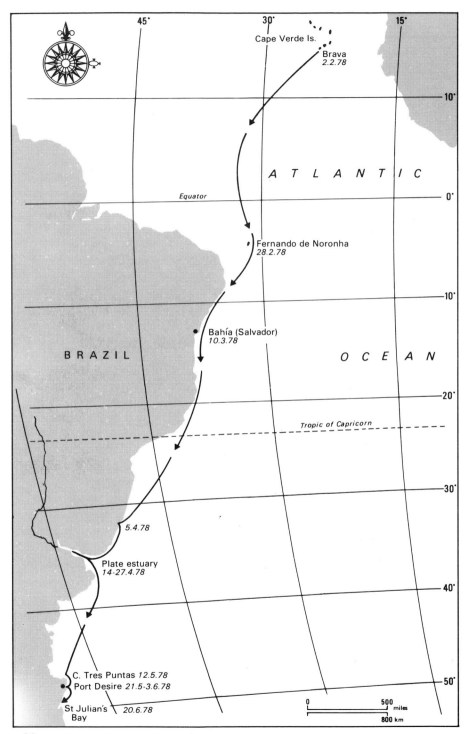

45°   30°   15°

Cape Verde Is.

Brava
2.2.78

10°

A T L A N T I C

Equator   0°

Fernando de Noronha
28.2.78

10°

Bahía (Salvador)
10.3.78

O C E A N

20°

Tropic of Capricorn

B R A Z I L

30°

5.4.78

Plate estuary
14-27.4.78

40°

C. Tres Puntas *12.5.78*
Port Desire *21.5-3.6.78*

50°

St Julian's
Bay   *20.6.78*

0   500 miles

800 km

diffidently, perhaps he should know that a charge, as yet unproved, had been made against a member of the *Mary*'s company. His name? Drake demanded. Doughty hesitated. The admiral must realise that nothing had been proved; that was why Doughty had not reported the man. Again Drake asked for the name, looking hard at Doughty past the cabin lantern swinging above the table. 'His name is Thomas Drake, your brother.'

The admiral was trapped. Having indignantly demanded an explanation from Doughty, he dared do no less with Thomas. The young man was called to answer the charges against him. To Drake's intense relief the accusation proved as groundless as that alleged against Doughty. The crisis had passed, but Drake knew that worse would follow if he could not disperse this atmosphere of accusation and counter-accusation. He decided to separate the contending parties. Doughty was sent to the *Pelican* and placed in charge of the gentlemen adventurers. It was a wise move, for it relieved the troublesome courtier of command over seamen without offering him any public slight. Drake himself remained on the *Mary*, as did his brother. With the admiral in command of the prize vessel there would be no likelihood of pilfering.

Solving problems quietly and unemotionally was not Drake's forte but in this instance he showed remarkable skill in taking the heat out of a situation. His wisdom deserved a more lasting success than it, in fact, achieved.

The ships creaked their sluggish way across the glassy calm of the Atlantic, their crews dispirited and fearful. But Thomas Doughty was far from dispirited. He was the hero of the gentlemen adventurers. He had stood up to the admiral—that lowborn, bumptious mariner—and had prevailed. Far from controlling the gentlemen he set them an example of swaggering braggadocio. He scoffed openly at Drake's recent discomfiture and boasted of the important—nay vital—part he, Doughty, had played in the organisation of the expedition. He regaled his friends with stories of how he obtained the backing of powerful men at court and pointed out, in case they did not know, that he was a friend and confidant of the great Lord Burghley himself. Whereas, this fellow Drake—who was he? A nobody completely reliant on the support of his social superiors. Moreover, Doughty assured his colleagues with nods and winks, he knew things about the admiral which would shock and amaze them. Of course, loyalty forbade him revealing any of Drake's guilty secrets, but he was by no means the straightforward, honest, Christian man he pretended to be. Scarcely a mealtime passed aboard the *Pelican* without jests and gibes being circulated at the expense of Francis Drake and his cloddish, wooden-headed sailors.

One day, as the vessels wallowed idly in a sultry calm, an opportunity for personal revenge and also for a capital joke against Drake presented itself. The admiral sent a routine message across to the *Pelican* and his chosen spokesman was John Brewer. Doughty and his friends saw the messenger approach. 'Here comes Master Brewer who trumpets loud and untrue!' 'Let's give him a welcome befitting so important a visitor.' 'A cobbey!' 'Yes let's give him a cobbey.' Laughing like a gang of bullying schoolboys, the gentlemen ordered the crew to assemble to meet the admiral's messenger.

When Brewer clambered over the gunwale he was confronted by the gentlemen in a semicircle and behind them the rest of the crew drawn up in two lines. He glanced nervously round. Then Thomas Doughty stepped forward and with an exaggerated bow, welcomed the visitor aboard. Brewer began falteringly to announce his business when a shout went up from one of the gentlemen, 'A cobbey!' With a whoop the others took up the cry. Brewer was seized by two embarrassed-looking sailors. His struggles and curses were in vain; the gnarled fingers bit into the flesh of his arms and neck, and forced him to bend over a barrel in the centre of the deck. Eager hands pulled his breeches down. Then, one by one, the entire company beginning with Doughty belaboured Brewer's buttocks, while he gritted his teeth so as not to give his tormentors the added satisfaction of hearing him cry out.

At last Doughty called off the pack. Brewer faced him. 'God's wounds, Doughty!' he shouted. 'Why do you treat me thus? You had better take care; the admiral knows you are not his friend.'

Doughty laughed in the man's face. 'What, fellow John, why do you use these words to me? I am as good and sure a friend of the admiral as any man in this fleet and I defy anyone who says otherwise.' A sarcastic sneer spread over his tanned features. He forced his voice into plaintive whine. 'But if what you say is true, fellow John, oh, I pray you, let me live to see England again.'

There was a roar of appreciative laughter from Doughty's cronies and with much cheering and backslapping they retired to the afterdeck. Brewer made his uncomfortable way back in the *Mary*'s yawl to report the incident to his master. He found the admiral in the grip of anxiety and frustration. Drake was worried about the effects of inactivity and lack of progress on the men. Every few minutes he cast his eyes aloft to the pennants at the masthead but there was no sign of motion. It would have taken far less than the trumpeter's story to set his temper aflame. Drake was not averse to sailors' horseplay. He had himself suffered the cobbey and helped to administer it on several occasions. But there was more than boredom or high spirits behind this affront to his messenger. The gentlemen were showing their contempt for the sailors and the Doughty faction—for that is what it was becoming—were cocking a snook at the admiral. A team of sailors were hauling the yawl inboard. Drake yelled at them to stop. Within minutes the boat was on its way back to the *Pelican* bearing a request that Thomas Doughty would report immediately to the admiral.

By the time the yawl was on its way back, Drake had cooled down. Once again reason prevailed. The admiral decided he would not risk precipitating a crisis by taking retaliatory action. Rather he would remove the troublesome gentleman to a place where he could do little harm. Meanwhile, the day's routine must not be broken. It was now time for the evening service and Drake called the crew together.

Some minutes later he was reading aloud from the Geneva Bible when the yawl bumped alongside. Doughty stood up and siezed hold of the *Mary*'s bulwarks to pull himself aboard. Scarcely pausing in his recitation, Drake called out, 'Stay there, Thomas Doughty, I must send you to another place.' He gave quick instructions to the oarsmen and continued his reading from the word of God. The *Mary*'s crew pretended to listen to the edifying Scriptures and furtively watched the humilated Doughty being rowed across to the *Swan*, the expedition's 50 ton supply ship.

Day followed oppressive day and there was no sign of land. Occasional rain storms helped to eke out the fresh water supply but every man was on short rations. It was this lack of food which gave occasion to yet another quarrel involving Doughty. That gentleman's tongue was now completely unbridled. Angry at Drake's ingratitude and the way he had been humiliated, he made no effort to conceal his feelings. Mealtimes in the after cabin became embarrassing affairs for the other officers. One of them, John Saracold, at last could stand Doughty's complaining no longer. 'The admiral might do well to deal with traitors as Magellan did—hang them up as an example to the rest,' he said. Fifty-eight years before the great Portuguese pioneer had run into a mutiny while his ships were harboured at Port St Julian on the coast of Argentina and had dealt swiftly and ruthlessly with the ringleaders. The incident had made naval history, and the spot where Magellan had meted out justice was still known as Gallows Point. It was this to which Saracold was alluding, with meaningful glances at Doughty. The gentleman was not impressed.

'Nay, softly!' he said, 'Drake's authority is not as great as Magellan's. I know his authority as well as he does himself and it does not extend to hanging.'

At that point the master jumped to his feet.

'By God, Master Doughty, I'll not stay to hear such talk. In future I mess with the men. I prefer the company of honest seamen.' So saying he left the cabin.

The master was as good as his word. But not only did he take his meals with the crew, he also used his position to gain extra victuals at the expense of the officers and gentlemen. Doughty could not have more effectively formented a dispute between the upper and lower decks if he had tried.

But life was not all tension and stress aboard Drake's vessels. There was much to interest and amaze those who had not travelled in these waters before. The strangest phenomenon was the flying fish.

Among the fishes of the sea, my opinion is that none are to be compared

Francis Fletcher's drawing of flying fish made during the voyage and later incorporated in his account of the journey

to this kind in freedom from corruption and slimy nature, and so in wholesomeness and purity of substance. The cause whereof I gather to be, their continual exercise and water and air; for in the seas they are for the most part pursued by the shoals of the dolphins, and bonitos are the chief whereof they live. So that if they have not another help by nature than to swim in the water, they were like to be consumed in a short time out of their kind, having such mighty and devouring enemies, by means whereof they are inforced to practise their flying in the air to free themselves from so present danger, which otherwise they could not scape; whose flight is wonderful both for swiftness and height, for it is equal to a pigeon in both, as also in distance or length; for it is at least a quarter of a mile at a time.'[1]

Many of these strange creatures fell onto the decks of the ships and the sailors discovered that by using them as bait they could catch dolphins and bonitos (striped tunny fish).

Another source of both interest and food was the sea birds which preyed upon the flying fish. For hours on end the travellers watched the lazy gyrations of these graceful creatures as they spiralled far up into the blue then swooped, hawk-like, to attack a shoal of flying fish skimming over the water's surface. It was not difficult to believe the story da Silva told about the birds. According to him they flew high into the sky in order to sleep. As they slumbered with wings outspread, their weight brought them slowly downwards until the proximity of the waves awoke them, when they climbed once again into the upper air. Sitting and watching these antics from the shaded areas of the deck, the sailors devised ways of snaring and netting the birds and succeeded in killing quite a few.

70

Flying fish and their predators—porpoises and sea birds

Not quite so diverting were the sudden, violent thunderstorms which punctuated the long, sultry days and nights. As the sky reverberated from side to side with the explosive peals and the forks of lightning shafted into the ocean, the old legends about devil-haunted seas seemed all too credible. The storms did, however, sometimes bring rain-water which was a welcome relief from the stale liquid in the ships' casks which had to be gulped down quickly so as not to leave a foul taste in the mouth.

Thanks to Nuño da Silva's expert navigation and experience of the South Atlantic the expedition was able to take advantage of every suitable wind and current. By the middle of March they were running southwards parallel with the coast of Brazil but well off shore and out of sight of land. Here the pilot's honesty was put firmly to the test. Drake wanted to find a landfall as soon as possible. Left to himself he would have run close inshore looking for a suitable bay. Nuño da Silva warned him against this course of action, pointing out on the charts the ports such as Bahía where Portuguese galleys were based. So, with the men increasingly fretful, Drake kept a constant course.

It was about three o'clock on the afternoon of 5 April that the long-awaited cry of 'land-ho' rang out from the crow's nest on the *Pelican*'s foremast. They were now in $31\frac{1}{2}$ degrees of latitude and admiral and pilot were agreed that it was safe to seek an anchorage. As the crew strained their eyes towards the land they saw a pleasant green strand edged with silver sand. Before long a friendly bay came into view. Now the mood of the men changed completely. They went cheerfully about their duties and some broke into song, for they knew they had safely crossed the Devil's Sea and come to haven without being sucked into mysterious whirlpools or attacked by monsters of the satanic deep.

The sea serpent

Rejoicing proved to be premature. They were within hailing distance of the shore when they were suddenly engulfed in a *pampero*, a sudden hazy fog for which those regions are notorious. Within minutes they were in a very dangerous plight. They were being swept onto an invisible lee shore and soundings with lead and line told them that the water was shoaling rapidly. With deceptive calm Nuño da Silva gave his orders. Slowly the *Pelican* came round. By shouting to the other vessels as they drifted in and out of the fog the whole fleet managed to follow the same course. At last, they reached open sunlit water but not before one of the ships had scraped her bottom on a sand bank.

Later that day, probably at supper in the great cabin, Drake questioned da Silva about this extraordinary weather. The Portuguese name for this region, the pilot replied, was the Land of Demons. The local people were powerful magicians who had preserved their independence from Portugal by calling up sudden fogs, by moving sandbanks and by hurling off-shore winds of hurricane force at the invaders. They sent spirits aboard unfamiliar ships to sieze them by the rigging and pull them on to rocks and shoals.

As if to support the pilot's tales the expedition now ran into two weeks of atrocious weather. Intermittent storms and fogs descended on them. They were scarcely heartened to obtain occasional glimpses of the shore and to observe groups of natives lighting fires on the beach. Da Silva assured his host that these men were making sacrifices to their gods, doubtless with the object of calling down fresh terrors on the strange ships. Very early on the *Christopher* was lost to sight and for days the *Pelican*, *Mary* and *Swan* cruised back and forth looking for her. The search could not continue indefinitely. The need to find an anchorage was now urgent and Drake ordered the fleet to make for the Plate estuary. This they reached on 14 April. They sailed well into the wide mouth of the river and eventually anchored off a promontory. They had scarcely arrived when the *Christopher* came sailing in after them. Drake's relief knew no bounds. He had feared the ship and its crew lost, either foundered on the fog-shrouded rocks or destroyed by the fearful Patagonian giants said to inhabit these regions. Such a loss and the resultant blow to general morale might have proved disastrous to the expedition. He, therefore, gave the nearby promontory a new name on his chart—Cape Joy.

Sheltered now from the foul weather outside, Drake's ships travelled further up the estuary, seeking fresh water. On 19 April they stopped in the bay of Montevideo, largely because a colony of seals was observed on a rocky island offshore. Ever eager for fresh meat, boatloads of sailors rowed to the island and began chasing the ungainly creatures. They did not have an easy time of it. Though largely defenceless against humans the seals had a way of scuffing up sand and stones with their flippers into the faces of their pursuers. Nor did the seamen find the animals, with their thick coat of protective blubber, easy to kill. Fletcher came to the opinion that the only sure way of despatching them was to hit them on the nose with a club. However, large numbers of seals were eventually caught. The men found their meat very good and the oil extracted from their blubber was very soothing when applied to sores and other external wounds, 'whereof', says Fletcher, 'divers of our men had good experience by my directions to their great comfort.'

Seals were not the only item of interest found in this bay.

Upon the mainland above this rock, we chanced with a plant very rare and strange to all herbals which I have seen in any language, having but one leaf, and the stem rising in the midst, with the fruit on either side of the stem and round about the edges of the leaf; the leaf is a gross and thick substance, at the least a hand's breadth, or rather half a foot, and in height more or less than half a yard; of the one side green and full of white specks, as the belly of a toad, and the other perfect green and freyed over with a kind of whitish small down or cotton, full of pricks of a poisoned nature, which, being but touched come off, and being touched of any cloak, convey themselves into it so close that they cannot be got out again: if they come to touch their body they convey their poison into the pores of the skin, and work there a most vile effect, raising red and fiery pimples, with extreme itching and burning, to the tormenting of the body in some extremity till they have consumed their full poison: wherewith divers of our men were mightily afflicted; for the fruit being pleasant they gathered abundance of it to bring on shipboard, and putting them in their bosoms within their shirts, or in their pockets, and some in their hats, they had sour sauce with their sweet meat, the fruit being wholesome.[2]

Passing further up the river the ships eventually found themselves in three fathoms of fresh water. At last Drake was able to refill the water casks.

Spanish map of America, 1562

But there was nowhere on the estuary to carry out other important tasks, such as the careening and repairing of the ships. Wind, tide and sandbanks permitted of no safe anchorage. Thus, on 27 April the voyagers put to sea once more.

No sooner had the fleet set sail again than a sudden storm sprang up. Sea and ships were lashed by a fierce off-shore tempest carrying stinging grains of sand which tore clothes and cut skin as the sailors scrambled aloft taking in sail. For a day and a night the hurricane raged. From the *Pelican* (to which Drake's flag had been restored) the storm lanterns of the other vessels were occasionally visible, but every ship was fighting its own battle with the wild, raging sea and when the tempest died as quickly as it had come to life the fleet was scattered once more. The *Pelican* went about to search for the others. Within hours all the vessels were accounted for except the *Swan*. At nightfall Drake called off the search. It was no longer possible to spend days looking for a missing ship; the food situation was desperate. The dried pork had been jettisoned days ago when its smell had become intolerable. The salt beef was almost inedible. The men had taken to saving their rations of biscuit until nightfall so that they could not see the worms. The cheese was finished and for weeks the only hot meal (apart from lucky catches of fish or fowl) had been lentil soup. Drake knew that they must find safe anchorage from which they could go in search of fresh vegetables, fruit and meat. Anyway, he mused, if the *Swan* had foundered or turned back one of his most pressing problems would have been solved.

But the *Swan* had neither foundered nor turned back and the Doughty problem was growing worse. The gentleman and the master were still at loggerheads over the issue of food. Doughty tried to enlist the support of Captain John Chester. He pointed out that now that the *Swan* was on her own there was a very real danger of starvation. Moreover, if the master had his way it would be the men of the after deck who died first.

'I marvel, Mr Chester,' he said, 'that you will submit to being so abused by him, since you are in command here.'

But the captain would not be drawn, and Doughty confronted the master once more.

'If you continue to show this partiality the admiral shall hear of it. I know that you hate the gentlemen and that is why you are happy to see us starve while you and your simple seamen eat your fill.'

'Gentlemen!' the seaman spat on the deck at Doughty's feet. 'Idle peacocks and villains more like! If you don't like your rations, go and take the thole pins from the boats. They are good enough for the likes of you.'

'Have a care, my man, I have a share in this venture and were it not for me the admiral would still be wandering the streets of Plymouth looking for money and ships. For that alone I deserve to be as well fed as the rest of you.'

The master flew into a rage.

'If you come safe home at the end of this venture I'll be hanged. You are the foulest traitor that ever cursed any ship.'

He strode away and Doughty went straight back to the captain.

'Master Chester, you cannot allow this knave to treat us in this way. Bring him to heel and you have my sword and many others to support you if there is any trouble.'

Chester had little sympathy for the master who had acted in a foolish and headstrong manner; but he had no sympathy whatsoever for the troublesome Doughty. It was Doughty's fault that the master had been goaded into his absurd attitude over the ship's rations; and the intransigent mariner still refused to change his mind. Chester was determined not to fall into the same trap; he would not allow Doughty to provoke him into an armed conflict aboard ship which could only have disastrous results.

It was not only in direct encounter with the *Swan's* superiors that Doughty showed his mounting anger and frustration. In every casual conversation with gentlemen, officers and crewmen he stressed his importance, his influence and his power. Perhaps he also intimated that his power was not limited to this world. Both he and his brother John (also aboard the *Swan*) boasted that they could 'Conjure as well as any man and that they could raise the devil and make him to meet any man in the likeness of a bear, a lion, or a man in armour.' There is little doubt that such loose remarks were widely believed by the intensely superstitious crewmen. They were quite ready to attribute the storms, the fogs and the other misfortunes which beset them to the 'Jonah' in their midst.

It was only with the greatest difficulty that Captain Chester kept the crew of his lonely and unhappy ship at their labours. He planted trusted mariners on every watch. If men gathered together in muttering groups he was quick to disband them and he kept the *Swan* always in sight of land. It was impossible to separate Doughty and the master within the narrow confines of the ship but he did his best to cool their tempers. He knew full well that a situation could easily arise which would give one or other of the contenders the leadership of a mutinous minority of his discontented men. As day followed day, Chester watched anxiously for some sign of the fleet but there was nothing to see except empty ocean and friendless coastline. How much longer, he wondered, could he force the crew to take the ship farther southwards, farther from home.

The situation was scarcely better aboard the other ships. Squalls and fog continued to separate them from each other, and the need to find fresh food was now desperate. Every time a promising bay or creek was sighted on that uncharted coast Drake had the *Pelican* brought close inshore. Every time the ship had to stand out to sea again because of hidden rocks, shoals or unfriendly natives. Then, on 12 May, he spied a wooded headland which reached its long curving arm towards the sea. Within the crook of that arm lay a wide harbour from which the land sloped gently into misty hills. It looked ideal. Drake ordered the fleet to drop anchor and had his boat lowered. With a small group of well-armed men he was rowed towards the shore. There was no sign of life and the only sounds were the cries of sea birds and the welcome liquid notes of a stream falling through the tangle of vegetation ahead. The bay was wide and the entrance channel seemed deep enough for the ships. As he gazed around Drake's optimism blossomed anew. Then he suddenly realized that the wooded slopes ahead were disappearing as the mist became a fog which rolled rapidly forward. Now he could not see the breakers. He shouted an order. The rowers back-paddled and turned the prow seaward. They had not pulled half a dozen strokes towards the ship before the fog engulfed them. And with the fog came a fresh wind. Suddenly they were quite helpless. Rocked by the growing waves they could only keep the boat head on to the weather and strain their ears for the awful sound of waves breaking on rock.

For half an hour they endured the buffeting of the elements, their clothes soaked, their eyes sore with peering through the fog. Then there came a sudden shout from seemingly close at hand. 'Ahoy!' As one man the boat's crew raised an answering shout. The disembodied call was repeated and Drake ordered the oarsmen to row towards it. Suddenly a dark mass loomed out of the pervading grey cloud. It was the *Marigold* nosing cautiously into the harbour.

The resourceful Captain Thomas of the 30 ton vessel had seen Drake's boat engulfed by the fog. Without hesitation he had weighed anchor and taken the *Marigold* inshore. It was a courageous action for he was sailing blind onto an unknown shore and had taken no soundings of the harbour entrance. The desperate gamble deserved to succeed and it did. The admiral and his companions went aboard the *Marigold* and spent the night safe within the harbour. The other ships' companies were not so fortunate. Being on a lee shore they had to beat out into the weather. By daybreak, when the storm had abated and the fog dispersed, they were scattered over the ocean miles from the haven. The *Marigold*'s crew built and lit beacons on the headland and over the next few hours the fleet re-convened and got under way again.

Within a couple of days they had been separated yet again. The two larger vessels, the *Pelican* and the *Elizabeth*, kept together, as did the *Marigold* and the *Christopher*. The *Mary* found herself quite alone and there was still no sign of the *Swan*. Once again it was Captain Thomas who took the initiative. On 14 May he discovered a fine natural harbour at 47°45'. So ideal was it that he called it Port Desire and anchored there. From this base the *Marigold* and the *Christopher* sallied forth each day in search of the other vessels. To everyone's surprise the first ship they found on the 16th was the *Swan*. Captain Chester was immensely relieved to drop anchor in the sheltered waters of Port Desire, to allow his men ashore and to share his problems with his colleagues on the other vessels.

'Port Desire', never had haven been more aptly named. The terrain was wild and rocky but there was fresh water and there were seals and birds in abundance. Within three days the entire fleet had gathered at the anchorage and the men were soon busy replenishing the ships' larders and carrying out necessary repairs. Two of the ships were beached for careening and re-caulking. Another, the unhappy *Swan,* had reached the end of its voyage. Drake was exasperated at the delays caused by trying to keep his fleet together and had decided to reduce its size. So the *Swan* was emptied of everything of any use, all her metal fittings were removed and her crew dispersed among the other ships. Then she was towed to the middle of the harbour and burned.

Here the travellers obtained their first real glimpse of the Patagonian 'giants'. Popular legend, reinforced by da Silva, attributed enormous size to these people. Fletcher, never one to miss a good story, said nothing to contradict this belief:

> ... their legs are all calves down to the ankles whose feet are like shovels & their hands like shoulders of mutton their ears most large & eyes in compass to a great hard bowl or ball or the inmost circle of a reasonable saucer their brows like the forehead of an elk. & under their chins a bag reaching to their breasts as if it were stuffed with bombast so that a camel should have much ado to carry one of them any long way.[3]

John Wynter in the brief mention he accorded the natives in his log was much more objective:

> Here I saw first this people which they call Giants, which indeed be not at all, though being afar off, for the greatness of their voice a man would think them so. Here six or seven of us went to see them, being a mile from us, because we would make true report of them, what people they are. The which we came nearer to them seemed rather to be Devils than men.[4]

Most of the Patagonian Indians were shy but one day a group of thirty or so came down to the beach and the Englishmen managed to establish contact. Drake's men offered rings, beads and other trinkets which the Indians seemed pleased to receive. Drake had his trumpeter and musicians play and this amused the natives so much that they began to dance, John Wynter joining in with them. One of them was so playful (or thieving) that he snatched from Drake's head a scarlet and gold cap the admiral was wearing. It was very jolly and friendly and Drake hoped that all the 'terrible giants' would prove to be so innocuous. These Indians were scantily clothed with skins, the rest of their bodies being painted, and they carried bows and arrows. The visitors were obviously able to examine the Indians quite closely for Fletcher made drawings of their arrowheads, fire sticks and musical instruments.[5]

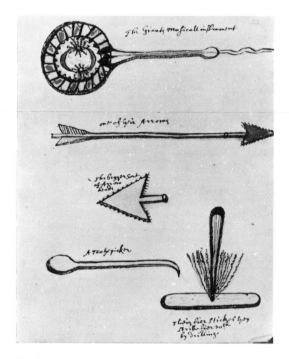

Tools and weapons of the Patagonian 'giants' according to Fletcher

This area yielded the expedition more fresh meat, most of which came from birds. The rhea (South American ostrich) was plentiful and, as Fletcher informs us, one should only eat 'the legs which are bigger than the greatest legs of mutton in the province of Peru [he is probably referring to Llama meat] & the meat thereof is equal to any red deer...'[6] A little farther down the coast there was another inlet swarming with sea birds which the sailors found,

> a store house of victuals for a king's army. for such was the infinite store of eggs, & birds that there was no footing upon the ground but to tread upon the one or the other. or both at every step. yea the birds was so thick & would not remove that they were enforced with cudgells & swords to kill them to make way to go & the night drawing on the fowls increased more & more so that there was no place for them to rest in. Nay every third bird could not find any room in so much that they sought to settle themselves upon our heads shoulders arms & all parts of our body they could in most strange manner without any fear. yea they were so speedy to place themselves upon us that one of us was glad to help another & when no beating with poles, cudgels swords. & daggers would keep them off from our bodies we were driven with our hands to pull them away one from another till with pulling & killing we fainted. & could

not prevail but were more & more overcharged with feathered enemies. whose cries were terrible & there powder & shot poisoned us unto even death if the sooner we had not retired & given them the field for the time. we therefore taking with us sufficient victual for the time present took fitter opportunity of time the next day. & at all other times to take revenge upon so barbarous adversaries & to weaken their power.[7]

During the two and a half weeks spent at Port Desire the admiral heard many versions of the trouble centring around the person of Thomas Doughty. He did not know what to do about the man. Doughty was a nuisance but was he anything more? Drake had already humiliated him; there was little else he could do. It was unthinkable to flog him like a common seaman: such action would have gone quite against the universally respected social distinctions of the age. And Drake always had to remember that Doughty did have important connections. There was considerable truth in the courtier's frequent taunt 'When we come back to England you will need me more than you will need any reward from this voyage.' Yet, on the other hand, Drake was committed first and foremost to the success of his venture. He had to ask himself, and often did so, 'Is Doughty a threat to my plans?' Soon they would be facing the terrors of Magellan's Straits. No Englishman had ever battled with the fabled, notorious storms of that passage or ventured into the unknown terrors beyond. It would be difficult enough to force his men to face these hardships; if there was a leader around whom malcontents could gather the whole expedition might peter out in dismal failure. Drake contemplated a 'final solution' to the Doughty problem but put the idea instantly from his mind. Instead he made it quite clear that the gentleman was still excluded from his confidence by assigning him to the *Christopher* the smallest member of the fleet, and by giving command of the *Christopher* to Doughty's enemy, Gregory, master of the *Swan*.

Doughty was by now bent upon challenging the admiral's authority. During the stay at Port Desire he put himself at the head of a deputation. He and his supporters came up to Drake on the *Pelican*'s main deck, demanding to know who Drake's deputy was; who would take over in the event of anything happening to the admiral. Only recently, they argued, he had been nearly drowned and many of their companions had already succumbed to fever and the bloody flux (dysentery). It was unreasonable of the admiral to make no provision for their future if the worst should happen. Drake was by now sufficiently wary of Doughty to realise that there was some subtle trap in his apparent concern for the success of the venture. For the moment he could not understand what was in the gentleman's scheming mind so he took refuge in a display of temper. Increasingly he found this a useful stratagem: it kept alive the awe and respect of the men and it gave him time to think. In a torrent of words which drove the deputation from the deck he upbraided them for their presumption. He

80

and he alone, Drake shouted, would make such important decisions; he needed no prompting from empty-headed popinjays and stupid sea-dogs.

Later, in his cabin, Drake reflected on Doughty's latest move and realised just how subtle it was. First of all the gentleman had already obtained a following among the men. Doubtless he had promised them that if they looked to him for leadership he would turn the ships round and get them all safely home. Had not one of Magellan's ships deserted in these very waters? It was clear that Doughty had his own reasons for wishing to frustrate the real purpose of the voyage. Probably he was working for Burghley, as Drake had once suspected. Doughty's approach had been so calculated as to force Drake into a dilemma. If he had named a deputy Doughty would have turned his attention to that man and tried on him the flattery and lies with which he had once beguiled Drake. If he refused to name an admiral elect Doughty could tell his followers that their leader cared nothing for their welfare, that he was only concerned with driving them as hard as possible in the pursuit of personal ambition and wealth. So indeed, it turned out. The next day Drake kept a careful eye on Doughty from the poop. He saw him going from group to group of men as they worked. Some paid no attention but an alarming number set their tasks aside and talked earnestly with him, risking the lash of the bosun's tongue—or worse—for slacking. Drake was afraid and, since fear was an emotion he despised, he was fiercely angry—with himself and with the man who had betrayed him into tasting fear. In a rage he descended to the main deck and confronted Doughty. But his angry demand to know why Doughty was interfering with the men's work failed to move the supercilious smile from the courtier's face. 'Very well' said Drake, 'we will see to it that you can meddle no more. You there!' He summoned two sailors, 'Fetch a rope and tie this gentleman to the main mast.'

This, at last, unlocked the finely polished lid and freed Doughty's fury. A stream of oaths and personal abuse poured from him as he was dragged struggling away. For two days he was lashed to the *Pelican*'s mast, an object of scorn and ridicule to all, only being released to sleep. He was set free when the fleet was ready to sail but he was not a whit subdued by his experience. He now refused point blank to rejoin the *Christopher*. With Gregory and his cronies aboard, he said, his life would be in constant danger. He raged, argued and pleaded in a most unseemly fashion for almost an hour. At last Drake ordered the boat tackle to be prepared so that Doughty could be bound and lowered ignominiously on to the deck of the canter. It was obviously no empty threat so Doughty shrank from this further humiliation and clambered over the side with what little dignity he could muster.

Problems now multiplied for the admiral. Despite every attempt to keep together, the ships of the fleet were immediately scattered by bad weather. More important than that, the crisis point of the entire voyage was almost upon him. They were only days away from the Straits of Magellan, the

Navigating by compass and quadrant

hazards of which were unknown and terrifying. Another difficulty drew just
as inexorably closer; the moment when Drake would have to take the entire
company into his confidence and reveal the real objectives of the voyage.
That moment would give Doughty his opportunity to point out he had
been right all along—Drake was bent on leading the men into all manner
of dangers and they would be unlikely ever to see their homes and loved
ones again if they followed him.

Drake thought much about his predecessor, Ferdinand Magellan, during
those anxious days. The *Pelican* was almost off Port St Julian where the
Portuguese pioneer had faced the main crisis of his great voyage. His entire
company was divided between those loyal to himself and the supporters of a
handful of malcontents who wanted to turn back. A running fight ensued
and valuable lives were lost. When Magellan sailed away from Port St
Julian he left the remains of Luis de Mendoza and Gaspar de Quesada
swinging from gibbets on Gallows Point. Was history about to repeat itself?
Drake forced the idea from his mind and gave all his attention to the
problem of regrouping the fleet. He turned the *Pelican* northwards and
went in search of his missing ships. It was the last time, he resolved, that
he would allow time to be wasted in this way. To minimise the risk of

ships getting lost again (or of their crews deliberately deserting the expedition) the fleet must be further reduced.

The first ship to be scuttled was the little *Christopher*. This immediately raised once more the problem of what was to be done with Doughty. The latest news was that he had been trying to bribe members of the canter's crew, offering one man £100 and another £50 for their support. Drake decided to house the miscreant on the *Elizabeth* but first he went aboard himself and summoned the whole crew together. He warned them that he was about to commit to their charge a couple of evil men. Thomas Doughty was a 'conjurer and very seditious lewd fellow'. His brother John was little better, 'a witch and a poisoner, the devil's own offspring'. No one was to speak to them and they were not to be allowed to read or write. Having thus prepared the *Elizabeth*'s company he sent the Doughtys across to her, rejoined his flagship and then went in search of the still missing *Marigold*. He found her at last on 19 June. The next day Drake led his little fleet to safe haven—in Port St Julian or, as it was also called, St Julian's Bay.

CHAPTER SIX

'The Island of Blood'

21 JUNE—2 JULY 1578

Port St Julian was the last anchorage on that desolate coast before the Straits were reached. A place of jagged rock, grey sky and frugal verdure, it breathed an atmosphere of violence and despair. And violence reached out to meet them. As soon as they had anchored Drake set out for the shore. He took with him his brother, John Brewer, Oliver his gunner and Robert Winterhey, one of the gentlemen. They all wore part armour and carried weapons, but they also bore presents with which to establish friendly relations with any natives they chanced to meet.

They had not advanced more than a few paces up the beach when six young Patagonians emerged from the rocks ahead. They were tall impressive warriors, each armed with a bow and arrows but their intentions were obviously friendly. Drake handed over the presents which were received with great excitement. Guests and hosts were soon conversing in sign language and when one of the Patagonians pointed to the bow which Winterhey was carrying the gentleman loosed a shaft along the beach. Laughing the young native did the same, his arrow slightly out-distancing the Englishman's. Within minutes a good-natured contest was in full swing.

It came to a sudden stop. With angry shouts a second group of Patagonians were making their way down the beach—older men whose frowns and gestures were far from welcoming. It was clear that they wanted the visitors to return to their ships. The Englishmen stood frozen, uncertain, on the shingle. Then Winterhey made a move. He fitted a fresh arrow to his bow. Probably he was intending only to continue nonchalantly with the contest but the action looked distinctly hostile. Drake called out but in the same instant the string of Winterhey's bow snapped. The aggressive gesture, the shout, the mishap, dispelled any uncertainty the Patagonians might have felt. Young and old ran together, charging their bows. A shower of arrows clattered among the stones around the Englishman and Winterhey fell backwards clutching his chest.

Between Drake's men and the boat there were fifty yards of empty beach with not a scrap of cover. Headlong flight would invite certain disaster. As usual, danger cleared Drake's mind. He called out a string of urgent, authoritative commands. As the fusillade of arrows continued his men spread out across the beach, presenting as difficult a target as possible. Those with shields sheltered their comrades. Every arrow which fell near them they picked up and broke. Inspired by the coolness of their leader, Drake's men stood their ground and waited for the natives to exhaust their ammunition. Had it not been for the wounded Winterhey the admiral would have ordered a slow retreat, but he would not leave one of his company to the mercy of these savages. Then Oliver decided to bring the conflict to a swift conclusion. Under cover he primed his fowling piece then stepped forth to fire it at the enemy leader. He squeezed the trigger but instead of an explosion there was only a splutter from the damp powder. Before he could pull back the serpentine for a second shot an arrow transfixed him through the heart. He fell forward, the arrow's reddened shaft protruding between his shoulder blades.

Holding his shield on his right arm Drake ran across to where Oliver lay. A glance told him that there was nothing he could do for the gunner. Angrily he siezed the matchlock, drew back the serpentine, checked the powder and fired at the natives' ringleader. This time there was a thunderous explosion. The pieces of shot tore into the man's chest and belly. He fell backwards screaming, blood pouring from his wounds. His horrified companions lowered their bows and stared open-mouthed at their leader's death agonies. Then they turned and fled. With a shout some of the seamen made to follow, but Drake called to them to stop. Little was to be gained by pursuing their advantage and Winterhey's wounds required immediate attention. The injured man was conscious but coughing blood from a pierced lung. Gently seamen carried him back to the boat. Aboard the *Pelican* he was tended by the surgeon, but he died an hour later.

Next day, while guards lined the fringes of the beach and Chaplain Fletcher read the burial service, Oliver and Winterhey were laid to rest in shallow graves upon the shore. Then the men divided into gangs for hunting, cleaning, repairing and loading. The *Mary* was systematically stripped and sunk in the middle of the harbour. Drake allowed plenty of time for relaxation; he wanted sound men as well as sound ships for the passage of the Straits. Early in their stay a party of sailors exploring the vicinity came upon a spruce mast embedded in the ground. Convinced that they had found Magellan's gibbet, they returned to the ship for picks and spades. Sure enough, a little digging unearthed a number of skeletons—the remains of rebels and loyal sailors who had died in the 1520 mutiny. With a curiosity which did not to them seem morbid they raked over the bones searching for personal items of value or interest. The *Pelican*'s cooper had the gibbet taken down and proceeded to saw it into short lengths from which he fashioned tankards.

One of the bizarre trophies was presented to Drake. It made no easier the decision over which he was brooding. Should he follow Magellan's example and make human sacrifice for the safety of his expedition?

Were Doughty's crimes worthy of death? Was it just that the gentleman should die, or simply expedient? No mutiny had yet occurred but it was only a matter of time if Doughty was not stopped. One man, as Drake knew, could split a ship from top-gallant to keel and transform a company of comrades into little groups of partisans. The germ of imagined grievance, once caught, could turn the most loyal seaman into a mutineer. Suspicion and mistrust always spread rapidly and could break the most efficient chain of command. Drake could honestly say that he had inflicted on Doughty every punishment short of the ultimate one—all to no avail. The arrogant gentleman was forcing Drake's hand and Drake was not the man to shrink from extreme measures.

If he still hesitated it was because some of Doughty's taunts were true. He did have powerful friends. How would Christopher Hatton react to the death of his secretary? And what if Hatton and his colleagues had already been swung out of power on the roundabout of court politics? If Burghley were in complete command and peace with Spain had been firmly established, Drake's situation on his return to England would be very precarious and the execution of Doughty would certainly count against him.

There were other reasons which made Drake shrink from the action he was contemplating. Doughty had, as yet, done nothing worthy of death. In the sixteenth century men loved justice as much as they do now but in the courts they often had to be content with far less. Yet, the forms were scrupulously observed even in the most blatantly rigged state trials. Even if justice was not done, it had to be seen to be done. What legal form could Drake devise for removing Thomas Doughty which would satisfy the gentlemen and the sailors? How could he possibly justify taking the life of one of the principal partners in this adventure?

Finally, and most important of all, did he have the requisite authority? On many occasions during the voyage Drake produced his 'commission'. He held it aloft for his men to gaze on. He waggled it under the noses of Spanish gentlemen who could not read English. He boasted that it was handed to him by the Queen. He claimed that it gave him complete power. But nowhere in the records of the voyage do we read that he allowed anyone to scrutinise that piece of paper. The inference is plain. However vaguely or specifically his instructions may have been worded, they did not give him power of life and death over all the other members of the expedition.

So Drake hesitated, but he could not go on hesitating much longer. Soon he would have to lead his men through the Straits. Then he would have to tell the gentlemen and captains that they were not bound for *Terra Australis* or for the Moluccas but that their target was the soft underbelly of the Spanish Americas. That would bring angry protest from Doughty and from Wynter and from all who shared their sensitivity about piracy. If there were enough of them and if they were firmly led they would be able to turn back or follow a different route home. It was not in the least unusual for great maritime enterprises to founder because of divisions among the leaders (the Fenton expedition is a case in point; see below p. 210). If there was one thing that Francis Drake was absolutely determined about it was that this expedition was not going to fail. He would break through into the South Sea. He would lay hold on the unprotected prizes afloat on those unprotected waters. He would revenge himself yet again on the agents of Philip of Spain. And not all the Doughtys in Christendom should stop him.[1]

By the end of June, Drake had steeled himself to have done with Thomas Doughty once and for all. He had carefully thought out how he meant to proceed. He had secured witnesses who would testify to the gentleman's ill intentions.

On the 30th he summoned all members of the expedition to a rocky island in the middle of the bay. When they landed they found the admiral seated in a chair set upon the summit of the isle. The company was drawn up in a square around and below him and given leave to sit. Then Thomas Doughty was set forth flanked by armed guards. Everyone fell silent. All shuffling and murmured conversation ceased. The admiral spoke.

'Thomas Doughty, you have sought by divers means, and as hard as you can, to discredit me to the great hindrance and overthrow of this voyage, besides other great matters I have to charge you with. If you can this day clear yourself of all these charges, well and good; you and I shall again be very good friends. If not you deserve to die. Say now, by whom will you be tried?'

The prisoner replied boldly and clearly. 'Why, good admiral, I will be returned to my own country and there tried by Her Majesty's laws.'

It was a good opening move. Doughty had, in the hearing of the whole company, appealed directly to the Queen. Drake must deny that appeal, for the only alternatives were unacceptable. They were an immediate return to England or a continuance of the existing situation with Doughty confined as a troublesome prisoner aboard one of the ships. Everyone waited for Drake's reply. The only sounds were the breaking of waves on the rocks beneath and the cries of sea birds.

'Nay, Thomas Doughty,' Drake said at last, 'I will empanel a jury to enquire into these charges.'

'Then I hope you will make sure your commission is sufficient.'

'You may be sure my commission is good enough.'

'I pray you, then, let us see it. It is necessary for it to be shown.'

Drake was completely outmanoeuvred. He had no written proof of his life-and-death authority over the members of his expedition. He resorted to blustering.

'Well you shall not see it. See how full of prating the desperate fellow is, my masters. Bind his arms; I do not feel safe with him unbound.'

While this was being done, the admiral appointed a jury of forty men under the leadership of Captain Wynter of the *Elizabeth*. Solemnly they took their places on one side of the square. Then the witnesses were called. One after another they came to tell of Doughty's seditious words, his threats, bribes and accusations. The prisoner scarcely bothered to answer them. They were, he said, 'unkind words spoken in anger'; in themselves they amounted to nothing.

Then Ned Bright one of the senior mariners was brought forward. He hated Doughty and believed he had evidence which would settle the swaggering courtier's fate once and for all.

'Nay, Doughty, we have other matter for you yet that will a little nearer touch you. It will, i' faith, bite you to the quick.'

The prisoner remained calm and dignified.

'I pray thee, Ned Bright, charge me with nothing but the truth and spare me not.'

Bright told of a number of conversations between himself and the accused in which Doughty had tried to persuade him of his vital role in planning the expedition and obtaining backing for it at court. Drake, he had declared, was of little consequence, indeed he (Doughty) wished he had undertaken the voyage by himself. There might yet come a time when he would have to assert his leadership. He would see to it that any who supported him were well rewarded. To underline his authority Doughty had told Bright that he was in Lord Treasurer Burghley's confidence.

'It fell out upon further talk that Master Doughty said that my Lord Treasurer knew the real purpose of the voyage.'

At this point Drake could not restrain himself from shouting out, 'No that he hath not!'

'He hath.' The two words were spoken quietly by the prisoner.

'How?'

'He had it from me.'

Was this really the first indication Drake had that Burghley was privy to the unwritten plans of the voyage? He must have known that the Lord Treasurer had tried to find out what the Queen and her more 'irresponsible' courtiers were up to in planning this voyage. Whether or not his outburst was one of genuine surprise and anger it was certainly vehement.

'Lo, my masters, what this fellow hath done!' he shouted. 'God will have all his treachery known, for Her Majesty gave me special commandment that of all men my Lord Treasurer should not know it. See how his own mouth hath betrayed him.'

To the seamen these issues of high politics meant nothing. What mattered it to them who among the great men of the land did or did not know the admiral's secrets? Indeed, it is difficult to see what difference it could possibly make to Drake now. It might give Burghley and the pro-Spain party an advantage they would not otherwise have possessed but the diplomatic manoeuvrings in distant London were so complex and would doubt-less change frequently during the course of the voyage. Drake may have felt a sense of great personal outrage, as though he had been used as a pawn in some Renaissance intrigue by a man he had once regarded as a friend. Yet making Drake feel small was no judicial cause for death. Rather, Drake's outburst was intended to overawe the jury. Like a practised barrister who has a weak case he feigned hot anger and he threw at the simple-minded sailors words designed to convey more than they actually meant—'treachery', 'Her Majesty', 'betrayed'.

Having thus planted the impression of high treason in the jury's minds, Drake, as both presiding judge and prosecuting counsel, proceeded to his summing up.

'My masters now you can see whether or not this fellow has sought to discredit me and overthrow the whole voyage. First he has tried to take away my good name. Secondly he has plotted against my life. And just think, what would become of you all if I were dead? You would fall to fighting among yourselves. And do not imagine that you would ever find your way home without me to lead you.

'Think carefully about this voyage we are embarked upon. So great an enterprise has never been sent forth from England. If it succeeds the humblest sailor here will return home a gentleman. But if we do not proceed with this voyage, if we turn tail for home think what a laughing stock we shall be and what dishonour we shall bring upon our country. But I tell you, I do not see how this voyage can continue if this fellow is allowed to live.

'Well my masters, what do you think? If you say that Thomas Doughty is worthy to die, hold up your hands.' [2]

What could the men do? They gave Drake the unanimous verdict he wanted. The admiral solemnly pronounced that the prisoner would be beheaded in two days time.

Doughty received the sentence without flinching. Might it not be com-muted, he asked; would justice not be served if he were set down on the coast of Peru with only a gun and some rations, to fend for himself? Drake replied that he could not risk Doughty's meeting up with the Spaniards and revealing his plans. This was reasonable; his reaction to John Wynter's suggestion was not. The captain of the *Elizabeth* volunteered to keep Doughty under hatches as his prisoner and return him safe to England to face trial there. The admiral refused bluntly. Wynter's suggest-ion smacked of collusion. Drake knew that the vice-admiral shared many of Doughty's views and he could not trust them together. He rose, declared the proceedings ended and made his way down to the boats.

But there were still more bizarre scenes to be enacted in the bizarre and tragic life of this complicated man. On the morning of 2 July the condemned prisoner and his judge met on the foredeck of the *Pelican* and there took Communion together. Fletcher had set up an altar and before the service he heard Doughty's confession. At that solemn moment Thomas Doughty declared himself before man and God innocent of the charges laid against him. Then he knelt side by side with Francis Drake and received the sacrament. It was an emotional moment and both men had tear stains on their faces when they rose from their knees.

Now the two men repaired to Drake's cabin for dinner. They sat talking cheerfully together while servants set the various dishes before them. Doughty proposed a toast to the success of the expedition and Drake drank to the more uncertain journey on which his companion was embarking. To all appearances the differences between the two men had been purged away and their friendship restored.

After the meal they were rowed across to the island where the execution was to take place. The entire complement was already there, forming a square around the block which had been set up. When the two principals appeared Doughty craved a few last words in private with Drake. They walked a short distance along the shore and no man has ever known what passed between them. At last they embraced and Doughty then placed himself in the hands of the Provost-Marshal. Coming to the block he kneeled and prayed aloud for the Queen and for the safety of the expedition. Then he turned to the executioner,

'Strike clean and with care, for I have a short neck.'

He laid his head upon the block and, a moment later, he was in eternity.

Thomas Doughty died with greater dignity than he had often displayed during the voyage. After the sword had fallen there was a long respectful silence. But Drake was not going to allow sympathy for the dead man to sieze the hearts of his company.

'Lo, this is the end of traitors,' he called out.

Apparently not all his men were disposed to agree with the admiral's interpretation of events. The place where the trial and execution had taken place was officially named 'The Island of True Justice and Judgement'. Many of the sailors called it, more directly, 'The Island of Blood'.

CHAPTER SEVEN

'A Palpable Darkness'

3 JULY — 25 NOVEMBER 1578

The days following the execution were the blackest of the whole expedition. Those who agreed with much of what Doughty had stood for had been provided with a martyr. Even those who had hated the arrogant 'necromancer' were alarmed at the ruthless power their admiral had displayed. The removal of Doughty had not eliminated dissatisfaction and discord; it had merely added fear. The weather was bitterly cold. Water froze in the butts and the decks were slippery with frost. The frozen halyards were like iron to handle and every chore became a torture, As if that were not enough the expedition was now desperately short of food. The frozen mainland offered little prospect of animal or vegetable life and there were few volunteers for foraging parties in the land of the hostile Patagonian 'giants'. Mussels and other small molluscs now became the men's staple diet and often that had to be eked out with seaweed. Working or relaxing round their fires, the mariners were cold, hungry and miserable.

Most of them lived in tents of Portuguese canvas or in makeshift huts and shelters on the Island of Blood. Much of the material for these buildings came from the *Mary* which was beached and broken up at St Julian's Bay. Drake distributed the prize's cargo, equipment and crew among the other vessels. The aggravating delays caused by waiting and searching for laggard vessels had already lost him much time and had resulted in his having to camp on this inhospitable coast until the southern spring brought better sailing weather. Drake was determined only to enter the Straits with good ships which stood some chance of being able to stay together.

Yet morale was now the admiral's biggest problem. Foraging for food, general repairs and the work on the *Mary* kept the men fully occupied for several days, but the bitter, stormy weather continued and jobs had to be manufactured to keep them busy. After the recent episode none of the men dared to voice open discontent but Drake knew that a large number, probably the majority, were for turning back. The longer they stayed at St Julian's with its gruesome reminders of violent death the worse the situation became. On the beach were the graves not only of Thomas Doughty but also of Oliver, Winterhey and other members of the crew who had died of disease. A stone had been set up with their names and an inscription in Latin giving details of the expedition.

Drake's first attempt to restore unity and harmony among the crew involved, characteristically, a resort to spiritual pressures. In the words of John Cooke, the admiral

> willed and straightly commanded the whole company to be ready to receive [Communion] the next Sunday following [6 July], saying that he would have all old quarrels whatsoever between any man to be forgiven, and that whatsoever he were that from that time forth should upbraid any man with any thing past he would lay such and so heavy punishment on him as should be a terrible example to the whole fleet ... and also every man commanded to confess him unto Master Fletcher ...[1]

The men obeyed, and doubtless the Sacrament uplifted some, but bitterness, frustration and quarrelsomeness seeped back into their souls as easily as the cold seeped in through their sea boots. They had to think and talk about something to take their minds off their aching bellies and the friends who were dying of disease and exposure.

They must have thought often of their families, have pictured their brothers working in the hot fields among the ripening corn while they themselves huddled for warmth around sputtering fires. The lure of booty was far less strong now; the men were more concerned about whether they would ever reach home than they were about the likelihood of returning as rich men. In such a mood they were ready to listen to their bolder or more foolhardy colleagues. The most talkative malcontents were John Audley and Edward Worrall. They let it be known that they were determined to demand their wages and a ship to take them home. Captain Wynter, they said, would take little persuading to turn the *Elizabeth* about and head for warmer, northern waters. It was in fact far from certain that Wynter would put himself at the head of the dissidents. After the Doughty incident no one was prepared to stand up to the admiral. Drake had promised death to any man who even whispered mutiny and there seemed no doubt he would be true to his word. Even the gentlemen went in fear of him. In fact, there was no difference between gentlemen and seamen now. The peacocks had long-since moulted and were only too happy to wear woollen caps and warm, coarse, heavy sea coats. They had also shed much of their arrogance. In fact the only real difference between the inhabitants of the main deck and the poop deck was that the latter were idle and useless. Drake knew about the mariners' fears, resentments and frustrations. He realised that they must be dealt with—quickly.

On 11 August he gave the order for every man to be assembled on the shore and to form up by ships' companies. When the men paraded they found themselves facing a tent, its front flaps drawn back to reveal Drake's great chair and a small table before it. For quite some time nothing happened. The men gazed morosely around, stamping their feet. They were cold—and apprehensive. At last the admiral arrived and seated himself. Behind him stood his black servant and he was flanked by John Wynter and John Thomas. The speech which follows is based on the only account we have of it, written by John Cooke. Obviously he did not take it down verbatim and Cooke was no lover of Drake, but in all its main points and in its general tenor the speech rings true. All fidgeting in the ranks ceased as Drake began to speak, referring to books and papers on the table.

'My masters, I am a very bad orator, for I was not brought up to be a scholar, but I want every one of you to listen very carefully to what I am going to say. Write it down, if you wish, for I am ready to answer for every word before her Majesty when we return safe to England.

'We are, all of us, far from our own country, our families and friends. We are in the midst of enemies and we are few in numbers. Every man here is precious; he cannot be replaced for ten thousand pounds. Yet some of you seem determined to die for you plot mutiny and spread discord and you know well what I must do to such men as that. God's life! I say there must be an end to plots and grumblings. There will be no more dissensions between sailors and gentlemen. I am thoroughly sick of your squabbles. You will all work together in harmony, gentleman with mariner and mariner with gentleman. There must be good order and discipline, that's why the gentlemen are here and all seamen will respect and obey them. But I have no room for any gentleman who doesn't care to get his hands dirty or won't take a pull on a rope next to a brother mariner. Let us prove that we are united and not give our enemies the satisfaction of seeing us destroy ourselves by our own arguments.[2]

'If there are any here who want to go home let them speak up now.' He pointed towards the harbour.

'There is the *Marigold*. I don't need her. I will victual her and send any deserters home with letters explaining to the backers of this voyage why they have run away.'

There was a murmur among the crew and many eyes turned to look at John Audley and Edward Worrall. Drake left the pause just long enough. His voice was heavy with menace as he went on.

'But if any of you do turn back take very good care of one thing. Keep out of my way. For if I find you on the open sea, as God is my witness, I'll sink you. Now, who is for going home?'

He stared hard at the ranks of shivering, dispirited men. It was the moment of truth. If one man stepped forward many would join him. If the potential ringleaders lacked the courage to take that vital step no man would be able to claim hereafter that he travelled unwillingly. The moment passed.... No one moved. Now Drake could go onto the offensive.

'Is there any man here who did not come on this voyage of his own free will?'

Silence.

'Who do you look to for your wages?'

A mumbled chorus of 'You, sir. We look to you.'

'Will you take your wages now or wait for your full share of the venture when we get home?'

They would wait.

'Good! Now we all know where we stand. Master Wynter, John Thomas, Thomas Hood, William Markham, Nicholas Anthony.'

Sharply he called the names of the captains and masters of the *Pelican, Elizabeth* and *Marigold*.

'You are all dismissed your posts!' . . . .

This bombshell had its desired effect. After a moment's stunned silence, the dismissed officers all began talking at once, demanding reasons for Drake's decision. With a wave of his hand he silenced them.

'Is there any reason why I should not dismiss you, if I choose? Did I not put Thomas Doughty to death, who was my close friend? Does any one say I had no right to do that?'

Now he was coming to the main point of this speech—his authority.

'Some people who want to discredit me say that Master Hatton sent me on this voyage; others that my master is Sir William Wynter or Master Hawkins. These are foolish stories conceived in idle brains which have nothing else to think about.'

Then he told them about his relationship with Essex and Walsingham, about his private interview with the Queen and how she had invited Drake to help her to be revenged on King Philip of Spain and how they had together decided that this could best be achieved by a surprise attack on his American empire. He held aloft a paper showing that the Queen had a stake of 1,000 crowns in the venture.

'You see, I have been plain and open with you. I have her Majesty's commission and you and I are here at her bidding. Think what it will mean if our enterprise fails. We shall be a laughing stock among our enemies in Spain and Portugal and we shall bring shame upon our own country.

'Now, by the authority vested in me, I restore every man to his office. Furthermore, I swear on my word as a gentleman that there will be no more killings . . .'

He scanned their faces slowly.

'. . . though some of you have deserved to die. Stand forth Edward Worrall and John Audley.'

The two men stumbled forward. For several minutes Drake harangued them calling them treacherous rogues and empty-headed braggarts. They fell on their knees and begged his pardon. Graciously the admiral forgave them and bade them return to the ranks. Their potential as ringleaders was broken. No one would follow them now.

'Well then, my masters, I have done. Remember this one thing: if any man says he has come on this voyage to serve Francis Drake, he will get no thanks from me. We are all here to serve Her Majesty. She it is who set this voyage forth and she expects every one of us to serve her faithfully until our journey is ended.'

No event in the whole of Drake's known career shows him more clearly as a brilliant manipulator of men than this speech. It was the culmination of seven weeks of intense psychological struggle for the mastery of an expedition that was disintegrating before his eyes. He had acted swiftly and ruthlessly. He had used lies, threats, bullying and bombast. He had chosen his moments with care. So much is obvious, and can only be explained by acknowledging that Drake had an intuitive feel for the man, the moment and the mood. But that should not blind us to the fact that during those weeks Drake was under an almost intolerable strain—the sort of strain which breaks lesser men and pinpoints the difference between great leaders and others. If, as seems very likely, the admiral's commission did not include the right to condemn members of his crew to death by military court, the strain must have been even greater.[3] It is worth noting that Thomas Cavendish, the second Englishman to circumnavigate the globe (1586–8), came to grief on a later expedition in these very waters and that his failure and death resulted in large measure from his inability to stamp his own will on the enterprise.

By now the weather was showing some signs of improving. Drake ordered camp to be struck and all gear stowed on board ready for departure. On Monday 17 August the signs at last seemed propitious, so Drake called the entire company together again for the last time. Francis Fletcher celebrated Holy Communion and preached once more on the subject of unity and duty.

This gracious exercise ended with prayer to God for her most excellent Majesty her honorable council and the Church & the common weal of England with singing of Psalms & giving thanks for God's great & singular graces bestowed upon us from time to time.

About noon the three ships made their slow way through the long entrance channel of St Julian's Bay, across the sand-bar and out into the Atlantic.

They were now well beyond the range of reliable charts and of Nuño da Silva's knowledge. The admiral apparently had some Spanish charts but these soon proved to be worthless because they were, perhaps deliberately, totally inaccurate. Drake's only guide was Magellan's book. It was therefore with great relief that after three days the ships rounded a pointed headland and found themselves in the mouth of a strait some twenty miles

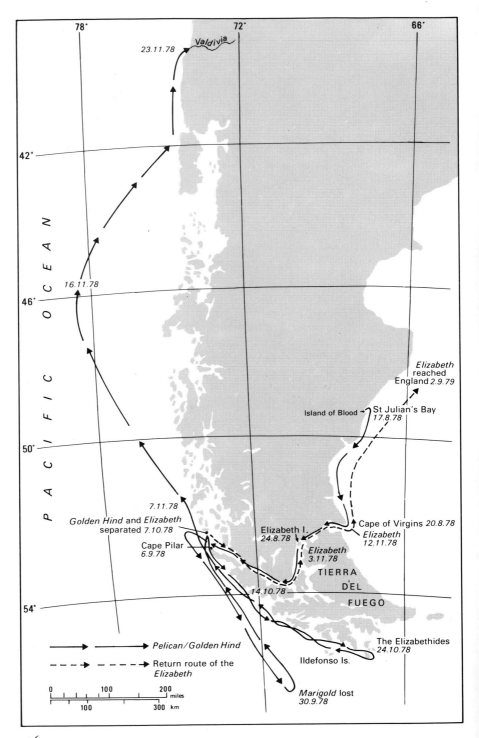

23.11.78 Valdivia

P A C I F I C   O C E A N

78°   72°   66°

42°

16.11.78

46°

Elizabeth
reached
England *2.9.79*

St Julian's Bay
Island of Blood   *17.8.78*

50°

7.11.78

Cape of Virgins *20.8.78*

Golden Hind and *Elizabeth*
separated *7.10.78*

Elizabeth I.
24.8.78

Elizabeth
12.11.78

Cape Pilar
6.9.78

Elizabeth
3.11.78

TIERRA

14.10.78

DEL

54°

FUEGO

The Elizabethides
24.10.78

Ildefonso Is.

→ *Pelican/Golden Hind*

- - → Return route of the
Elizabeth

Marigold lost
30.9.78

0   100   200
        miles
    100   300   km

across. It was Magellan's Strait, the gateway to the South Sea, and the land mass to larboard was the unexplored continent of *Terra Australis*.

The *Pelican* struck sails and the other vessels followed suit. On each ship prayers of thanksgiving were said. Every man was aware that this was a historic and solemn moment. It was the turning point of the voyage; ahead lay the unknown half of the world. It may well have been this occasion on which Drake chose to rename his ship the *Golden Hind*.[4] It was a gesture made in honour of Sir Christopher Hatton whose coat of arms bore 'a hind trippant or'. Probably Drake felt that, having recently put to death Hatton's secretary, some indication of his loyalty to the powerful captain of the guard was called for. Perhaps he was already worried about the interpretation which would be placed on the Doughty episode when the expedition's survivors returned to England. In any case it was a modest enough demonstration on Drake's part.

Having found the strait they were unable to enter it. For two days winds and currents were unfavourable and all the masters could do was tack to and fro between the gaunt grey cliffs with nothing to look at save the windshorn landscape. On the north it rose steeply to snow-capped peaks against the grey sky. To the south lay the drab lowlands of Tierra del Fuego. However, on the 23rd they were able to move forward, threading their way carefully between the towering cliffs which in places squeezed the channel through gaps less than a mile across. There was no question of night sailing and the water was too deep for the ship's anchors. Before dark, therefore, the masters had to select a spot carefully and moor close in to the channel's wall held by cables tethered to the rocks.

On 24 August, St Bartholomew's Day, the travellers came to a group of three uninhabited islands. The small fleet tied up once more and on the flagship Drake and his nephew carefully added the islands to the new chart they were compiling. The rocky islets were not impressive but they were fresh discoveries, hitherto unrecorded, so they had to be named. Drake wrote beside the three marks on his map 'Elizabeth Island', 'St Bartholomew's Island', 'St George's Island'. Elizabeth Island may have lacked human habitation but it had a population the sailors were delighted to see. It was swarming with thousands of flightless birds. Magellan had called them geese, and the taste of their flesh was certainly not dissimilar to that of the fat farmyard ganders. But some Welsh sailors aboard the *Golden Hind* gave the birds a new name; they called them 'whiteheads'— *pen gwynns*.

The men, who had not tasted fresh meat for months, scrambled quickly ashore and ran eagerly among the thousands of waddling panic-stricken creatures. With hooks tied to poles they prised the birds out of the holes and clefts where they hid and battered them to death with cudgels. The poor animals put up a fierce struggle, nipping hard with their beaks and gripping the weapons of their assailants. Nevertheless the hungry sailors inflicted a wholesale slaughter, killing, on one estimate, 3,000 birds, enough for the expedition's needs for many weeks.

Thus provisioned, Drake plunged deeper into the desolate strait. During the next few days the seamanship of his masters was put to the test. Blustering, icy winds cut down at the little ships from the towering glaciers and through the maze of tortuous channels. Though the water beneath them seemed fathomless and there was little danger of running onto unseen rocks, there was every danger of being spun suddenly off course into the steep walls of the canyon or into one another. Sometimes the ships would make excellent progress for several hours only to meet a sudden headwind and be swept miles back down the strait. As they travelled westwards the voyagers moved into the belt of rain and snow which lies almost permanently over this region and gives Chilean Tierra del Fuego an annual rainfall of 200 inches.

Preparing to cook

Yet this bleak and inhospitable climate was not without its advantages, as Francis Fletcher, whose eyes were ever open to the marvels of Providence, recorded

The trees of the islands near adjoining to the roots of these mountains feel the force of the freezing streams which descend from them for the snow which falleth upon them & rain which cometh down do both freeze as they light upon the trees & with their continual increase there is such a huge weight that the main arms & boughs are couched down so close together that no art or labour of man can make closer & sweeter arbours than they be: under the which the ground being defended from cold is engendered such temperate heat that the herbs may seem always to be green & flourish as if it were in our summer. Amongst other the simples we had in this place many being to me very strange & unknown...were...Thyme, Marjoram, Alexanders Scurvy Grass as seamen call it...& divers others well known to us all whereof were more excellent in their natures than we find them in these parts in our gardens. And for other strange plants they were so gummy & full of fatness that touching them the fat and gum would stick to our hands being so pleasant that it yielded a most comfortable smell to our senses whereby we received great help both in our diet, & physic to the great relief of the lives of our men...

The travellers saw little of the indigenous people of this region, the Ona and Alacaluf Indians, but that little was enough to reveal to them the utter simplicity of these hunter-gatherer communities. They wandered the mainland and islands in large extended family groups, scantily clad and living on berries, plants and small rodents. Their fires were often visible at night and at one point Fletcher and other curious Englishmen went ashore to examine one of their temporarily deserted settlements. They found a huddle of simple huts and such belongings as bowls and cups made of bark, axes, knives made of mussel shells, cooking utensils and 'boxes of stuff to paint'.

According to all the charts and maps of the region Drake had ever seen, Magellan's Strait divided South America from the great antarctic continent of *Terra Australis*. Already he had proved the old geographers wrong on that point. Whatever lay to larboard it was not part of a solid land mass. It was a rag-bag of islands. The mainland of *Terra Australis*, if it existed at all, must be still farther south.

Despite their difficulties and setbacks the Englishmen completed their transit of the straits in the good time of seventeen days. On 6 September they saw beyond the rocks off the starboard and larboard bows not more cliffs and promontaries but the flat, unbroken horizon of the sea Magellan had called *Mar Pacifico*.

But the great Portuguese pioneer had rounded Cape Pilar in the southern midsummer. When Drake arrived in the new ocean he found is anything but peaceful. It should for him and his men have been a very special moment. They had unlocked for England the treasure chest of the South Sea which the Spaniards had so long kept for themselves. Drake had planned another ceremony to mark this great occasion. He was going to land his men at the cape and, midst prayers and loyal speeches, erect a brass plate in honour of the Queen. But a sudden offshore wind carried the fleet out into the open ocean. As if that were not a sufficiently rude introduction to the South Sea the next day Drake's flotilla ran into the full fury of a Pacific tempest.

The storms that infest 'the Horn' are the most notorious in the world and Drake's three tiny ships now faced their full terrors. With all sails furled the bucking vessels were driven relentlessly south-eastwards along the craggy shore. Black cloud turned all time into a universal night in which only the lurid phosphorescence of the wave crests was clearly visible. In such peril the men could well do without omens but on the night of 15 September, during one of the few clear spells, they observed an eclipse of the moon, a sure portent of disaster. On and on went the ships. Day after day the winds and sea roared till the mariners, unable to sleep and scarcely able to eat, believed themselves confiined to an eternal watery hell.

> The day being come the sight of Sun & land was taken from us so that there followed as it were a palpable darkness by the space of 56 days without the sight of sun moon or stars . . . we thus . . . continued without hope at the pleasure of God in the violent force of the winds intolerable working of the wrathful seas and the grisely beholding (sometimes) of the cragged rocks & fearful height, & monstrous mountains being to us a lee shore where into we were continually drawn by the winds & carried by the mountain-like billows of the sea . . . If at any time we had a little opportunity to seek some harbour for refuge to come to anchor & rest till God in mercy might . . . give us more safe sailing at the seas such was the malice of the mountains that they seemed to agree together in one consent & join their forces together to work our overthrow & to consume us so that every mountain sent down upon us their several intolerable winds with that horror that they made the bottom of the seas to be dry land where we anchored, sending us headlong upon the tops of the mounting & swelling waves of the seas over the rocks the sight whereof at our going in was as fearful as death.

At length the storm carried them far away from land, a hundred miles or more to the south of Tierra del Fuego into 57 degrees of latitude (see Appendix). Incredibly, the ships stayed together. In the small hours of 30 September those keeping watch upon the *Golden Hind* and the *Elizabeth* heard a terrible sound above the caterwauling of wind and sea. It was the despairing cries of their comrades on the little *Marigold*. She had taken all the punishment she could endure. The storm had already torn great holes in her. She keeled over and slipped in to the less turbulent depths. She took with her her entire complement of twenty-nine men.

Then, as if fate had done its worst for the time being, the wind abated. Drake and Wynter were able to bring their ships about and steer a northerly course to regain the land. A week later they found themselves back near the entrance to the Straits. The crews were in a desperate state; many men were ill with scurvy and those that were not were half dead with fatigue. As they patrolled the tattered fringe of fiords and islands Drake strained his eyes through the mist and spray and driving rain. He had to

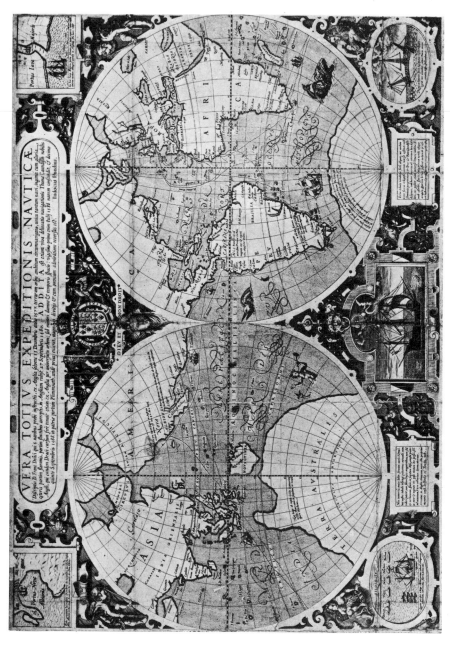

Map by Hondius showing Drake's journey

find an anchorage. His men simply could not go on. At last, seeing an entrance that looked wider than the others, he ordered the helm hard over and the *Golden Hind* limped into a wide bay. (They were in 51 degrees, just north of the entrance to Magellan's Strait.)

It was almost night and the *Golden Hind* dropped fore and aft anchors as soon as she reached a sheltered spot—or what seemed to be a sheltered spot. The illusion did not last long. A wind bore down from the mountains and churned the harbour waters into a frenzy. The anchor cables snapped and the ship was flung towards the rocky walls of the bay. There was no staying here. Wearily Drake gave the order to bear out to sea. Wearily the crew responded. The *Elizabeth* had not had time to anchor and she hauled out first. As darkness fell the two ships lay hove to well beyond the breakers within about two leagues of each other, the men on watch taking comfort from the occasional glimpse of the partner ship's light. But some time during that squally night the light disappeared. When dawn came the watchers on the flagship's deck looked in vain for the *Elizabeth*. It was 8 October.

Before Drake could make a search for the missing vessel the tempest was on him again. Once more the *Golden Hind* was driven south-west before a wind which howled through the rigging, bent the empty masts and avalanched water onto the deck. Once again the ship ran past the islands bordering Tierra del Fuego. Fortunately the fury of the gale was now

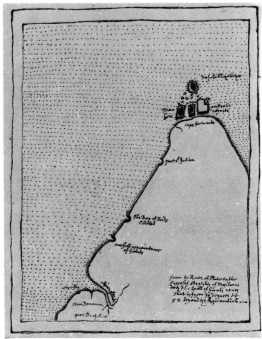

The southern tip of South America and the Elizabethides. Francis Fletcher's drawing

intermittent. On three occasions Drake was able to anchor and send a boat ashore in search of water and food. But there was still no going back. That persistent north-westerly continued to dominate. Rocks, islands, snow-capped mountains slipped past to larboard in monotonous succession. The exhausted crew watched in vain for a friendly, sheltered anchorage or some sign of their missing comrades. Nothing, only the unending combat of sea and land.

Until the 24th. On that day the sun showed itself for the first time in forty-eight days, the wind dropped and the *Golden Hind* found herself bobbing in an easy sea in 57 degrees of latitude near the southernmost tip of America—Cape Horn. They were amongst a group of islands which Drake entered on his chart with the almost inevitable name, the Elizabeth-ides. The ship found a good anchorage and, though there were hundreds of minor repairs to be done, Drake allowed the crew to relax. Some were too ill or exhausted to move, some wanted nothing more than to fling themselves down in their bed space and sleep. However, there were a few men with sufficient stamina and hunger to accompany the ever inquisitive Fletcher ashore next day. They found the islands sparsely populated but not unfriendly. The small Stone Age Indian communities wandered from settlement to settlement eking out a meagre existence from the restricted flora and fauna of the isles. The Englishmen found little to replenish their empty larder but there was 'wonderful plenty of the small berry with us named currants, or as the common sort call them small raisins'. Fletcher and his companions walked to the southern tip of the furthest island* and erected a simple monument: '. . . having set up on end a stone of some bigness & with such Tools as I had of purpose ever about me when I went on shore had engraven her Majesty's name her kingdom the year of Christ & the day of the month.'

Drake was anxious to return as soon as possible the way they had come. He wanted to take full advantage of what might prove to be only a break in the weather in order to get back on course and he wanted to rendez-vous with the *Elizabeth*, if indeed she was still afloat. Wynter's orders were that if the ships separated he was to make for the 30th parallel and there meet up with the flagship. This was close to the latitude where Magellan had picked up a favourable wind to carry him across the Pacific. It was therefore the point at which options for the rest of the voyage would have to be examined again. Two and a half weeks had elapsed since the *Elizabeth* had been lost and it might take the same amount of time to regain the point where she had last been sighted. Even then the *Golden Hind* would be 1,500 miles from the rendezvous point.

Yet there was no question of setting sail immediately. Food and water had to be found. His men had to be given time to build up their strength.

*No other islands were visible to the south but it is by no means certain that the travellers were at Cape Horn.

The next five days were, therefore, devoted to cruising among the islands, filling the water casks from rivers and springs, gathering edible plants and berries and catching birds and seals. On board there were broken spars to replace, rotten and frayed lengths of rope to be cut out and new sections spliced in, the bilge to be pumped, gaps which had appeared between timbers to be caulked. When it came to examining the storm damage Drake was relieved to find that his ship had stood up to her buffeting remarkably well. The men, too, had personal chores to attend to—jackets and shirts to be dried out, torn jerkins to be patched.

For the admiral and his nephew there was the task of entering on their charts all that they could recall of the delineation of land and sea. The one vital discovery which they had to set down was the junction of the oceans. Geographically speaking, this was Drake's greatest achievement. His discovery of the Cape Horn islands proved conclusively that Magellan's Strait was not the sole passage between South America and the supposed *Terra Australis*. The myth of the great southern continent was also exploded, at least in so far as the region to the immediate south of America was concerned. As Fletcher somewhat ruefully remarked:

> We altered the name of those southerly islands from terra incognita (for so it was before our coming thither & so should have remained still with our good wills) to terra nunc bene cognita. This is broken islands, which in coasting it again on that side in returning to the Northward we proved to be true, & were thoroughly confirmed in the same.

Whereas many of his countrymen had been searching for a north-west passage for some decades Drake had now shown that the south-west passage was much wider than had previously been supposed. His only fundamental mistake was his failure to recognise the size of Tierra del Fuego and his insistence, therefore, that Magellan's Strait was merely one among several channels through the southern isles. The way for English, French and Dutch poachers into the Spanish and Portuguese preserves was now, in theory, wide open, though, in fact, the atrocious weather round the Horn would prove almost as formidable a barrier as the solid mass of *Terra Australis*. Yet Drake, good Calvanist that he was, when he had time to reflect on the ordeal through which he and his men had passed, could only regard it as a proof of divine favour bestowed by a sovereign God. Without the storm they would never have made the great discoveries in which Drake henceforth took such pride. The admiral might put this interpretation on events but the expedition did not lack those who saw the storm and all its attendant horrors as a visitation of God's wrath following the murder of Thomas Doughty. Francis Fletcher was already inclining to this view. In his account of the loss of the *Marigold* he was careful to point out that its recently-appointed master was Ned Bright, one of Doughty's principal accusers. Another incident off the Elizabethides also struck him as significant. John Brewer, Drake's trumpeter and a devoted enemy of Doughty, was knocked overboard by a stray rope and very narrowly escaped drowning. 'Mark God's judgement against a false witness', wrote Fletcher in the margin of his journal. The would-be mutineer might be dead but his ghost vigorously haunted the decks of the *Golden Hind* and the *Elizabeth*.

On 1 November the *Golden Hind* turned to the north-west in weather which was now as pleasant as it had previously been intolerable. Drake was able to keep the broken coastline in view for hundreds of miles, but he only stopped once to call at an unnamed island (perhaps one of the Ildefonso Islands) where a large colony of sea birds had been spotted. Her deck heaped with dead birds and a pile of eggs, the *Golden Hind* was quickly under way again. With favourable winds she regained the mouth of Magellan's Strait by about 7 November. Drake's Spanish maps and charts showed him that from about this point the coast of Chile curved away to the north-west. Being anxious to make the rendezvous as soon as possible Drake therefore stood out to sea altering his course several points to westward, planning to make a landfall at about 45 degrees.

Nine days later an astrolabe sighting on the sun at midday showed the *Golden Hind* to be in $45\frac{1}{2}$ degrees. There was not the remotest sign of land. In fact the ship was 250 miles or more out in the Pacific. The charts were obviously wrong—deliberately wrong as Drake and his gentlemen believed. There seems little doubt that their suspicions were right. Ever since Magellan there had always been a possibility that captains of other nations might enter by the South Sea's 'back door', and what motive could they possibly have other than the desire to tap the silver trade at source? The Pacific coast of Spanish America was virtually unfortified against seaborne attack. The only way the colonial power could protect its possessions from a remotely possible raid was by spreading inaccurate information about the Americas—such as false charts and stories about the violent current which raced westwards through Magellan's Strait making a return voyage quite impossible.

Drake altered course to north by north-east and once more made contact with the Chilean coast, where the Valdivia river poured itself into a wide bay. At last they were on course. The horrors of the Horn were behind them and, in the mercy of God, the crewmen of the *Golden Hind* looked to be reunited with their colleagues in a few days. But their colleagues on the *Elizabeth* were at that moment in mid-Atlantic ardently steering a course for home.

When Wynter discovered that he had lost the flagship on the morning of 8 October his first thought was for the safety of his own vessel. He ordered the master to make for the comparative shelter of the Straits. He found a safe anchorage in a wide bay and immediately sent a party of men ashore to gather wood for a fire. For two days the fire was kept burning on the shore as a signal in the hope that the *Golden Hind* had also found a nearby haven. When there was no sign of the other ship it was obvious that the *Golden Hind* had been forced to run before the storm. On 10 October Wynter climbed to the highest point of the nearby land, 'in the top whereof I engraved her Majesty's name, and we praised God together for the great danger we escaped.'[5]

The next day the storm penetrated their anchorage and they were driven out, losing their anchor. They retreated further into the Straits and found a fresh haven, which this time served them for 22 days. The same wind which drove the *Golden Hind* to Cape Horn prevented the *Elizabeth* going in search of the flagship or setting off for the rendezvous.

When it came to discussing what course of action they should pursue next, captain, master and crew were at loggerheads. Accounts survive by both Wynter and one of his men, Edward Cliffe, and the historian has to steer his way to the truth through their mutual recriminations. Wynter says he was all for continuing with the voyage but was forced to turn back by a mutinous crew. Cliffe insists the decision to return home was taken by the captain 'full sore against the mariners minds'.[6]

Wynter's account was set out in a report he made to the navy board on his return. At that time the vice-admiral had two concerns; to explain his 'desertion' and to dissociate himself from the plunder of Portuguese and Spanish vessels. Clearly Wynter was very worried about being branded as a pirate. He was, after all, captain of a Queen's ship and was closely related to high officers on the navy board. He was the centre of a great deal of attention; the Council and every foreign diplomat wanted to know all about the voyage. If Wynter gave the impression that he was a willing participant in a gigantic freebooting exercise the embarrassment to the government might be considerable. Therefore, in his report he insisted that the seizure of shipping off the African coast was carried out against his will. He produced an inventory of all the *Mary*'s cargo brought home in the *Elizabeth* and accounted for items used on the voyage (e.g. canvas for sail repairs)'* so that restitution could be made to the Portuguese owners.

About the decision to bring the *Elizabeth* home he had this to say. First of all he had been successful in persuading the master and some of the crew to continue with the voyage. It was agreed, first of all, that they would sail back through the Straits as far as the Island of Geese (i.e. Elizabeth Island) where they could replenish their stock of penguin meat. On 8 November,

> ...calling my whole company together, I made my determination generally known, which was for the east parts of the world, using what persuasion I could. And protested unto them upon the Bible that Mr Drake told me that he would go thither when I was last aboard of him.

*For a detailed account of Wynter's return see below pp. 193–4.

But all was in vain, for the Master did utterly dislike of it, saying that he would fling himself overboard rather than consent to any such voyage. Sometimes he wished himself whipped at a cart's [tail] in Rochester. He said Mr Drake hired him for Alexandria, but if he had known that this had been the Alexandria, he would have been hanged in England rather than have come in this voyage.[7]

This brings up another related problem. According to Wynter, Drake had already decided to make for the Moluccas. What weight should we give to this contention and how does it affect our understanding of the whole plan of the voyage? One can only attempt a reconstruction which at least fits all the known facts.

Before leaving the Straits, the admiral told the captains of the other two vessels to rendezvous with him at 30 degrees on the coast of Chile if the fleet was separated. At such a point there would still be three options open as far as the Captains knew. First Drake could continue along the coast of Spanish America picking up whatever loot might present itself and seek a return route round the north of the continent. Or he could find the trade winds and follow Magellan's route to the Spice Islands. Or, thirdly, he could return home via the Straits. Knowing Wynter's opposition to piracy, Drake deliberately soft-pedalled on the first option, though he certainly had no intention of committing himself to a circumnavigation route at this stage. He was determined to make each decision as necessity arose or, as he certainly would have said himself, 'to follow the guiding of divine Providence'.

When, at the crucial *Elizabeth* debate on 8 November, Wynter presented the Moluccas plan to the crew there was, understandably, little enthusiasm for it. Most of his men would willingly have followed Drake on a pillaging expedition up the Peruvian coast, with its prospect of a share of booty, but this option was never presented to them. They had already had one taste of what the South Sea could do and had no desire to sail right across it even though Wynter produced his copy of Magellan's book to prove that it was possible.[8]

Thus a disgruntled Wynter set sail for England on 11 November with his disgruntled men. Seven months and three weeks later the *Elizabeth* reached Ilfracombe, where captain, master and crew hastened to exonerate themselves from all blame for their expedition's failure. The navy board, the powerful men who had sunk good money in the venture and, above all, the Queen were not pleased. John Wynter had made a mess of his big chance and his inadequacy was shown up more clearly the following year when the *Golden Hind* returned triumphant. He was punished with a long spell in prison and might have fared even worse if Drake had not put in a good word for him.[9] Thereafter, not all Wynter's excellent contacts could prevent him from sinking into oblivion. His last appearance in the annals of naval history is during the Armada campaign of 1588. At that time of crisis when England needed and used all her available maritime talent and when Drake played such a vital role, his ex-vice admiral sailed on the Queen's galleon *Vanguard*. But not as captain, as lieutenant.

> There is a tide in the affairs of men,
> Which, taken at the flood, leads on to fortune;
> Omitted, all the voyage of their life
> Is bound in shallows and in miseries.

CHAPTER EIGHT

'Like a visitation from heaven'

26 NOVEMBER 1578—15 FEBRUARY 1579

Don Francisco Alvarez de Toledo was a man of rare talents in the prime of life and the plenitude of power. For ten years he had been Viceroy of Peru—ten years of remarkably constructive energy. Inheriting a province torn apart by bands of rival *conquistadores* and trembling with potential Indian revolt, Toledo had established royal authority, disarmed revolution by murdering Tupac Amaru, the last Inca, established sound judicial and administrative patterns, brought a new, ruthless efficiency to the collection of taxes and the organization of forced labour and begun a programme of public works which was slowly transforming a land of isolated settlements into a colonial civilisation.

When he looked from the windows of his splendid new palace high above the port of Callao, he could see the visible proof of his firm but wise dictatorship. The bay was full of shipping. There were vessels from Arica on their way to Panama bearing the silver which flowed in an unstanchable stream out of the Potosí mines in the high Andes. There were others carrying the gold and silver which found its way to the Peruvian and Chilean coasts from the host of small, private workings which had brought sudden wealth to many enterprising and lucky prospectors. There was the usual gaggle of ships from bullion-hungry New Spain, laden with all the merchandise of the old world and also silks and spices from the Philippines. All was activity and peace and wealth. His Most Catholic Majesty had every reason to be pleased with Don Francisco Alvarez de Toledo.

In 1578 the potential of Spain's westward-facing colonies was just being realised. Peru had taken over from Mexico as the main source of precious metal and this had stimulated a vigorous coastal trade. Ships were laid down at Guatulco and other Nicaraguan ports where there was a plentiful supply of timber and fibres from the *pita* and *caguya* plants for rope-making. In the second half of the century a shipbuilding industry was established at Guayaquil. The original objective of this trade was to convey the gold and silver of Peru to Panama and New Spain. From Panama it was carried across the Isthmus to Nombre de Dios for shipment to Spain. But a growing volume of bullion ended its journey in Mexico where a flourishing colonial society needed it to pay for the European-manufactured necessities and luxuries of life.

A Spanish galleon

A proportion of these articles—carved chairs, tapestries, pots and pans, paintings, ploughs, candlesticks, olive oil, wine—found their way to the small but growing communities of Peru and Chile. By 1560 the *conquistadores* Pedro de Valdivia and García Hurtado de Mendoza had made Spanish might felt as far south as the Straits of Magellan, although for all practical purposes Concepción marked the farthest point of effective colonial occupation. Chile never fulfilled the hopes of the early pioneers who were looking for an *Otro Perú*, another Peru, but small settlements were able to eke out a living based on plantation agriculture and panning for alluvial gold. These settlements had to be served and so the trading system was extended further south. By 1578 it covered over 6,000 miles of Pacific coastline.

But a more recent development had overshadowed this coastal trade and was on the point of eclipsing the commerce with mother Spain. In 1565 Miguel López de Legazpi had sailed from New Spain to establish the first colonies in the Philippines. Within a decade, despite resistance from the natives and Portuguese rivals, the Spanish conquest was complete. In 1567 Alvaro de Mendaña discovered the Solomon Islands and another step had been taken in the transforming of the southern Pacific into a Spanish lake. Toledo took as much interest in these ventures as the Viceroy of New Spain.

One of his senior officers and a personal friend was Pedro Sarmiento de Gamboa who had been the captain of Mendaña's flagship. Sarmiento was a remarkable man of diverse talents. He was a traveller and soldier and also a man of culture who wrote the first history of the Inca nation. He was an expert in navigation, cartography, cosmography and, according to the Inquisition, he was also a dabbler in forbidden arts.

Hispano-Portuguese rivalry in the Philippines soon gave way to commercial co-operation. At Manila Spanish merchants did a thriving trade in silk, paying their suppliers in Peruvian silver. The home base of this trade was Acapulco, the best harbour on the Pacific coast of Spanish America. From there ships had an easy run of eight to ten weeks before the trade winds to Manila. The return journey was slower and more hazardous. Captains had to steer a north-easterly course through the typhoon belt in order to pick up a westerly air current between thiry and forty degrees north. They made a landfall on the coast of California and from there they could reach home without losing sight of land. Despite the hazards, this was a highly profitable trade. Portuguese demand for silver was insatiable and, by the 1580s, much more was finding its way across the Pacific than was going home via the Atlantic route.* The demand for silk both in the colonies and Europe was equally strong. New Spain was thus in the enviable position of a middle man controlling the market in two highly saleable commodities.

The Pacific coast colonists enjoyed other blessings apart from a thriving commerce. They had no trade rivals and they had complete security. Their colleagues in the West Indies and along the Atlantic seaboard were perpetually on the alert for French, English and Dutch pirates but no unwanted sea raiders upset the thriving luxury trade of the South Sea. John Oxenham's audacious raid across the Isthmus in 1575 (see above pp. 34–7) had brought swift retribution. The pirate and two of his colleagues were now in the Inquisition's prison at Lima undergoing the periodic torture considered appropriate to heretics. The rest of his crew were dead. It was very unlikely that any other foreigners would try to break into the South Sea via the land route. As to Magellan's route through the Straits, that was so hazardous as to be discounted completely. There was therefore no prospect of trade ever being stopped. Well-laden ships would continue to sail in and out of Callao. The viceregal palace and the homes of other notables would continue to fill with obsidian mirrors, lacquered gourds, and feather-work tapestry from the traditional craftsmen of New Spain, oriental silk and porcelain as well as inlaid oak and walnut furniture, bejewelled daggers, lutes, spinets, bales of brocade and all the other desiderata of the homeland. The only threat to Peru's peace came from the sporadic and easily-crushed revolts of natives who had escaped from their bondage in the mines and on the *haciendas* and

*The astronomical figure of 12,000,000 pesos has been quoted for the year 1597. cf. J. H. Parry *The Spanish Seaborne Empire*, p. 132.

had formed outlaw bands amidst the Andean clefts and ridges. Don Francisco Alvarez de Toledo therefore had some justification for any complacence he may have felt as he gazed daily on the peaceful and prosperous bustle of Lima and its port of Callao. He was about to receive a shock.

In mid-November the *Golden Hind* was far to the south of Callao de Lima and just entering the area of Toledo's administration. Drake's main concern was to rendezvous with the *Elizabeth* and, perhaps, the *Marigold*, for although those on watch had claimed to have heard cries of distress from the bark there was no proof that she had, indeed, foundered. The crew of the *Golden Hind* simply did not know what had happened to their colleagues and were hoping against hope to meet up with them in the appointed latitude.

But the admiral had other problems on his mind. There was, of course, the perpetual headache of food and water. Scurvy has many symptoms. When Drake saw men suffering form lassitude, depression and physical weakness he probably assumed that they were simply being lazy. But when sailors stumbled about the deck with glazed eyes sunk deep in their sockets, lost their teeth when they bit on ship's biscuit, and moaned because of the pain in their arms and legs he knew they were sick men. He also knew that even those who showed the most distressing symptoms made a remarkably rapid recovery as soon as they were fed with fresh plants or fruit.

If some of the men were sick so was the ship. She moved sluggishly through the water and was in desperate need of careening to strip off the clinging barnacles and weed. The bilges now had to be pumped at least once a day and always yielded a quantity of clear sea water which meant that there were gaping timbers in need of recaulking. Drake knew that at any time from now on he might encounter Spaniards by land or sea. Then he would have to have a fast and efficient ship.

He would also need a fast and efficient crew and that he had not got. Even among the fit members morale was at a low ebb. The atmosphere had improved slightly since they had left behind the frightening storm belt but the men were very conscious that they were now further from home than they had ever been and that they were entering a region dominated by the notorious Inquisition. Already they had lost the greater part of the company and, for all they knew, their shipmates were rotting at the bottom of the ocean. They were in a hideous limbo between the freezing horrors of the South and the untold horrors to the North. Some sailors were convinced that their plight was the result of the admiral's murder of the sorcerer, though whether it was Doughty's ghost or the Lord of Hosts who was exacting vengeance was not clear. Drake kept a sharp ear open for seditious talk and a sharp eye on known malcontents, particularly on John Doughty who was never allowed to leave the ship.

On 25 November the island of Mocha hove into view. It was pleasantly

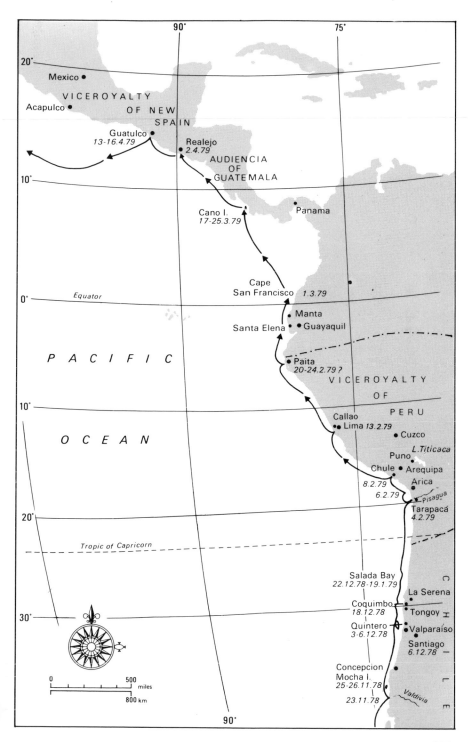

20°

Mexico •

VICEROYALTY
OF NEW
SPAIN

Acapulco •

90°

Guatulco •
13-16.4.79

Realejo
2.4.79

AUDIENCIA
OF
GUATEMALA

10°

Cano I.
17-25.3.79

Panama •

75°

Cape
San Francisco *1.3.79*

0°   *Equator*

Manta •
Santa Elena • • Guayaquil

P A C I F I C

Paita
20-24.2.79 ?

VICEROYALTY

OF

10°

O C E A N

Callao
• • Lima *13.2.79*
• Cuzco

PERU

L.Titicaca
Puno •
Chule • Arequipa
8.2.79   • Arica
Arica
6.2.79   Pisagua
Tarapacá
4.2.79

20°

Tropic of Capricorn

Salada Bay
22.12.78-19.1.79

La Serena

Coquimbo
18.12.78

• Tongoy

30°

Quintero
3-6.12.78

• Valparaíso

Santiago
6.12.78

0   500
         miles
    800 km

Concepcion
Mocha I.
25-26.11.78

23.11.78

Valdivia

90°

wooded and seemed to offer the possibility of food and water without the danger of encountering any Spaniards or allies of the Spaniards. Drake anchored well off shore and himself took a boat to the island. As it approached the beach, a group of Indians appeared, smiling and waving a welcome. They had offerings for the strangers, offerings which set the Englishmen's mouths watering—maize, root vegetables (including potatoes), chickens and two fat sheep. The prospect of roast poultry and mutton was ravishing and that night there was feasting aboard the *Golden Hind*. By signs interspersed with a few Spanish words Drake made clear his need for water, and the natives promised to lead him to a spring the next day.

While Drake and his crew were making merry that night the people of Mocha Island were seriously debating what to do about the white men. They had no reason to love these Spaniards (and to them all white men were Spaniards). Many, perhaps all, of the natives had fled to Mocha from the mainland where the colonists were killing and enslaving their people. They probably feared that the *Golden Hind* was full of armed soldiers come to invade their sanctuary. Or perhaps they were just determined on revenge for past wrongs. The impromptu offering of food had probably been made in the hope that the white men would take it and go. When Drake announced his intention of actually coming ashore with more men next day he seriously alarmed the people of Mocha. And so they decided on a show of strength to rid themselves of the hated Spaniards.

Early next morning the unsuspecting Drake returned to the island with a dozen man and steered for a narrow, reed-fringed creek to which the people had directed him. As they neared the land the visitors saw a small reception committee of smiling Indians. Thomas Flood and Thomas Brewer jumped out and ran through the shallows with the painter to beach the boat and make fast. Before they could do so they were seized and dragged off by their hosts who were no longer smiling. Another Indian grabbed the painter. From the reeds on either side there now appeared scores of warriors armed with spears, bows and arrows. They loosed a torrent of missiles on the trapped and helpless Englishmen. There was not a man who was not wounded. Some lay slumped over their oars, their bodies sprouting thick clumps of arrows. Drake himself was struck many times and nearly lost an eye, one arrow piercing his cheek. If he had any time at all for reflection he may well have seen his fate following an earlier pattern: had not Magellan died in precisely these circumstances, though on a different shore? The landing party was saved from annihilation by the quick thinking of 'one of the simplest of the company', as Fletcher calls him. This man cut the painter with his sword. Seeing their victims escaping, a few warriors waded into the water and seized some of the oars but they were beaten off. With frenzied strokes the boat pulled away from the shore while spears and arrows splashed into the water.

The ten men who were helped aboard the *Golden Hind* were a sorry, bloody sight. The surgeon and his assistants set to immediately, stanching and bandaging wounds. Fortunately, most proved to be superficial. Only one man, the Danish gunner Great Nele, died from loss of blood. When his own cuts had been attended to Drake distributed arquebuses to several men and despatched them in the boat to try to rescue Brewer and Flood. It was a hopeless task. As soon as the boat came close to the beach hundreds of natives appeared brandishing their primitive weapons. There was no chance of the Englishmen regaining their two lost comrades if, indeed, they were alive without losing many more of their number.[1]

Admiral and crew were united in a desire to put as much distance as possible between themselves and Mocha Island. Drake steered for the coast some eighteen miles off and followed it northwards. He was seeking a quiet cove far from Indian or Spanish habitation. Therefore, he sailed straight past Concepción and Valparaíso. On 3 December he dropped anchor in a wide bay at 33 degrees. The only sign of life was a solitary Indian fishing from a canoe. He hailed the ship and was brought aboard. Drake made a great show of friendship, presenting him with linen (probably part of the *Mary*'s cargo), 'butcher's chopping knives' and other 'trifles'.[2] He undoubtedly thought Drake and his men were Spaniards and, since he was not frightened, he obviously belonged to a people who were allies of the conquerors. But he did not speak Spanish and was therefore of little value to Drake. However, he paddled back to the shore and returned almost immediately with a friend.

The friend spoke to Drake in quite good Spanish and proudly announced that his name was Philip, the same as the big white king. Obviously he was a baptised convert who had received some education from Catholic priests. He told Drake all about the activities of the Spaniards and asked why the *Golden Hind* was not anchored in the harbour of Valparaíso. All the big ships called at Valparaíso, Philip said. Why, even at this very moment there was a rich merchantman loading there. This was the best news Drake had heard in months. He pressed Philip for more information and learned that there were few houses and fewer soldiers in Valparaíso. There was only one or two ships in the port. It all sounded too easy and Drake was convinced that this was the change of fortune he had been waiting for. After a couple of days to allow the wounded to recover and to take on water the *Golden Hind* left the place which was entered on the charts as 'Felipe's Bay' (Quintero). The Indian guide was aboard as the ship made the fifteen-mile journey to Valparaíso.

The visitors discovered a cluster of some nine dwellings around an ample anchorage. Valparaíso existed only as an outpost of the capital, Santiago, seventy miles inland at the base of the Andes. There was, as Philip had said, only one major ship in port, the *Capitana Grande de Los Reyes*, more popularly known as *La Capitana*. She was a famous ship: ten years before she had been Mendaña's flagship under the command of Pedro Sarmiento on the historic expedition to the Solomon Islands. But now she had left her exciting youth behind and settled to the more sedate life of a coastal trader. In December 1578 she was on her way home to Callao de Lima from a voyage to the Chilean settlements. She carried wine, maize and gold from the Valdivia region.

The only crew left aboard were eight Spaniards and three negroes and the prospect of company from the new ship beating into harbour was heartening. They brought up a butt of wine and made preparations for a convivial evening. They watched the *Golden Hind* anchor and as a boatload of men pulled across the bay towards them one of them beat a welcoming tattoo on the ship's drum. They were still smiling when Tom Moon scrambled over the side at the head of the boarding party, swung a fist into the pilot's face and shouted out '*Abaxo, perro!*' 'Get below, you dog!' The astounded crew were soon herded below decks but one Spaniard had the presence of mind to make a break and fling himself into the water. He soon reached the quay and raised the alarm. The reaction of the populace was to flee. The invaders now had the run of the town as well as of the ships.

Pirates attacking a Spanish settlement

Having secured the *Capitana*, Drake filled his own boat and the Spanish ship's with men, and rowed ashore. The sailors rampaged exultantly through the settlement. Here, at last, it seemed, were real action and tangible rewards. The houses yielded a variety of household goods of no great value but there was a warehouse full of cedar wood and Chilean wine and the church supplied the raiders with a silver chalice and cruets, vestments and an altar cloth. Some of these latter were destroyed as 'papistical' and others were given to Francis Fletcher. Drake then turned his attention to the other vessels in the harbour before returning to the *Capitana*. There, he examined the crew and deciding that only one was of any use to him, he set nine of them ashore. The exception was the pilot, Juan Griego (so named because he was a Greek). He was a middle-aged man, a master of his craft and one who knew the coast of Chile and Peru intimately. As such he was far too valuable to be allowed to go free.

Drake now gave the order for the *Golden Hind* and the prize to set sail. Once out at sea he had the chance to examine the *Capitana*'s cargo at leisure. The inventory was impressive: 1,770 jars of wine, sacks of maize, a stack of fine cedar wood (which the English cook subsequently used for his fire), gold to the value of 25,000 pesos and a large gold crucifix set with emeralds. It was a splendid haul; at one stroke Drake had covered all the costs of the expedition and had a small profit to show for all his sufferings and difficulties. Equally important, the Valparaíso raid had put fresh heart into his men. All in all, it had been a highly auspicious start to a momentous visit to King Philip's American dominions—a visit that would stir alarmed officials into sending frenzied reports to Lima, Mexico, Panama and Madrid.

One of these officials was Don Rodrigo de Quirega, Governor of Chile. News of the raid took some time to reach him as he was away in the south quelling a native revolt. As soon as he heard about Drake he returned to Santiago and gathered a small force, planning to embark with them at Valparaíso and go in pursuit of the corsair. Unfortunately, he fell ill with dropsy and had to entrust the quest to a subordinate, Gaspar de la Bareda, who set sail early in January. Another ship was sent to Callao to warn the viceroy. Both ships unaccountedly failed in their mission. Bareda never made contact with the *Golden Hind*, though as we shall see, it was not far up the coast at the beginning of 1579. Callao was certainly not forewarned of Drake's approach. There was little more that Quirega could do but he did send out messengers by road to order coastal communities to withdraw inland so that the English marauders could not land to buy food. The governor was more worried at the prospect of Drake encouraging native revolt than in the looting of a few ships. Nor was his concern without cause; the corsair was enthusiastically urging Philip to promise his people that if they would cast off the Spanish yoke they could count on English help.

Drake obviously discounted the possibility of pursuit for he allowed the *Golden Hind* and the *Capitana* to drift serenely before a southerly wind with only half their sails hoisted. He was looking for a quiet haven on or near the thirtieth parallel so that he could careen his ship and search for his support vessels. He returned Philip to his own village with presents and solemn entreaties to take note from all he had seen and heard as to whose side the white man's God was really on. He spent some days searching the coast around Tongoy, without finding any trace of the *Elizabeth* or the *Marigold*. With every day that passed his anxiety about the other ships grew. Nor could he find a suitable harbour; every bay seemed to have its Indian settlement and he could not risk a prolonged stay in any refuge which might be revealed to the Spaniards. He explained his position to the gentlemen but some of them were all for risking a trip ashore. It was very tantalising, they said, to be so near to abundant supplies of fresh food and water without being able to take advantage of them.

On 18 December Drake yielded to persuasion—and his caution was immediately justified. The two ships anchored at evening off La Herradura, a bay lying just to the south of Coquimbo which was the port for the Spanish town of La Serena. Drake agreed to let a foraging party go ashore the next morning. Fourteen men landed under the command of Richard Minivy. They found water and they managed to catch some wild pigs. While they were all engrossed in getting these provisions aboard the boat there came the sound of a sudden explosion. It was the *Golden Hind*'s signal gun. The men looked up but could see nothing. Nevertheless, they hastily responded to the pre-arranged signal. While the others manhandled the last casks and carcases Minivy kept watch. Suddenly a large force of mounted Spaniards and Indians on foot came into view and charged down the beach. Minivy's arquebus was already primed and the tow lit. Now he fired it into the advancing ranks in the hope of slowing their advance. This brought an answering fusilade and Minivy fell dead, shot through the temple. The remainder of the Englishmen made good their escape.

The alarming fact to be learned from this incident was that the garrisons at Coquimbo and La Serena had obviously been warned about the 'pirates'. They would not otherwise have turned out so promptly and in such large numbers (300 to 500 according to the various accounts). Nor would they have directed such intense hatred against the body of poor Minivy. For, in the sight of his compatriots, they cut off his head and his right hand and plucked out his heart. Then the Spaniards stripped the body and ordered their Indian companions to shoot it full of arrows. When, in the afternoon, Drake's men returned to the shore to give Minivy a decent burial there was little but a gashed and pulpy mess to be interred. This object lesson in gratuitous Spanish cruelty and violence was not lost on the Englishmen. Henceforth there were very few men on the *Golden Hind* who did not share Drake's crusading zeal against the papists. The crew regarded Minivy, a man of pronounced Protestant opinions[3] as a martyr and they determined to extract full vengeance for his death.

Three more days were spent searching for a haven. The Englishmen's northward progress was not unobserved. Frequently the lookout reported groups of horsemen who were obviously watching the ship closely. Whenever Drake sent the boat off in search of water it had to return without landing because Indians or Spaniards were spotted ashore. It was 22 December before the travellers found an uninhabited cove in 27 degrees 35 minutes. Here Drake decided to stay. But if he had hopes of hauling the *Golden Hind* ashore for proper careening he was soon disappointed; every day groups of natives came to the beach. The place was probably Salada Bay, a harbour on an arid, rocky stretch of the coast.

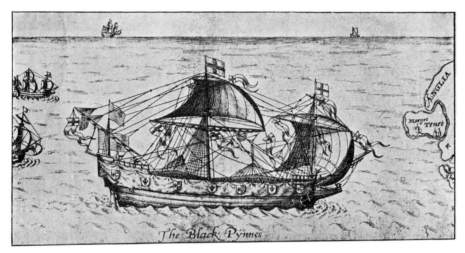

A pinnace, c. 1585

The first task to which Drake addressed himself was the erection of his last pinnace. The timbers were removed from the flagship's hold and transferred to the *Capitana* for the first stages of construction but work became more and more difficult as the vessel grew and it was obviously desirable to tow her ashore for the final stages of construction. Reconnaissance parties had by now established that there were no Indian settlements nearby and had probably discovered lookout points from which any large movement of men could be observed. After some days, therefore, Drake decided to risk completing the work ashore. The carpenters and those drafted to assist them set up their benches on a part of the beach which could be easily protected. Guards were posted on the surrounding rocks. With bare backs sweating under the sun's midsummer glare, the men set to work. It was a nerve racking business. On more than one occasion natives were seen, the alarm was sounded and the workers scrambled quickly into the boat. On the evening of 7 January a small group of Spaniards appeared and fired two arquebus shots before departing. At last, on 9 January, the work was complete and the pinnace, with one of the flagship's bronze demi-culverin mounted in the bow, was launched.[4]

The Englishmen did not spend their four weeks at Salada Bay in unrelieved drudgery. There was excellent fishing to be had and hunting for wild animals ashore. Doubtless these activities furnished part of the New Year's feast which Drake gave on the first day of 1579. There was also plenty of wine for all by courtesy of the Chilean vineyard owners and the admiral shared out some of the preserved fruits and other delicacies brought from England.

When the pinnace was ready Drake divided his complement into two parties. The larger was entrusted with the task of preparing the *Golden Hind* for careening. The remainder set out in the pinnace with Drake to search for their lost comrades. They swept an area some sixty miles to the south, prodding into every likely bay and inlet. Neither the *Elizabeth* nor the *Marigold* were anywhere to be seen. Then the south-west wind increased in strength and the pinnace could only make headway with difficulty. Sadly, Drake abandoned hope of finding his lost fleet and steered course for Salada Bay. He could not devote any more time to the search. He would have to concentrate all his efforts now in getting his one remaining ship home.

Back at the expedition's base the *Golden Hind* had been emptied of much of her cargo. Everything of value had been temporarily removed to the

Preparing to careen

Capitana and what remained aboard had been lashed down. Drake was doubly glad of his Spanish prize now. It would provide quarters for the crew while the flagship was beached and in the event of their being surprised before the *Golden Hind* was ready it would afford a means of escape.

On 14 January five days hard work began. No one liked careening; it was hot, dirty, back breaking labour. At high tide the *Golden Hind* was brought as far as possible inshore, sideways on to the beach. Wooden ramps were hammered into the sand close under her side and a system of ropes and pulleys attached the mast heads to stakes farther up the beach. As the water receded teams of men hauled on the ropes until the ship was listing at an angle which made it possible to get at her sides and bottom. Then began the scraping to remove all the limpet-like accretions covering every square inch below the waterline. Behind the cleaners came the carpenters, carefully examining the timbers for damage, worms and shrinkage. The fact that the *Golden Hind* was double-sheathed with timber probably meant that no planks needed replacing but there would be worm holes to be drilled out and plugged, gaps to be caulked, loose caulking to be prised out and replaced, damaged areas to be patched with lead. Soon the beach was alive with activity—men staggering under heavy kettles of molten tar, others minding the fires over which fresh supplies were being melted, carpenters drilling and sawing, others forcing oakum between the timbers and hammering it home. Even unpleasanter work was reserved for those labouring inside the hold. Slipping and stumbling over the slimy boards, they bucketed out the stinking, green water, pursued rats with marlinspikes by the dim light of lanterns, and peered closely at the timbers for signs of leakage or weakness. When all discoverable defects had been dealt with the external surface was given a good coating of tar and brimstone. For good measure, a layer of grease was applied on top. When all that had been done the crew retired wearily to the *Capitana* and sleep, knowing that the next day the *Golden Hind* would have to be turned round and the entire process repeated.

There was now nothing to detain Drake in this latitude and every reason for him to be gone. Cargo and equipment were quickly re-assembled on the *Golden Hind*. Two spare cannon which had been in the ballast were lashed on deck now that there was a real prospect of action. The ship was so full of stores and loot that Drake was forced to make some interesting choices. Six pipes of tar, for instance, were jettisoned to make way for some of the captured wine. On 19 January the three ships weighed anchor and sailed away northwards on a voyage of undisguised pillage.

As they proceeded the pinnace kept close inland, ever on the watch for fresh water or small groups of natives who might tell them where water was to be found. The novelty of an unlimited supply of wine had long since worn off and the men longed to slake their thirst with real Adam's ale. But this was a barren coast; most of the streams that broke through its sheer walls were drunk up by the parched earth before they reached the sea. On more than one occasion the Englishmen followed trails indicated by the Indians only to discover dried up or inadequate springs.

They were more fortunate with fish and other foodstuffs. It would be pleasant to be able to record that, whatever his attitude towards Spaniards, Drake treated the Indians fairly. This was not always the case. Sometimes he bartered for supplies with groups of natives; on other occasions he simply took what he wanted. One coastal village was relieved of half its store of fish. Later a fishing boat was captured and simply hitched to the *Golden Hind*, crew and catch remaining aboard (these fishermen did not remain captives for long: they escaped by the simple expedient of casting themselves adrift during the night).

A. The mountain. B. The Town of Potosi. C. The Royal mill for grinding the Ore. D. Watermills for cleaning the Ore.

Silver mining at Potosí

Such escapades did not delay the expedition long. Within a fortnight of quitting Salada Bay the three ships had left Chile and were coasting off Peru. They were now very close to the great source of Spanish wealth, the silver mines of Potosí. Most of the precious metal was carried by the long route which ran north-westwards along the Andean ridge to Puno on Lake Titicaca, thence down to Arequipa, where private exporters were taxed. Most of it then travelled to Arica for shipment, though some went down to

122

the smaller port at Chule. It goes without saying, however, that many Spanish businessmen found the payment of tax an inconvenience and devised their own means of conveying silver to the port. Drake was about to benefit from this illicit trade.

At the mouth of Pisagua river he noticed the small Indian village of Tarapacá and went ashore in the pinnace to see if there was anything worth having. All was quiet and the village seemed at first sight deserted but entering one of the huts they found a Spaniard sleeping soundly. He was worn out after making the journey from Potosí by tortuous mountain tracks. Beside him, in a nonchalant heap on the bare earth, lay thirteen bars of silver, which he had unloaded from his llamas so that they would be safe. If the English accounts of the incident are to be believed, Drake's men managed to remove the silver without disturbing the courier's repose. If that is true it would be interesting to know how the unfortunate fellow explained the loss to his master, or, indeed, if he ever had the courage to do so.

Drake's good fortune was not over for that day. Landing again a few miles further up the coast he encountered another Spaniard with an Indian boy driving eight llamas carrying another eight hundred pounds of silver. Both silver and llamas were brought aboard the *Golden Hind*, the one destined for the hold, the other for the pot. This was a very welcome addition to the expedition's profit but it was, Drake believed, merely a prelude to what was to come. His ships were only a matter of hours away from Arica and, if Juan Griego was right, the royal storehouse there should be stacked with silver bars.

Drake's flotilla slipped quietly into the harbour of Arica in the warm dusk of a February evening. There were only two small ships riding at anchor and Drake repeated the tactics which had been so successful at Valparaíso. Without any overt show of military strength he boarded the Spanish vessels. One of them was unmanned. On the other, a ship belonging to Philip Corso (a Corsican), they found a solitary Fleming, Nicolas Jorje. It was this ship which also carried the only cargo of interest—thirty-five bars of silver and a chest of silver coins amounting to some 500 pesos.[5] The silver was quickly trans-shipped as was some wine aboard the other vessel, a general trader from Lima.

It was now dark and Drake decided there could be no question of attacking before morning a strange town about which he knew nothing. Then he heard a most unwelcome sound; the church bell clanging an excited alarm. When it stopped other noises drifted across the water—the shouting of men, the clatter of horses' hooves, the metallic sounds of military preparation. Would the people of Arica attack him at night? Drake decided to deter them from such an action. He called for his gunners and loosed off a few rounds of cannon fire towards the shore. He ordered his trumpeter and even his musicians to perform at intervals through the hours of darkness to let the

Spaniards know the English were not asleep. And in case the enemy should risk an attack he doubled the watch aboard the *Golden Hind* and ordered all the crew to sleep with their weapons beside them.

Early next morning he filled two boats with armed men and rowed towards the town. But a couple of hundred yards short of the beach he stopped. There, drawn up in front of the houses and public buildings, was a formidable reception committee of armed and mounted men. Drake had made a tactical error. If the silver warehouse was his objective he should have raided the town immediately on arrival while he still had the advantage of surprise. Now he would have to be content with the loot in the ships. He cursed his ill fortune. If the voyage had gone according to plan he would now have had three ships, with their boats, more pinnaces and well over a hundred men. With such an assault force, Arica and all the treasure depots of the Pacific coast right up to Panama would be at his mercy. Now fate or, possibly, human cowardice—for Drake must have had at the back of his mind the suspicion that Wynter and Thomas had deserted him—had robbed him of all these rich prizes.

He was angry and he left Arica a symbol of his anger. As he sailed away with the *Golden Hind*, the *Capitana* and Corso's ship, he left the Lima merchantman ablaze in the harbour.[6]

The next port of call on the silver route was Chule, the harbour for Arequipa, over a hundred miles up the coast. It was, therefore, Drake's next port of call also. The admiral now travelled close inshore in the pinnace, leaving the *Golden Hind* in charge of the two prizes. From information he picked up on the coast it appeared that a large treasure ship had very recently passed. On all the ships an eager lookout was kept. A day and a half's sailing brought them to Chule. And there she was. The silver ship lay at anchor and seemed deserted. Judging from the crowd of people on the shore all her crew must have left her. With the thrill of the huntsman who has just had his first sight of the quarry, Drake steered the pinnace into the harbour. It was only as he drew closer to the treasure ship that Drake began to realise that something was wrong. The sides of the vessel were glistening in the sunlight. They were still wet. That could only mean one thing—she had just discharged her cargo. Shielding his eyes against the midday sun, Drake saw an ominous line of llamas making their way up into the hills. There was the silver. To emphasize his failure the townsfolk now began jeering and shouting at him that he had missed 500 bars of silver by two hours. He boarded the vessel and searched from stem to stern. Nothing. Dejected and frustrated, he ordered his men to set sail in her and bring her out to join his growing fleet.

When he stepped back aboard his own ship he was still in a rage. Searching around for someone to vent his wrath on, he saw the Fleming, Jorje. He grabbed the man, swore at him and threatened to kill him for not telling him about the silver ship. What was as worrying as the loss of a valuable haul was the fact that Drake had now lost the advantage of surprise. Chule had been warned of his approach by messengers galloping along the valley road from Arica. With the increasing uproar that he was creating as he progressed along the coast it was certain that the authorities would try to send warning messages by land and sea to overtake him. Speed was therefore essential and Drake, accordingly, decided to get rid of the prize ships.

It was not an easy decision and it was one that was certain to provoke discontent among the crew. It meant jettisoning ships and cargo of known value. There were many gentlemen and sailors who preferred to stand by the old adage that a bird in the hand is worth two in the bush. But Drake was probably already thinking ahead to the homeward journey. Whichever way he went he would have to face a hazardous ocean crossing and the prospect of assaying it with a fleet of undermanned ships was not attractive. The next day (9 February), therefore, having removed all he required from the captured vessels, he cast them adrift far out to sea. If they were ever found it would be too late for anyone to use them for pursuit.

The *Golden Hind* was now in a busy shipping lane. Twice in twenty-four hours she overtook merchant vessels and the admiral sent boarding parties to capture them. But both vessels proved to be carrying only wine and Drake let them go.

Dawn on Friday the thirteenth found the *Golden Hind* a few miles short of Callao de Lima. Many superstitious Spaniards and Englishmen would have cause to reflect on their luck before that auspicious day drew to a close. At first fortune seemed to be on Drake's side. Standing cautiously out to sea, he saw three vessels leave Callao on the morning tide. He apprehended one, a bark headed for the small port of Cañete. She carried nothing of value but it was information that Drake was principally after and with that her captain, Gaspar Martín, was well furnished. Alone on the *Golden Hind*'s poop deck encircled by unpleasant-looking English gentlemen the poor man readily answered all the questions fired at him. There were, he said, many fine ships in Callao of which two were loading up with large cargoes of silver. Unfortunately, Drake had missed the greatest prize, for the magnificent *Nuestra Señora de la Concepción* had left Callao a fortnight before with one of the year's major consignments of silver.

For the rest of the day the English ship kept well out to sea and, of course, they did not release Martín's vessel. Drake formulated his plans. They were essentially the same as those followed at Valparaíso and Arica: he would go in at nightfall, cut out the silver ships with as little fuss as possible and sail them out of the harbour. There was no question of attempting a shore raid with the large garrisons of Callao and Lima so close at hand.

Shortly after 10 p.m., guided by men taken off Martín's ships, the pinnace, followed by the *Golden Hind*, slipped through the narrow Boquerón channel between the mainland and San Lorenzo Island. Disaster almost struck when

CALIOV DE LIMA

The port of Callao

the leadsman called out that they were running into shallows. Drake seized the pilot by the throat and threatened to hang him if the ship grounded. But the *Golden Hind* passed over the bar into deeper water and safely entered Callao harbour. He moored and sent some armed men off in the boat to enquire for the ship of Miguel Angel (the vessel reputedly carrying the largest cargo of precious metal). He took some more men in the pinnace and set off on the same errand. It took little time to discover the silver ship, clamber aboard and swiftly silence the guard. Impatiently, but quietly, the hatch covers were removed and a lantern thrust down into the hold. Empty! The cargo had not yet been loaded.

A quick search of several of the other vessels revealed the same disappointing fact. All the silver in Lima was still ashore and safely under lock and key. After disabling the merchantmen by cutting their cables Drake returned to his own ship but was allowed no time to consider what to do next. The harbour authorities had noticed the newcomer. A boat drew along-side the *Golden Hind* and a Spanish voice called out of the darkness.

'What ship are you and where are you from?'

Quickly Drake grabbed one of his Spanish prisoners. With a sword point in his back the frightened man made answer, probably with the first words which came into his head.

'Miguel Angel's ship from Chile.'

The puzzled official was understandably dissatisfied. Instead of rowing back across the harbour, he began to pull himself aboard. The Englishmen stood, hands on weapons, frozen into inaction. The Spaniard's face appeared above the rail. It looked around. It saw the cannon. It stared. It disappeared.* Drake's men rushed to the side to see the dim shape of the rowing boat merging into the gloom. Quickly Drake ordered his men to fire their arrows. The only response was the sound of more frenzied rowing and the agitated cry of 'Frenchmen!'†

There was nothing to be done now but leave. There was plenty of time for that. With the shipping drifting anchorless about the harbour it would be daybreak before a pursuit could be organised. Then a vessel passed close by the *Golden Hind*, sails set, lamps blazing, orders being shouted. It was the one ship Drake's men had missed because it had entered harbour after them. It belonged to Alonso Rodríguez Bautista of Panama and it was heading out to sea. Drake sent a pinnace full of men after the runaway and they caught up with her in the middle of the wide harbour.

'Heave to and receive boarders!' one of Drake's men called in Spanish.

The answer was a volley of arquebus shots and one of the Englishmen fell dead in the boat. Drake weighed anchor immediately and soon caught up with the sluggish, laden merchantman. Now it was the turn of the Spaniards to receive a taste of gunfire. Rodríguez himself was among the men who fell wounded. Seeing this the crew lost whatever small appetite they may have had for a fight. They rapidly departed in the ship's boat, leaving Drake to put his own men aboard and sail her out past San Lorenzo's Island into the black, empty ocean. As the Englishmen quitted Callao after their brief two-hour visit they heard the bells ringing out their strident alarm.

It was not the bells which woke Don Francisco Alvarez de Toledo. The English pirates had already been gone an hour before he was aroused. As soon as he had made sense of the garbled, excited accounts of the men who had galloped up from Callao he acted swiftly and decisively. He was no cowardly petty official like his subordinates along the coast who took des-perate panic measures when their towns were attacked only to slump back

---

* No Pacific coast merchant ship carried cannon.

† Most of the pirates operating in the Caribbean at this time were French and France was Spain's most powerful enemy. The mistake was therefore a natural one.

into comfortable sloth as soon as danger was passed. He gathered a force of *caballeros* and sent some on ahead to mount guard over 200,000 pesos worth of bar silver in the royal store. Then he issued a general call to arms, sending his servants to knock up all the able-bodied men in Lima. When they had assembled in the plaza he distributed arms and set out immediately for the harbour.

A Peruvian woman

Dawn was breaking as Toledo marshalled his troops on the quay. He commandeered two of the larger merchant ships and embarked three hundred men under the command of General Diego de Trias Trejo assisted by the adventurous Pedro Sarmiento de Gamboa. The prospects of catching up with invaders were excellent for the very good reason that the *Golden Hind* and the captured vessel were still in sight. On leaving the harbour they had run into a flat calm. Now, though an offshore morning breeze had arisen, Drake's ship had got into the lee of San Lorenzo Island.

The pursuing vessels, all sails hoisted to the breeze, drifted slowly across the bay. When Drake saw them his first thought was to rid himself of Rodriquez's ship. He sent the pinnace across to her with all his Spanish prisoners, including Juan Griego, for whom he had no more use. Drake watched as the pinnace nudged the other ship and unloaded its human cargo. He had ordered that this was to be done and the prize crew brought off as quickly as possible. But the pinnace still had not started back and the pursuers were gaining. Abruptly he ordered the boat to be brought alongside. He had himself rowed across to the Spanish ship, where, shouting and swearing at the men, he chased them into the pinnace. Back aboard the *Golden Hind* he hoisted every stitch of canvas and, at last finding a breeze, pulled away to the north-west. The two Spanish ships followed throughout the day but the corsair steadily increased his lead and, by the next morning, he had disappeared from view.

Sarmiento, contemptuous of this humiliating failure to capture the pirates when they were almost within their grasp, thought that the ships were largely to blame: 'With the movement of the people and being narrow they were very crank and could not carry sail, on which account they went like drunken men and were much hindered in sailing.' But it was not only the ships which were at fault. Pedro de Arana, in charge of one of them, had intercepted Rodriguez's ship and spoken with Juan Griego. From him he had learned alarming facts about Drake's weapons, manpower and armament, which made him think very carefully about the whole enterprise.

Pedro de Arana, having learned this, went to the *Capitana* at night with some of those from his ship and discussed with the General and many other gentlemen whether they should continue following the enemy or return in better shape and with more force to follow them. The General was of the opinion that they should follow the pirates, but there were many of the contrary opinion, pointing out that it was advisable to return to the port, giving in support the reasons which then occurred to them, especially the bad plight of the ships and the fact that they carried no food, guns, munitions, nor engines to throw fire to oppose those of the Englishmen which were many. For this reason, our people incurred much risk as the ships were unballasted, on which account it would not be possible to catch up with the enemy, and even if we did, the damage which our people would receive from the guns was a certainty as our ships had nothing except their arquebuses with which to defend themselves. What appeared to be the most forcible argument was that many gentlemen were very seasick and not able either to stand on their feet or fight...[7]

These arguments prevailed and the ships returned to Callao where the gentlemen soldiers soon had cause to regret their lack of zeal. The viceroy was furious when he heard that his ships had not even engaged the enemy. No one was allowed to disembark and, after a preliminary hearing, many of the leading officers were placed on trial and either fined or exiled.

But Toledo's reactions were far from being all negative. He questioned Drake's released prisoners, particularly the Greek, and from them he obtained full details about the voyage of the *Golden Hind* and her sister ships. Now he learned, for the first time, just who it was he was dealing with—Francis Drake, the English pirate whose name was so well known on the Atlantic seaboard. Such an audacious and dangerous criminal Toledo was determined to apprehend. He summoned a meeting of the Royal *Audiencia* (the governing council of Peru) on Monday 16 February, and they agreed that Drake's appearance on their coast was a major emergency which justified a lavish expediture of royal funds. Toledo proposed to send a bark immediately to call at every port as far as Panama warning the officials to keep a watch out for the Englishman. She was also to overtake the two treasure ships currently *en route* for the Isthmus (the *Nuestra Señora de la Concepción* and a vessel commanded by Sebastian Pérez) and order them to land their bullion. A royal galley lying at Guayaquil was to embark on a search of all the creeks and inlets of the coast while from Lima two fully equipped and armed ships were to be despatched in pursuit of Drake.

It was in connection with this expedition that Don Francisco approached Juan Guttierez de Ulloa, Chief Clerk to the Holy Inquisition, ordering him to make available for interrogation John Oxenham and his two colleagues currently being held in the Inquisition's prison at Lima. Four days later the dishevelled captives were, accordingly, led forth one at a time for examination by the civil authorities. Each was asked the same questions. First and most urgent, the viceroy wanted to know if they knew anything about the manufacture of ordnance and incendiary devices suitable for use at sea. Clearly the complete lack of cannon on most ships based in Peru and New Spain was a major drawback when attempting to combat piracy. The fact that Toledo was prepared to contemplate setting up a gun foundry is a proof of his imaginative grasp of the problem if not of his realism.

The next thing Toledo wanted to know was whether Drake's voyage was the prelude to a deliberate English colonial invasion. Did the English Queen contemplate such a policy? Were her subjects equipped with the knowledge, ships and skill to pass at will to and fro through the Straits of Magellan?

Finally the prisoners were questioned as to what they knew about Drake. How good a sailor was he? Did they think he would return home via the Straits or seek some other route?

Having satisfied the authorities to the best of their ability on all these points, the prisoners were returned to their cells. They were to be kept in miserable confinement for a further twenty-one months. Then, despite having satisfied the Inquisition by confessing and abjuring their 'heresies', they were executed on criminal charges by the civil authorities.

By 27 February the two ships were fitted out and provisioned ready for departure. 120 well armed soldiers were embarked under the viceroy's most trusted captains and command was entrusted to his own son, Don Luis de Toledo. The hunt was up.

CHAPTER NINE

'This man . . . is a devil'

20 FEBRUARY—16 APRIL 1579

The hunt was up in another sense also; while Don Luis de Toledo was pursuing Drake, Drake was pursuing the *Nuestra Señora de la Concepción*. He had decided that if the voyage was going to make a large profit it would be made at sea. To attack any Spanish settlement was now far too risky but a floating treasure chest like the *Nuestra Señora*—that was another matter. San Juan de Anton's ship had a two-week start but Drake had discovered that she was making a leisurely progress along the coast to take on consignments of flour. By making all possible speed the *Golden Hind* was rapidly closing the gap on her unsuspecting quarry. If all the accounts Drake gathered were to be believed the capture of the *Nuestra Señora* would prove the greatest *coup* of his piratical career. She was one of the finest ships in the coastal trade and she was very heavily laden with silver. She also carried armament in the form of several cannon—a precaution unusual in these trouble-free waters. This was why she was nicknamed the *Cacafuego*, the Spitfire. Such a prize was worth making a great effort to outpace but there were other considerations which also urged haste: the further north the Englishmen went, the closer they were drawing to danger. The coast of what is now Ecuador and Colombia was more densely populated than the coast further south and news of the corsair would certainly be following rapidly. If he did not apprehend the *Cacafuego* long before she reached the Gulf of Panama, Drake knew that he would have to let her go.

Drake needed every scrap of information he could gather and he did not want to go ashore to gather it. He travelled in the pinnace and explored the harbours and inlets while the *Golden Hind* followed a parallel course in deeper water. A keen watch was kept for the treasure ship and the admiral had promised a gold chain to the first man to sight her. A couple of days out of Callao an excited cry came from the masthead. A sail had been sighted on the horizon. Drake sped towards her but soon knew she was not the *Nuestra Señora*. She was small—the sort of ship classed vaguely as a frigate—and she was travelling in the opposite direction. He boarded her and while his men rummaged through the cargo he questioned the captain and pilots. He gleaned little from them; one man thought that the *Cacafuego* was about three days ahead. Drake decided to waste no more time with the frigate. Having selected a few trifles from her cargo of general goods he let her go. Doubtless she made straight for the nearest harbour to report the alarming news that there were English pirates about.[1]

A few more days brought the travellers to the small harbour of Paita. Drake knew that this was one of the *Nuestra Señora*'s ports of call and that he would be able to find out how far ahead she was. As Drake's two vessels sailed in they saw a single ship anchored in the bay. And that ship's crew saw them. From the panic which gripped the sailors it is obvious that news of the Englishmen's approach had gone before them. Completely disregarding the master's orders, the men clambered into the boat and rowed towards the shore. Others flung themselves into the water in their frenzy to escape from the pirates. When Drake climbed aboard he found only the master, the pilot and a few negro slaves. The usual search of the ship began and she was found to be carrying wine and wax. The pirates took sixty jars of wine, two boxes of wax and whatever food they needed, including bread, chickens and a pig. Drake also transferred the pilot, Custodio Rodríguez, to his own ship and then sailed away. From Rodríguez he learned that San Juan de Anton's vessel was little more than two days ahead. When he relayed this information to the crew there was great excitement and every man went about his tasks with renewed vigour.

As they rounded Parina Point just to the north of Paita another vessel came into view sailing towards them. The normal procedure was followed— minute search and close questioning of the officers. Neither yielded anything of value and the ship was allowed to go. Within a few hours the English-men were sailing across the wide Gulf of Guayaquil from which issued the merchant and royal vessels launched from the thriving dockyards. Drake had no intention of rushing into populous, well fortified Guayaquil. In any case, he probably already knew that San Juan de Anton was not calling there.

Sailing on past Manta, Drake's ships rounded Cape Pesado on the last day of the month. Immediately, the cry of 'Sail ho!' came from the hopeful watcher in the crow's nest, forty feet above the main deck. Ahead lay a well-laden merchantman travelling northwards. She was fast and it took Drake some time to overhaul her in the pinnace. When he did so he discovered that she was not the *Nuestra Señora* but a vessel belonging to Benito Díaz Bravo carrying ship's tackle and provisions to Panama where the new governor of the Philippines, Gonzalo Ronquillo de Peñalosa, was fitting out his expedition to Manila. Also aboard were several wealthy passengers headed for Spain.

The crew were swiftly brought under control and locked up. Then Drake turned his attention to the more distinguished company on the poop deck. His menace was tinged with faint politeness as he asked the group of gentlemen and friars for their money and valuables. The captives exchanged anxious glances. Then they slowly produced their treasures—a bag of silver coins, gold crucifixes, a jewelled pendant. Díaz Bravo told Drake where to find forty bars of silver and some gold. The pile in the middle of the main deck grew most gratifyingly but Drake could tell from the faces of his prisoners that some of them had not revealed all their valuables. Drake waved his sword towards them.

'Gentlemen, in a few moments I shall have you all conveyed aboard my ship. Then my men will search this vessel from stem to stern. If they discover any hidden items which you have not told me about I will have you all hung.'

It was mere bluff. Drake wanted to extract everything of value from Díaz Bravo's ship without having to go through the time consuming process of searching it thoroughly. The bluff worked. His prisoners scuttled to their quarters and returned with more money, a large gold cross and a bag of exquisite emeralds some as long as a man's finger.

As the passengers were rowed across to the *Golden Hind* Drake turned his attention to the ship. He had already been appraising her carefully. She was fast and trim and she might serve him well in his race with the *Nuestra Señora*. He ordered his men to run up full sail and the Spanish ship leaped forward before the freshening offshore breeze. His mind was made up, Díaz Bravo was about to lose his vessel and his livelihood. Drake promised to return the Spaniard his ship in Panama (where he certainly had no intention of going) or to pay for it with some of the captured gold (which he probably had no intention of handing over). His men now threw overboard most of the tackle Díaz Bravo was carrying and fetched a couple of cannon from the *Golden Hind*. He also rid himself of the passengers by having them rowed ashore.

During their brief stay aboard the flagship these dignitaries had chatted with the English gentlemen. It had been the first chance Drake's companions had had to catch up with news from Europe. They learned that King Sebastian of Portugal was dead and succeeded by his grand uncle, the elderly Cardinal Henry. They learned that politico-religious conflict continued in France. Most important of all they learned that Don John of Austria, the Catholic champion, the victor of Lepanto, the hammer of the Dutch Protestants, the potential leader of a crusade against heretical England, was dead. When Drake heard this he asked Díaz Bravo to confirm it and when the Spanish captain had done so Drake 'at once called all his men together and told them this in his language. They all received the news with great pleasure and began to dance'.[2] There was nothing feigned about the joy or relief of the Englishmen. They all knew that political events in Europe were critical for them. A Catholic triumph resulting in an enforced *rapprochement* between England and Spain or a Spanish-backed revolution in England would mean that they would be branded as pirates, disowned by their government, have their booty confiscated and be thrown into prison. As it was, Catholic Europe was in disarray and the Queen's greatest enemy had been removed by the hand of God.

It was news worth celebrating and celebrate they did. The elated English commander jovially informed Díaz Bravo, 'you must know that my men are going to have a great banquet tonight'.[3] The Spaniard tried to force a smile while ruefully reflecting that he was to be the provider of the feast. As darkness fell the poor man sat at Drake's right hand, an unwilling guest, and watched the English gentlemen and sailors gorge themselves on his chicken, ham and wine. He must have been puzzled by their jubilation but then he had not been fourteen and a half months away from home with no means of receiving news of his own land.

Apart from the encouraging tidings they had heard, the Englishmen had been in the company of men who were actually on their way to Europe by a regular route. That very fact made home seem much closer. So they ate and drank and sang and danced and Drake's musicians played and everyone, except poor Díaz Bravo, was happy. The corsair was in very high spirits, telling Díaz Bravo about his journey and indulging in a few travellers' tales for the gullible Spaniard's benefit, as the captive later reported:

> He now had come with five galleons, in which they had left the coast of Guinea and entered by the Strait by a country in 55° where he found people of one eye, one foot, and one hand. He said that he had all the vessels in this South Seas at his command . . .'[4]

In the morning Díaz Bravo was surprised to discover that the mood of his captors had changed drastically. Drake was now as ill-tempered as he had, twelve hours before, been jovial. Whether he was suffering from a hangover or whether some, unrecorded, event had soured him we do not know. We do know that he had made two important decisions. He decided not to use the captured ship. According to Díaz Bravo the reason for Drake's change of mind was that he did not have enough crew to man both vessels (his total complement was by now reduced to about eighty) but it is difficult to see why he had not thought of this before. His other decision was that the Spaniards were deceiving him; they still had silver concealed aboard the ship. Perhaps some Spanish sailor in his cups had boasted about how the English had been fooled over the real quantity of bullion aboard. However the, quite erroneous, idea was propagated it threw Drake into a rage. He was intensely jealous of his own and his country's reputation and the thought of being made to look stupid by foreigners—particularly Spaniards—angered him beyond measure. He questioned every member of Díaz Bravo's crew, swearing and threatening death and every kind of torture. The foreigners were terrified but they could tell Drake nothing. The corsair was not satisfied. He ordered ropes to be thrown over one of the spars, and a noose put round every man's neck. Now would they tell him the truth? The gibbering Spaniards swore by all the saints that there was no concealed silver. Drake gave the order for the ropes to be pulled tight. The horrified sailors felt themselves lifted off the deck. They choked, fought for breath, thought their last moment had come. Then they were lowered again. Now

134

would they talk, the corsair demanded. No? Very well, he would hang them, one by one, until the whereabouts of the hidden treasure was revealed. He pointed to Francisco Jacome, the clerk. A fresh hangman's rope was thrown over a spar so that it dangled above the blue water. Jacome was taken to the ship's side; the noose was placed around his neck; and he was once more ordered to reveal what he knew. He knew nothing. A push from behind and he was swinging by the neck above the Pacific. But only for an instant. The rope was cut and he plunged, bound and unconscious, into the water. English sailors were waiting in the ship's boat and Jacome was soon fished out and returned to his shipmates.

All this cruel sport had used up valuable hours of sailing time to no effect. Yet, in his rage, Drake seems to have been oblivious of his prime objective, the pursuit of the *Nuestra Señora*. Nor had he yet finished with Díaz Bravo's ship. He stripped it of all its provisions. He cut off the foresail and foresail yard. He wrapped some of the other sails round the anchor and cast it into the sea. He helped himself to clothing and other goods from the passengers' chests. Only then did he put the crew back aboard and, sailing away to northward with his own vessels, leave Díaz Bravo to make port as best he could. Well might the Spaniard claim on reaching Manta, 'truly it was our Lord who brought us here, and no other'.[5] Once ashore, his crew told terrifying stories of the cruelties practised by the English pirates, stories which spread an incredible panic among the small coastal communities. When Don Luis de Toledo arrived at Santa Elena twelve days later he found the town deserted and a note left by the innkeeper to say that everyone had fled for fear of the Englishmen.

The *Golden Hind* and the pinnace resumed their patrol of the coast. They rounded Cape San Francisco and just before noon the optimistic cry once more rang out from the crow's nest. John Drake, taking his turn on watch, had spied a three-masted ship travelling north, twelve miles ahead and slightly to leeward. This time, surely it was the *Cacafuego*. In this belief Drake laid careful plans. Normally he would have sped after her and taken her with the pinnace. But the *Cacafuego* was reputedly well armed and that called for different tactics. Drake transferred to the *Golden Hind* and kept the pinnace alongside with sails furled. He ordered the cannon to be run out, loaded and primed. The armoury was opened and weapons distributed. The gentlemen donned their helmets and part-armour. Then Drake resorted to a well-known ruse among pirates. He ordered full sails to be hoisted and at the same time he ran out to the stern a line of water-filled wine jars. These acted as a drag so that the *Golden Hind* looked for all the world like a well-laden merchantman who could only make slow headway even with all sails set.

The trick worked admirably. Sighting the stranger, San Juan de Anton aboard the *Nuestra Señora* changed course towards her. All through the late afternoon and evening the two vessels drew closer together. Not until nine

Caca Fogo.

Caca Plata.

The attack on the Cacafuego

o'clock did the treasure ship draw alongside and hail the *Golden Hind* demanding her name and destination. He did not receive the answer he expected.

'Strike sail, Mr Juan de Anton, or we will send you to the bottom!'

It was obviously a joke.

'What old tub is ordering me to surrender? Come aboard yourselves and strike sail.'

The elegant captain's laughter soon stuck in his throat and he stared incredulously as in answer to a trumpet blast a line of men suddenly appeared above the *Golden Hind*'s deck rail, levelling arquebuses and bows. There was a flash, a roar and his mizzen mast slewed round and fell over the stern, dragging a tangle of rigging. At the same moment shot and arrows came whizzing across the deck. One man fell with a howl of pain. The rest rushed to take cover. But the fusillade was not repeated. Instead the *Cacafuego* was boarded by a band of ruffians from her port side. The pinnace had come round unobserved and her complement was now scrambling up the channels of the shrouds.[6]

San Juan was hustled aboard the *Golden Hind* and presented to Drake on the poop deck. The corsair smiled reassuringly as he removed his helmet.

'Don't distress yourself, such are the fortunes of war.'

Drake embraced his defeated enemy and then ushered him to the poop cabin. But there was no time for courtesies and once in the cabin San Juan was locked up and placed under guard. Having secured the Spanish crew in the *Cacafuego*'s poop cabin, Drake ordered both ships to crowd on sail and make away from land north-westwards. All that night there was suppressed excitement among the Englishmen. Was the *Nuestra Señora* as richly laden as they had been led to expect? Had this single capture made them all rich men?

Early next morning the admiral went across to have breakfast aboard the *Cacafuego*, having left orders that San Juan was to be well fed from Drake's own silver at his own table. Drake's considerate, even generous, treatment of San Juan was not prompted solely by his desire to impress his enemies or to display the attributes of a gentleman, strong as these tendencies were in the low-born seaman. He was drawn to this other captain because he, too, was an Englishman. 'San Juan de Anton' was the Spanish version of St John of Southampton and identifies the captain as a member of an ancient Hampshire family. Nuño da Silva commented that he spoke English and had been brought up in England though he was, in fact, a Biscayan.[7] This probably indicates nothing more than that San Juan spoke Spanish with a heavy accent. There was nothing unusual about this; foreign merchants and captains often settled in the Spanish colonies and were quite unmolested as long as they remained good Catholics. However, San Juan very sensibly played down his English connections when giving evidence before the royal court in Panama.

Drake's own breakfast aboard the *Nuestra Señora* was a hurried one; he was impatient to count the loot. It was a fantastic haul: 1,300 bars of silver, fourteen chests of silver coins, and an unspecified quantity of gold and jewels. Checking the ship's register, Drake noted that the value of the silver and gold listed in the name of the king and other individuals was 362,000 pesos. But in addition the *Cacafuego* carried a large quantity of unregistered treasure, the value of which has never been known. San Juan reckoned it at 400,000 pesos but this is probably an underestimate. Whatever its precise value, the cargo of the *Nuestra Señora de la Concepción* represented for the admiral and his men a treasure beyond their wildest dreams. It was a very genial Drake who with mock solemnity ticked off the items on the ship's cargo list and presented San Juan de Anton with a receipt for them. Then he lined his sailors up and distributed to them all the silver and gold plate. Each man put his mark on his own booty and returned it to the admiral for safe keeping but it is doubtful whether this prevented many of them dicing away their share of the prize as they lay on the bleached boards in the equitorial sunshine.

A Spanish silver coin of 1557 with Philip II's image, and its reverse

This was an important moment for Drake. It was the moment when he proved to his own crew that he was a man worth following. It was the moment when he recompensed himself handsomely for the losses sustained at San Juan de Ulua. It was the moment when he could feel confident about his reception in England. Whatever the political situation in Europe, whatever the balance on the royal Council between the pro- and anti-Spanish factions, he would be able to show the Queen and his influential backers a profit of several thousand per cent on their investment. Francis Drake could easily be thrown to the wolves if political expediency required it, but it was difficult to see Elizabeth disowning her pirate and returning all his booty to the Spanish government.

All Drake's prisoners remarked his jubilation and confidence during the next few days. The ships sailed north-westwards before a fresh wind and, on 3 March, when they were well away from land Drake had the sails struck while the treasure, provisions, tackle and other items that took his fancy were transferred to his own vessel. Then they resumed their course for another three days. During all this time Drake showed San Juan and the *Cacafuego*'s passengers elaborate courtesy and the most lavish hospitality.

As they ate well of the salt pork, chicken, bread and fish that the corsair had taken from various prizes, they were impressed by the man's fastidiousness and style of living. He was attended by nine or ten gentlemen who would not dream of seating themselves at table before their leader. He dined off silver gilt plate engraved with his arms. He ate to the sound of violins and 'carries all possible dainties and perfumed waters. He said that many of these had been given him by the Queen.'[8] Drake showed his 'guests' the ship's armament, the goods he had for trade and the equipment he carried for repairing the ship and establishing fortifications ashore. With especial pride he displayed his charts and the paintings he and John had made of landmarks and stretches of coastline. They observed with interest, but with outward disapproval, the daily gatherings for prayer. Remembering the Inquisition, they were thankful that their captor allowed them to remain aloof in the fore part of the ship during these services.

And Drake talked to them, these inquisitive, apprehensive, stiffly formal Spaniards, talked not unguardedly but certainly affably and volubly. He told them how he had found his way into the South Sea and warned them they could no longer regard it as a Spanish lake. He told them that he came with the direct and explicit authority of his Queen. He warmly threatened the Spanish authorities with retaliation if they did not allow English merchants to trade in the Americas. He spoke of old scores still to be settled and fresh grievances which made him angry. He complained of the behaviour of the Viceroy of New Spain at San Juan de Ulua and he became most heated when he spoke about John Oxenham and his colleagues who were being held by the Inquisition in Lima.

> He said he cared nothing for the Viceroy of Peru nor for all his people. He charged San Juan de Anton to beg the Viceroy of Peru from him not to kill the English prisoners, and said that if they were killed, it would cost more than two thousand heads, not those of people of Spain, but of these parts, adding that if he reached England alive, there would be no one there who would attempt to hinder him from carrying out his threat.[9]

San Juan tried to pacify Drake by assuring him that the Viceroy would not kill the prisoners but would more likely send them to Chile to serve in military garrisons fighting against the Indians.

When the Spaniards cautiously pressed him about his plans concerning the return home to England Drake showed little reticence. He told them there were four ways out of the South Sea—the Straits of Magellan, the Moluccas route, Norway (presumably northwards up the west coast of America to the Arctic regions and then westwards around the north of Asia), and a fourth route he refused to divulge. It was not difficult to conclude that Drake was referring to the fabled Straits of Anian, the western end of the north-west passage.

Drake's skill as a navigator and the supreme confidence he displayed at sailing in these unfamiliar waters impressed and worried the Spaniards. Drake knew very well that this would be the case. He knew his prisoners would be questioned by the authorities on their return to the coast and he fully intended to create among those authorities as much confusion and anxiety as possible. In this he was abundantly successful: for months the reports would be flooding back to Spain from Mexico and Peru. Everyone who had met the corsair would be questioned and their depositions forwarded to Madrid. Throughout Spanish America from Lima to Guatemala alcaldes and captains would be reinforcing local defences and contributing ships and men to search for the pirates. Then they would hasten to explain their failure in complaining officialese. Appeals for more armaments would be despatched to the Council for the Indies. Pedro Sarmiento de Gamboa would lead an expedition back through Magellan's Strait with a view to establishing garrisons to protect the 'back door' to the South Sea. For years the merchants and officials of Peru and New Spain would live in fear of another visitation by Englishmen. And all because of one man—Francis Drake.

On 6 March the corsair concluded that he could safely rid himself of the *Cacafuego* and her crew. He also decided to bid farewell to his captives with a generous gesture (which he could well afford).

> Before the Englishmen turned loose my ship, [San Juan reported] he gave certain articles to those whom he had robbed. In money he gave thirty and forty pesos to each one, and to some, pieces of Portuguese linen and tools, such as pick-axes and pruning knives, and two of his own decorated coats. To a soldier named Victoria he gave some side-arms, to me a musket which he said had been sent him from Germany, for which reason he esteemed it highly, and to the clerk, a steel shield and a sword, telling us that he gave us these so we should seem to be men-at-arms. To me he gave two pipes of tar, six quintals of German iron and a barrel of powder, and to a merchant named Cuevas he gave some fans with looking-glasses in them, telling him they were for his wife. To me, he gave a basin of gilded silver with a name written in the middle of it which said, 'Francisqus Draques', and at the time he turned me loose, he gave me a safe-conduct in English, signed with his name, telling me that he gave it to me so that if the other two English ships, which had been reported to be behind him, should fall in with me they would not do me any harm, nor rob me again. He said he was the Captain-General of all of them and they would comply with his orders. He made very much of the favour which he did me in giving me that passport, telling me that the captain of one of the ships was a very cruel man and that if I should fall in with him he would not leave a man alive, but with that document from him, I would be safe from them.[10]

The safe conduct fell into the hands of the Spanish authorities and a copy of it was sent to the Viceroy of Peru. He forced one of the imprisoned Englishmen, John Butler, to translate it into Spanish for him. Re-translated into English it reads as follows:

Mr Winter. If it please God that by favourable chance Your Honour should meet Sant Juan de Anton, I pray you to treat him well, in accordance to the word I have given him. If Your Honour should be lacking in any of the things that Sant Juan de Anton carries, pay him double the value in the merchandise that Your Honour carries. Give orders that none of your soldiers are to do him harm or wound him. What we determined about the return to our country will be carried out if God so wills, although I greatly doubt whether this letter will reach your hands, I abide as God knows, constantly praying to the Lord who holds you and me and all the world in His keeping to save or to damn. I give him thanks always. Amen.

This my writing is not only for Winter but also for Mr Thomas, Mr Arle [Charles] and Mr Coube [Caube] and Mr Anthony and all the other good friends whom I commend to Him who redeemed us with His Blood. I have faith in God that he will not inflict more toils upon us but will help us in our tribulations. I beseech you for the love of Jesus Christ, that if God permits you to suffer afflictions you do not despair of the great Mercy of God, for the great Prophet says that the Lord grants and gives new life. May God thus have mercy and show his compassion—to Him be glory, honour, power and empire, for ever and ever, amen, amen.

I, the mournful captain whose heart is very heavy for you,

Francis Drake[11]

This safe conduct served more than one purpose. There is no reason why it cannot be taken primarily at face value but it was also a means of conveying a message to his separated colleagues. Drake knew that San Juan would soon be returning to Callao and Arica and it was just possible that he might run into the *Elizabeth* or the *Marigold*. If so, the other captains would discover that Drake had gone on ahead by a homeward route already discussed (whatever that might be). This was all conjectural but one certain result of that letter would be the panic it engendered in Spanish America. Drake knew that if the authorities believed the letter San Juan showed them they would not know whether to pursue him or guard their own coastline from the fresh waves of English pirates about to attack. Drake certainly added to the letter's effectiveness with his talk of the 'very cruel' captain of one of the other vessels. The tactics worked. Before long 'sightings' of the *Elizabeth* and *Marigold* were being reported from several points on the coast and whenever a strange or unexpected vessel entered a harbour of Peru or New Spain the cry of 'Englishmen' was raised.

San Juan and his passengers and crew were set aboard the *Nuestra Señora* as were Nicolas Jorje, Custodio Rodriguez and other prisoners Drake had taken along the Peruvian coast. One negro slave went on his knees before the admiral begging to be allowed to return to his master in Arica. This request Drake granted with a great show of graciousness, loudly declaring that he had no desire to keep a man against his will. This striking of a virtuous attitude must have caused some wry amusement to the victims of Drake's piracy. The negro was, accordingly, handed over to San Juan's safe keeping. In the last conversation between the two captains Drake made a final attempt to sow false information in the minds of the Spanish authorities. Pointing out to San Juan that the *Golden Hind* was in need of careening, he asked if Lobos harbour near Paita would be a suitable spot. He also parted company with the *Nuestra Señora* at nightfall so that the Spaniards should not see in what direction he set sail. The ruse did not work. In his testimony before the court San Juan declared that, in his opinion, Drake had no intention of returning southwards but would sail along the coast of Nicaragua.

As the *Cacafuego* merged into the darkness Drake had to give serious attention to the course he really was going to take. His only objective was to get home as quickly as possible. He had told San Juan that he proposed to return to England in six months. Though this was clearly impossible by any known route the declaration may well indicate Drake's genuine desire. There were now only two possible routes available to him. To return the way he had come would be to risk capture somewhere along the coast of Peru and total disaster in the stormy region of Cape Horn. He must either travel home via the Moluccas or seek the as yet undiscovered Straits of Anian. The former route was full of possible hazards. As well as involving long ocean crossings it would mean calling at islands in the Philippines (where his illustrious predecessor had been murdered) and the East Indies which were dominated by Spain and Portugal. On the other hand this was now a well-used trade route and he had picked up considerable information about it with which to augment his charts and the report of Magellan's voyage. The northern route via the Straits of Anian was more appealing for, though no one knew whether a passage, in fact, existed, if it did exist it would provide a very short way home and its discovery would be an immense boon to English mariners. By the Grace of God Drake had already discovered a narrow back door to the land of silver and gold. Might not the Almighty also use him to reveal a wide open front door? The enormous success of the expedition so far must have tempted Drake to answer that question with a confident affirmative. Whichever course he adopted he must first find a safe haven where he could replenish his water supply and set his ship in good order for the return voyage. He set sail nor'-nor'-west in search of a landfall and reached Caño Island off the coast of Nicaragua on 16 March.

It was about the same time that Drake's pursuers caught up with definite information about him. In order not to waste time, Don Luis did not call at Guayaquil to collect the royal galley as he had been instructed. He sailed past, called briefly at deserted Santa Elena and dropped anchor at Manta on 17 March. There he found Díaz Bravo still recovering from his experience at the hands of the corsair. The terrifying stories told by captain and crew did not fail to have an effect on the less stout-hearted members of Don Luis' following and, in all probability, on Don Luis himself. The command of the expedition disintegrated in a welter of conflicting opinion and mutual recrimination. Some officers, among whom Sarmiento was the most outspoken, urged the bold course of striking out north-westwards. Sarmiento brought forward every argument he could muster to show that Drake must go in that direction. Others countered by affirming their belief that the corsair would only return home by a route he knew—by the Straits of Magellan or across the Isthmus of Panama. The truth was that they had little stomach for a fight with the well-armed English vessel far out at sea and wished to keep open their lines of communication. They were backed up by the officials along the coast who wanted the Viceroy's ships to stay close at hand for the protection of themselves and local shipping.

The leaders spent two days arguing in Manta and had still not reached a decision when they again set sail. Indeed, it may well be that Don Luis commanded the ships to leave in order to cut short the persistent arguments of Sarmiento and his supporters. Shipboard conferences took place off Cape San Francisco and again off Cape Manglares. At last Don Luis made up his mind. To shouts of protest he declared his intention of sailing for Panama. The ships reached this destination on 31 March and were able to question San Juan de Anton about the latest news of the pirates. Even now that they had a clearer picture of Drake's whereabouts and some clue as to his plans the Spaniards were quite unable to take firm, decisive action. They stayed in Panama two full weeks and spent the time arguing among themselves and with the judge of the royal court about what should be done. Everyone was highly nervous. Stories and rumours flashed round the settlements of the Isthmus. It was confidently asserted that two more English ships had now appeared off Peru. Some of the Viceroy's men were thus for returning to guard their own territory. Others still wanted to pursue the corsair. The officials of the royal court divided their time between close questioning of Drake's released prisoners and demanding that the viceregal expedition stay to defend Panama. Then, while all the Spanish leaders were behaving like chickens in a fox-haunted farmyard, the order for the expedition's recall came from Lima. With ill-disguised relief the general sent the two ships home on 13 April under the command of Diego de Frias. He, himself, awaited a vessel which would take him to Spain so that he could report personally to the king.

Meanwhile Drake was making sure that Peru's sister state had her fair share of alarm. His arrival at Caño Island was unobserved and beyond it he found a creek admirably suitable for careening the ship. The fact that the *Golden Hind* was in need of fresh attention after only four months does not indicate that the careening carried out at Salada Bay had been inadequate, for Drake only cleaned her now above the water line. He was simply making sure that everything was in order before putting forth into the open ocean. Five days were devoted to doing all the necessary repair work.

But before the task was even begun fate threw another prize across Drake's path. The pinnace, patrolling outside the harbour, took a bark bound from the busy dockyard and port of Nicoya to Panama. She was carrying maize, honey, sarsaparilla and lard but, far more important from Drake's point of view, she had aboard the pilot who was to convey the new governor of the Philippines safely across to Manila. The man, Alonso Sánchez Colchero, had with him all his charts and rutters and Drake fell to examining these eagerly aboard the captured vessel while his own was beached, scraped and recaulked.

Drake welcomed the sudden appearance of the pilot as a further proof of divine favour and an indication of the route he was now to take. He decided that Colchero should fulfil for the Pacific crossing the role that da Silva had performed for the traversing of the Atlantic. He reckoned without the mule-like determination of Colchero. For the first time on the entire voyage Drake had met his match. Colchero simply refused to provide any assistance to men who were pirates, heretics and enemies of his country. First of all he claimed that he did not know the China route. Drake told him he was a liar. He threw open a chest of bar gold and offered the pilot a thousand ducats. When that failed he simply informed Colchero that he was going to take him to the Moluccas by force. The pilot showed little emotion. He simply asked permission to write two letters; one to the viceroy explaining that he was being taken under duress, the other, a letter of farewell to his wife and children.

Drake must have sensed in that moment that he was beaten. Colchero's armour of honesty and dignity had no flaw, no chink. Neither bribery nor threat could penetrate. Yet he had to go through the motions; had to convince himself that, given time, Colchero would crack; had to avoid losing face before his crew. So he kept the pilot close by him all the time and when, on 27 March, he released the rest of his prisoners Colchero remained aboard. The *Golden Hind* had left Caño Island two days before, accompanied by the prize ship and towing the pinnace. Now Drake decided that the newly-captured bark was more use to him than the pinnace so he put his prisoners into the little ship which had seen so many adventures in its brief life and, despatching towards the shore, sailed on to the northwest.

He was approaching the heart of the Spanish colonial empire, the Viceroyalty of New Spain. And now a new passion seized Drake, or rather an old passion intensified and was allowed to rule over better judgement and finer feelings: revenge. Secure in his capital at Mexico sat the one man Drake hated above all others, even above King Philip II. Don Martín Enríquez, Viceroy of New Spain, was the man whose perfidy had caused the deaths of so many brave Englishmen at San Juan de Ulua. Drake could not drag the grandee out by the beard from his viceregal palace and plunge a sword into him, as he would dearly love to have done, but he was determined to give Enríquez ample cause to remember his visit. The captain who had fled the slaughter of San Juan de Ulua and had returned to inflict his vengeance on Nombre de Dios was back once more in fulfilment of his self-imposed pledge to make Enríquez pay for his treachery.

The first chance came at the small port of Realejo. There a merchant ship was being built. It was the property of Diego García de Palacios, the licentiate, the judge of the royal court, and a personal friend of the Viceroy. Drake decided to burn the ship, destroy the town, and hang the judge (the latter declaration was probably a threat made in a moment of anger rather than a considered declaration of policy). There was a sand bar across the entrance to the harbour and Drake called upon Colchero to pilot him in. Colchero refused. He did not know the harbour, he said, and, therefore, would not dare to take the *Golden Hind* in. Drake was in no mood to argue.

'You will take us in or hang!'

Colchero repeated that he could not.

Drake ordered the rope to be made ready and then placed it round the pilot's neck.

Colchero was frightened but inflexible.

Drake had him hoisted off the ground. After a minute or two he ordered the rope to be slackened.

Now would Colchero do as he was told?

He would not.

Furious, the admiral ordered the rope to be tightened once more. This time Colchero was left hanging until almost unconscious before he was cut down. Drake stormed away to his cabin. The *Golden Hind* did not put in to Realejo.

As the ships slipped past the grey-green forested slopes of Guatemala Drake had two thoughts in mind: to find a watering place and to reach Acapulco, the nearest port on this coast to Mexico City, with the object of razing it to the ground. Late on 3 April an approaching sail was observed and at dawn she appeared again, much closer. Drake had the crew roused. Arms were issued but the men were not allowed to show themselves on deck. The helmsman steered a course which would bring the *Golden Hind* across the other's bows. From the light of the rising sun behind him Drake could see that only the men of the dog watch were on the deck of the Spanish ship.

'Give way! Give way!'

145

Drake ignored the command. Let the other helmsman believe his crew were only half awake.

By now the two vessels were very close. The same voice hailed the *Golden Hind*, even louder.

'Keep away! Who are you? Where are you from?'

Drake had his answer ready. Colchero, with a sailor's knife at his throat, called out, 'Miguel Angel's ship from Peru.'

The two ships slipped past each other. Then the English helm was put hard over. The *Golden Hind* swung across the other's stern. Her deck suddenly flooded with armed men and the air was filled with the sound of arquebus shots.

'Strike sail!'

The confusion and alarm on the Spanish deck was only momentary. Soon the six Spaniards were laughing at this 'joke'.

Their merriment was equally brief. Within seconds they were surrounded by murderous-looking Englishmen brandishing swords and bows. They were quickly herded below while the pirates roused the captain and his passengers. The most distinguished of the passengers was Don Francisco de Zarate, a member of the Spanish aristocracy and cousin to the Duke of Medina, one of the richest noblemen in Europe. Drake who was always very conscious of rank and title made a great show of refinement for Zarate's benefit. The extreme formality and high etiquette of Spanish élite society was a byword throughout the civilised world. Captain Drake was determined to give Zarate no excuse to dismiss him as a rough, uncultured clod. For the next two and a half days the corsair showed his guest the most elaborate courtesy, while at the same time making it quite clear that the nobleman was his prisoner.

As soon as Zarate had been aroused Drake had him rowed across to the *Golden Hind*, where he received him on the poop deck. There the cousin of a Spanish grandee knelt and kissed the hand of the son of a heretical English preacher. Drake was graciousness itself. He conducted Zarate to his own cabin assuring him that he would be well treated.

'One thing you must know,' he said when they were seated in the cabin, 'I am very friendly towards those who tell me the truth. With those who do not I am inclined to lose my temper.'

Zarate, who was fully expecting the demand of a heavy ransom for his release, nodded. Drake continued.

'Now, if you wish to travel by the shortest road to my good favour, tell me how much gold and silver your ship is carrying.'

'None.'

Drake's smile had a glint of menace.

'I see I must repeat my question. On your word as a gentleman how much gold and silver is your ship carrying?'

'On my word as a gentleman, none, except a few plates and cups from which I am personally served.'

Drake searched the other's face for several moments before deciding to let the point drop.

'Tell me, do you know the Viceroy of New Spain?'

'I know His Excellency very well.'

'Do you carry aboard any relative of his or anything belonging to him?'

'No, nothing.'

'A pity. A pity.'

Drake frowned and fixed his companion with an earnest stare.

'It would give me more pleasure to come face to face with "His Excellency" than to have all the gold and silver of the Indies. Then I would show him how a gentleman should keep his word.'

This conversation, faithfully recorded by Zarate, provides us with one of the clearest windows into Drake's mind. The sense of personal vendetta was strong. Time and time again he lamented the fact that he had lost two of his ships and their crews, a fact which prevented him flailing the coastal settlements of New Spain and Peru like the scourge of God. Quite what he would have attempted in the territory ruled by Don Martín Enríquez had he had a full complement of men and ships with him we can never know. But it is certain that New Spain would not have escaped so lightly from the corsair's visitation.

Drake next escorted his guest to the cabin below decks which was used as the ship's brig. The only occupant of this damp, stinking cell was Colchero. Zarate, treading carefully across the slimy boards and perhaps holding a pomander to his nose against the obnoxious smell, peered at the prisoner. Drake waved an arm towards the filthy, cramped cabin.

'These are your quarters,' he said, and enjoyed the nobleman's involuntary recoil.

Zarate recovered his dignity and went inside to sit on the bench, but Drake laid a hand on his arm.

'I don't intend you to try out this accommodation—yet. But, tell me, do you know this man?'

Zarate peered forward in the poor light.

'No.'

'His name is Colchero and "His Excellency", Don Enríquez, sent him to Panama to convey Don Gonçalo to China. He is not being very cooperative, which is why you see him here. Perhaps you can persuade him to a more sensible frame of mind. Guard!' Drake turned to one of the sailors, 'let the prisoner on deck for some fresh air.'

During the following forty-eight hours Don Francisco de Zarate had ample opportunity to observe the corsair and his crew. What he saw both impressed and depressed him. He saw a man who was an expert mariner, well acquainted with charts, navigational instruments, winds and currents. He saw a ship as well found and heavily armed as any he had ever seen.

147

He saw sailors under strict discipline, who yet admired their leader and believed him to be fair and just. That leader was a fanatical enemy of Spain and throughout his journey he deliberately made charts and drawings which would certainly make it easy for any of his countrymen to follow him into the South Sea. What was even worse, the corsair came with the full backing of his Queen, as he frequently boasted.

For Zarate, Francis Drake was the dreadful omen of the end of an era, as he intimated a few days later to the Viceroy:

> I beg of your Excellency to consider the encouragement that his countrymen would receive if this man should arrive at his own country. If up to the present time they have sent their second sons [a reference to Drake's gentleman adventurers], from now on they will come themselves, seeing the schemes which this Corsair has made under cover, and that all his promises have turned out so true for with such a great sum of gold and silver he will have proved his plan.[12]

It is not surprising that to a man whose prime concern was the continued welfare of the Spanish colonies Francis Drake and his crew should have appeared as a terrible threat. But all was not brotherhood and unity of purpose aboard the *Golden Hind*. The signs were there for anyone to see who was sensitive to atmosphere and human stress. Why did Drake make a point of telling Zarate all about the Doughty incident, extolling the virtues of the dead man and excusing his execution by saying the Queen's service demanded it? Why was John Doughty never free to leave the ship like the other gentlemen? Why was the corsair so concerned to stress that he was merely a man under orders? According to one of his other prisoners, Drake took him aside after a shipboard service and justified himself in the most earnest tones:

> You will say that this man who steals by day and prays by night in public is a devil, but what I do, is because, just as King Philip gives a written order to your Viceroy Don Martín Enríquez in which he tells him what to do and how to govern, so the Queen, my mistress, gives one to me to come to these parts. Therefore, I am doing so, and if it is wrong she knows it and I am not to blame for anything, although it gives me pain to make his vassals pay, as I would not wish to take anything except what belongs to King Philip and Don Martín Enríquez. I am not going to stop until I collect two millions which my cousin, Juan de Aquines [John Hawkins], lost at San Juan de Ulua as the record shows.[13]

Despite Drake's protestations about not wishing to rob private citizens, he and his men went through the cargo and personal belongings on Zarate's ship with obvious relish. They found mostly Chinese goods; silk, porcelain and linen while the passenger's chests yielded clothing, money and jewellery, and they took all they required. Drake made a great show of consideration towards Zarate, suggesting that he send a page with the looting party so that the nobleman's chest could be pointed out and remain untouched. For this 'kindness' Zarate presented his captor with an exquisite gold pendant in the form of a falcon. Drake also took from Zarate a slave, a negress called Maria, for the pleasure of himself and the crew.

After dinner on Monday 6 April Drake told his prisoners to prepare themselves for departure. The crew of the Spanish ship and the other passengers were conveyed aboard without ceremony. Among them was Alonso Sánchez Colchero whom Drake had tired of bullying (he departed, of course, without his charts and navigational aids). Drake had decided on a last display of formal pomp for his most distinguished guest. The boat was brought alongside and manned with a guard of honour of two dozen archers. Drake and Zarate took their places and were conveyed across to the other ship. On deck he called the Spanish crew together and gave to each man a handful of coins. Finally, he called for a volunteer to go with him to show him where he could find water. The result of this appeal was a vigorous shaking of heads and a gabble of excuses. At last Drake selected one man at random, Juan Pascual, countering the man's screams and protests with threats of a hanging if he did not do as he was told. Thus, with rather less dignity than he had intended, did Francis Drake bid farewell to Francisco de Zarate.

The *Golden Hind* together with her one prize sailed on along the dry, sparsely-inhabited coast for a week, Drake still intent on finding water and making one last demonstration of his feelings towards the Viceroy before leaving New Spain. He had decided not to visit Acapulco. It was too far up the coast, the winds were becoming contrary and he had learned from Zarate that the town was well garrisoned. Thus it was the waterside village of Guatulco, reached on 13 April, which eventually served his purpose. This small huddle of a few houses and a church was the port of a town of the same name a few miles inland. It was occupied by a priest, five other Spaniards and some Indians. When Drake arrived there was one small merchant ship in the harbour.

The *Golden Hind* anchored. Drake sent the bark and a boatload of men ashore. After a token resistance on the beach those inhabitants who were fortunate fled to the woods. Drake and his men went on a rampage through the houses, taking anything of use or value they could find. They enjoyed themselves enormously in the church. They swaggered around smashing crucifixes and images, tearing the frontal from the altar, laughing as they slashed pictures and put on chasubles and vestments over their rough seamen's jerkins. One man climbed to the belfry to prize loose the bell. Tom Moon the boatswain broke into one house and, before the eyes of the terrified owner, splintered a large crucifix against the table. 'Well may you be upset,' Moon laughed. 'You are no Christian. Only idolaters worship sticks and stones.' It did not take long. Soon the exultant sailors were sauntering back down the beach with their booty and prisoners.

Drake now took possesion of the anchored ship, which turned out to contain little of value. Then he summoned the men together for a service. No doubt it was nothing more than their usual evening devotions. Drake knelt at a table on the poop deck and read from the Scriptures and, probably, Foxe's *Actes and Monuments*.* Then everyone intoned a psalm. Yet it also seems to have been something of a demonstration for the benefit of the huddled Catholic prisoners in the bow of the ship who tried not to hear the Protestant 'blasphemies'. After the service Drake showed them the lurid woodcuts in his copy of Foxe's book—pictures of Protestant martyrs being burned in Castile. If they thought him a cruel, heretical pirate, Drake seemed to be saying, here was proof that papists were far more inhuman.

Among those who escaped Drake's clutches was the local alcalde, Gaspar de Vargas. He reached Guatulco town and from there despatched urgent messages to the Viceroy and the alcalde of Acapulco to warn them of the pirate's appearance and urge them to take action. Later, having heard from people who had been taken aboard the *Golden Hind*, he was able to report Drake's boast that he would destroy Acapulco. It seems certain that Drake had, in fact, already abandoned this plan; he would hardly have announced his intention beforehand. However, Vargas' letters certainly had an effect and one of which Drake would have thoroughly approved. In Mexico Don Enríquez was thrown into a state of near panic. He despatched all the forces he could muster to Acapulco and other points on the coast. He sent a flurry of letters off to King Philip lamenting the unsatisfactory state of coastal defences. He dispiritedly opined that the corsair would certainly have destroyed the shipping and town of Acapulco long before he could put it in a state of readiness to repel invaders.

But long before the Viceroy had bestirred himself Drake was away, nevermore to trouble Don Enríquez. By threatening to burn the town and the ship he had forced the local people to provide him with firewood and show him where he could find fresh water. By the 16th Drake had all he needed. He released his prisoners and keeping only two negro slaves, he sailed away.

Among the ex-prisoners he left behind him was one man who had no desire to stay; a man who feared the Spaniards and who knew what tortures lay ahead in the sound-proof vaults of the Inquisition; a man who had helped the corsair and would be punished for it; a man who was tainted with the Englishman's heresy and would be punished for it. But Nuño da Silva had outlived his usefulness to Drake and so, suddenly and unceremoniously, he was put aboard the ship in Guatulco harbour an hour or so before the Englishmen left. It was Maundy Thursday—an appropriate day for betraying a friend.[14]

* Sometimes known as the *Book of Martyrs*.

150

CHAPTER TEN

'I take possession of this kingdom'

17 APRIL—26 JULY 1579

When Drake left Guatulco he had provision and water for fifty days and he set out on a route which took him south-west by west. This does not mean that he intended to find the Acapulco-Manila route which his confiscated charts and manuals described. Drake had studied Colchero's papers very carefully and had questioned the pilot closely. He had discovered that one reason why Colchero was unwilling to take him across the Pacific was that it was the wrong time of year. To leave New Spain in April was to court trouble: it would mean reaching the area of the Philippines in July, the beginning of the typhoon season, and Colchero knew from personal experience just how devastating a Pacific hurricane could be. Drake realised that if he were to go home by way of the Moluccas he would have to wait until the end of the summer. To dally on the coast of New Spain for three months would be to place far too much reliance on the inefficiency of the Spanish authorities. No, he must at least try the northern route and seek the Straits of Anian. Why, then, head directly away from the continent? The answer is that Drake was seeking a favourable wind. The summer north-westerlies had already set in along the coast of New Spain. Only painfully slow progress could be made by sticking close to the shore and that again would be to invite pursuit.[1] They headed first of all west-south-west and then north-west by west until, by 5 June, they were in about 40°N latitude.[2] Still no sign of land. Drake consulted his maps. According to Ortelius (and Drake probably did not have any more up-to-date map conveying more accurate information about the Pacific coast of North America) they should by now have found land, for the cartographer showed the coastline turning sharply westward in this latitude. In fact, the ships were some two hundred and fifty miles off Cape Mendocino in northern California, a point on a north-south coastline. Once more the map makers had played him false, though not this time with deliberate malice. This was one of the many areas of the world's surface about which geographers could only conjecture. This did not prevent them producing maps on which the outlines of continents and islands were depicted with bold conviction.

It was not the only frustration Drake had to suffer. Since leaving Guatulco everything seemed to have gone wrong. Just when the end of a triumphant voyage was in sight, when he had cocked a snook at mighty

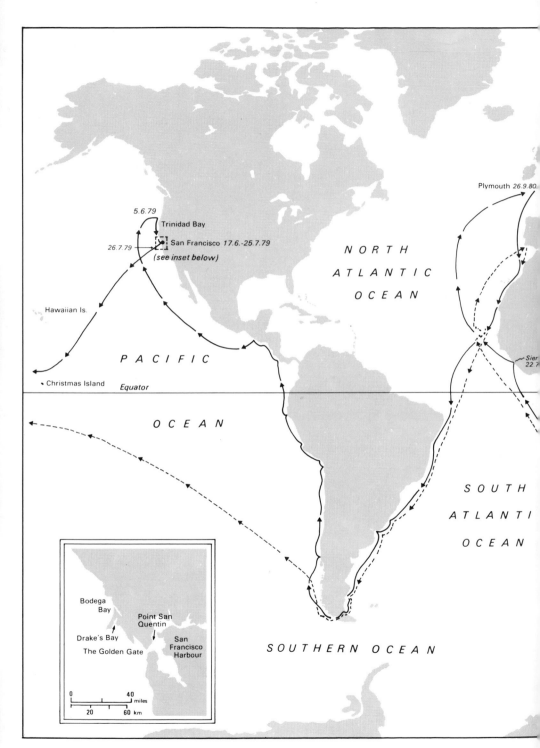

5.6.79

Trinidad Bay

26.7.79

San Francisco 17.6.-25.7.79
(see inset below)

Hawaiian Is.

Christmas Island

PACIFIC

OCEAN

Equator

NORTH

ATLANTIC

OCEAN

Plymouth *26.9.80*

Sier
22.7

SOUTH

ATLANTI

OCEAN

SOUTHERN OCEAN

Bodega
Bay

Point San
Quentin

Drake's Bay

The Golden Gate

San
Francisco
Harbour

0   40
              miles
   20   60 km

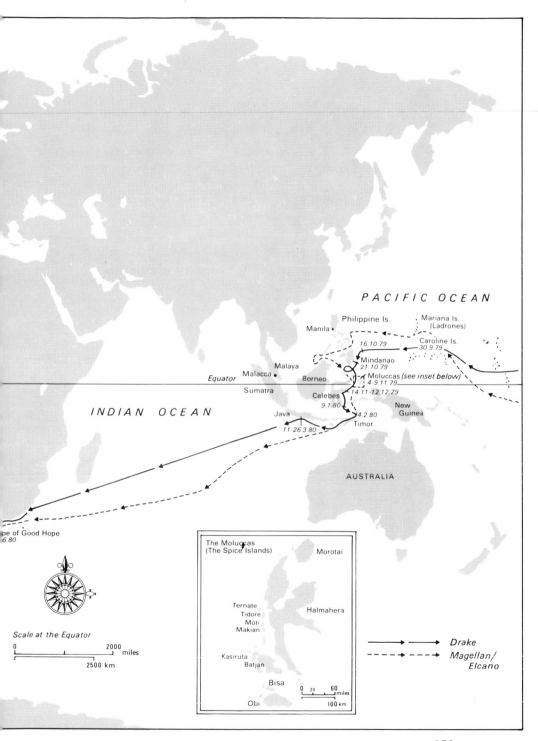

PACIFIC OCEAN

Manila •

Philippine Is.

Mariana Is.
(Ladrones)

Caroline Is.
30.9.79

16.10.79

Malaya

Malacca •

Borneo

Mindanao
21.10.79

Moluccas (see inset below)
4-9.11.79

Equator

Sumatra

14.11-12.12.79

Celebes
9.1.80

New
Guinea

Java

4.2.80

INDIAN OCEAN

11-26.3.80

Timor

AUSTRALIA

pe of Good Hope
6.80

Scale at the Equator

0   2000
|_____|_____| miles

2500 km

The Moluccas
(The Spice Islands)

Morotai

Ternate
Tidore
Moti
Makian

Halmahera

Kasiruta
Batjan

Bisa

Obi

0   20   60
|__|____| miles

100 km

Drake

Magellan/
Elcano

Spain and stuffed the *Golden Hind* with all the treasure she could hold, the elements began to conspire against him. He was beset by storms and fog and his laden ship began to take in water. After the months of easy sailing in tropical waters the men found the cooler climate and difficult weather hard to cope with. Drake coaxed and bullied them to work and encouraged them with the promise that they were taking the shortest way home. He and they watched anxiously for the coastline which they would be able to follow west and then north-east and finally, in about 60°, due east. It did not materialise. By 5 June they had been at sea for fifty days. Food was running low and, though rain had augmented the drinking water, this, too, was now rationed. Then the ships began to encounter strong head-winds. Drake could no longer maintain the struggle to seek a strait which

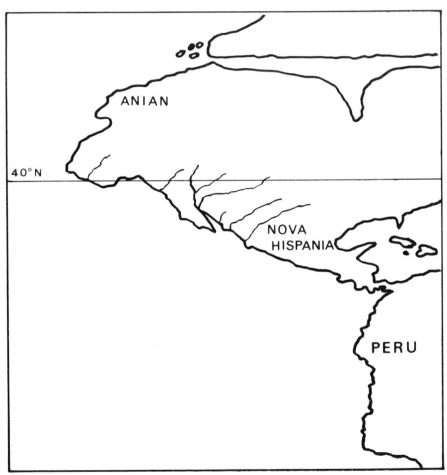

The coast of North America and location of the Straits of Anian according to Ortelius, 1570

might not even exist. He had to look for a haven. He ordered an easterly course and, with some relief, came up with the coast, probably in the region of Cape Blanco.[3]

Misfortune continued to dog the expedition. Their first landfall was in a bay which gave them no protection from the gale. Then, when the storm had blown itself out, a thick fog descended which prevented the ships leaving harbour. It was some days before Drake could break out of the unwanted anchorage. He ran his ships south before the prevailing wind. Scanning the low-lying shore for a suitable bay he at last discerned, on 17 June, 'a convenient and fit harbour' and, putting his helm over to larboard, ran into a sheltered cove in the region of 38 or $38\frac{1}{2}$ degrees.

Which cove was it? The question has perplexed historians for a century. Champions of various locations have fought for their convictions with vigour and even, at times, verbal violence. As San Francisco grew in sophistication and respectability after its brash, gold-rush beginnings there was an attempt to gain for it a far greater degree of antiquity than any other American city could boast by claiming Francis Drake as its founding father. In 1936 a young man walking across the inner headland near San Quentin State Penitentiary stumbled across an old brass plate which, it was subsequently asserted, was the plaque erected by Drake when he claimed this region for the English crown (see below, p. 163). Unfortunately none of the original records supports the contention that Francis Drake made the momentous discovery of the Golden Gate, through which no European passed for almost two centuries after 1579.* The bay described by early accounts and maps was a much more modest affair than magnificent San Francisco harbour, so young Beryle Shinn's discovery, even if accepted as genuine, cannot be said to have settled the problem or even simplified it. The point where the plate was found was twenty-five miles or more from any haven that Drake can have used.

The nearest anchorage which answers the very vague description in the documents is the one usually accepted as the true one and, indeed, known as Drake's Bay. Bodega Bay, twenty miles up the coast, is another possibility. This has the added advantage of being closest to the latitude specified in *The World Encompassed*. Its entrance lies in 38 degrees 18 minutes and *The World Encompassed* placed the anchorage in 38°30'. But it must be admitted that the lack of precision in sixteenth-century latitude calculation and the notorious inaccuracies rife in *The World Encompassed* prevent us making confident identification based on this evidence alone. Beyond Bodega Bay the only harbour which will serve is Trinidad Bay but this lies in 41°07' and can only be accepted as Drake's anchorage if we are prepared to jettison completely the location mentioned in *The World Encompassed*.[4]

* It was in 1775 that Juan Manuel de Ayala brought the *San Carlos* into San Francisco harbour.

At either Drake's Bay or Bodega Bay, then, the weary travellers found shelter and anchored preparatory to cautiously exploring the country. The next morning they had their first sight of the inhabitants. A man came out in a canoe, stopped at a safe distance and addressed them with shouts and signals. Three times this performance was repeated. When Drake saw the Indian paddling towards the ships for the third time he sent some men in the boat to meet him. But the native would not allow himself to be conveyed on board. From a short distance he threw into the boat some presents he had brought—a headdress of black feathers, a rush basket and a bag of herbs. Nothing would induce him to receive anything in return. The sailors tried throwing presents into the canoe and into the water. They even contrived a little raft loaded with gifts which they floated towards him. He ignored all these offerings, except a hat which he retrieved from the water, probably in return for the headdress.

The man never returned and Drake's shore parties completely failed to make contact with the local people. These were Miwok Indians—a linguistic description which covers many groups who spoke related languages. Precise customs varied from group to group but as a whole the Miwok were Stone Age communities, innocent of agriculture, pastoralism and metal. They collected shellfish, hunted small animals and sea mammals, and caught fish with spears and nets. Their staple diet was a meal made from pulping acorns. The Englishmen soon discovered the local settlement, about three quarters of a mile from the harbour. It was a village of circular huts each constructed by digging out the earth and setting a roof upon the rampart thus created. The timber roof was sealed with mud and the single door was the only ventilation. Since the fires were lit indoors, the houses were very warm and 'giveth a marvellous reflexion to their bodies to heat the same'.[5] The chief and his braves wore feathered headdresses and skins, but most of the other men went naked. The women, however, covered themselves with skins and loin cloths.

For all the attempts of the Englishmen to establish friendly relations, the Indians remained non-hostile, but shy—until they realized that the strangers had come to stay. The repairs which the *Golden Hind* now needed meant that it had to be raised out of the water on chocks, so that faulty timbers could be replaced and all joints thoroughly recaulked. Everything was taken out of the ship and a depot was built on the shore. The crew gathered rocks and built a stone-walled enclosure within which they erected their tents and temporary storehouses. When the Indians saw this they all rushed down to the beach brandishing their bows. But they were obviously perplexed as to how to deal with their visitors, for the 'attack' petered out rapidly. It says much for Drake's judgment that he did not over-react. The experience of St. Julian's Bay must have been very vivid and it would have been entirely understandable if he had seen off the natives with a round of arquebus fire. Instead, he motioned to the braves. He tried to show them that he was a man of peace and that they should lay down their arms. He was completely successful. The sand was soon littered with bows and arrows, and the whole people stood gazing with awe at the white men.

Fletcher was convinced that the Indians regarded Drake and his company as gods come from the sea—a blasphemy which appalled him. He urged the admiral to try to disabuse them of their error. The Englishmen took food and drink and tried by every means to show the goggle-eyed Indians that they too were men. They also presented the people with clothing and lengths of cloth, 'teaching them to use them' 'to cover [their] shame'. Apparently the indigenes missed the point; they immediately took off their own clothes and offered them in exchange for the proffered garments. At length the crowd dispersed and shortly afterwards the Englishmen heard from the direction of the village a 'most lamentable weeping and crying out'. Doubtless the baffled Indians were calling upon their gods for assistance in this strange situation.

As the days passed, confidence, if not understanding, grew between visitors and visited. More and more people congregated on the bay; as the word spread Indians from far inland set off for the coast anxious to see the strangers. Drake and the gentlemen were very interested in these friendly, simple people, for they were potential new subjects for Her Majesty Queen Elizabeth. If and when the secrets of the north-west-passage were finally laid bare Englishmen would have easy access to these shores and, since Spain's Colonial arm did not reach this far, they would be able to establish their own settlements. Thus every demonstration of honour and courtesy made by the Indians was interpreted as conveying worship and fealty, the wish, doubtless, being father to the thought.

Against the end of two days (during which time they had not again been with us), there was gathered together a great assembly of men, women, and children (invited by the report of them which first saw us, who, as it seems, had in that time of purpose dispersed themselves into the country, to make known the news), who came now the second time unto us, bringing with them, as before had been done, feathers and bags of *Tobàh* for presents, or rather indeed for sacrifices, upon this persuasion that we were gods.

When they came to the top of the hill, at the bottom whereof we had built our fort, they made a stand; where one (appointed as their chief speaker) wearied both us his hearers, and himself too, with a long and tedious oration; delivered with strange and violent gestures, his voice being extended to the uttermost strength of nature, and his words falling so thick one in the neck of another, that he could hardly fetch his breath again: as soon as he had concluded, all the rest, with a reverend bowing of their bodies (in a dreaming manner, and long producing of the same) cried *Oh*: thereby giving their consent that all was very true which he had spoken, and that they had uttered their mind by his mouth unto us; which done, the men laying down their bows upon the hill, and leaving their women and children behind them, came down with their presents; in such sort as if they had appeared before a God indeed, thinking themselves happy that they might have access unto our General, but much more happy when they saw that he would receive at their hands those things which they so willingly had presented: and no doubt they thought themselves nearest unto God when they sat or stood next to him. In the mean time the women, as if they had been desperate, used unnatural violence against themselves, crying and shrieking piteously, tearing their flesh with their nails from their cheeks in a monstrous manner, the blood streaming down along their breasts, besides despoiling the upper parts of their bodies of those single coverings they formerly had, and holding their hands above their heads that they might not rescue their breasts from harm, they would with fury cast themselves upon the ground, never respecting whether it were clean or soft, but dashed themselves in this manner on hard stones, knobby hillocks, stocks of wood, and pricking bushes, or whatever else lay in their way, iterating the same course again and again; yea women great with child, some nine or ten times each, and others holding out till 15 or 16 times (till their strengths failed them) exercised this cruelty against themselves: a thing more grievous for us to see or suffer, could we have helped it, than trouble to them (as it seemed) to do it. This bloody sacrifice (against our will) being thus performed, our General, with his company, in the presence of those strangers, fell to prayers; and by signs in lifting up our eyes and hands to heaven, signified unto them that that God whom we did serve, and whom they ought to worship, was above: beseeching God, if it were his good pleasure, to open by some means their blinded eyes, that they might in due time be called to the knowledge of him, the true and ever-living God, and of Jesus Christ whom he hath sent, the salvation of the Gentiles. In the time of which prayers, singing of Psalms, and reading of certain Chapters in the Bible, they sat attentively: and observing the end at every pause, with one voice still cried, Oh, greatly rejoicing in our exercises. Yea they took such pleasure in our singing of Psalms, that whensoever they resorted to us, their first request was commonly thus, *Gnaáh*, by which they entreated that we would sing.[6]

The climax of all this came on 26 June when, at the head of a large concourse of people and attended by a hundred or so braves, the local chief arrived. Drake and his companions watched, fascinated, as the procession appeared. They could only understand it in terms of English royal ceremonial. When the accounts of these events came to be written the royal sons who preceded the chief were designated 'ambassadors'. Another who carried presents for Drake was the royal 'sceptre bearer'. As they approached all

Drake 'crowned' by the ruler of Nova Albion while a sailor fixes the plaque laying claim to the territory, a fanciful reconstruction from a collection of voyages published in 1655

the men, including the chief, broke into a dance which continued until they were inside the English camp. Then the chief motioned to Drake to be seated and, after various speeches by himself and his tribal elders, he set a feathered headdress on Drake's head. Other Indians came forward to deck the white man with necklaces and other offerings. What was probably happening was that the English leader was being made an honorary chief of the tribe. That is not how Fletcher chose to interpret it.*

> ...the king and divers others made several orations, or rather, indeed, if we had understood them, supplications, that he would take the Province and kingdom into his hand, and become their king and patron:

* This passage in *The World Encompassed* bears the unmistakable stamp of Fletcher.

159

making signs that they would resign unto him their right and title in the whole land: which that they might make us indeed believe that it was their true meaning and intent, the king himself, with all the rest, with one consent and with great reverence, joyfully singing a song, set the crown upon his head, enriched his neck with all their chains, and offering unto him many other things, honoured him by the name of *Hyóh.** Adding thereunto (as it might seem) a song and dance of triumph; because they were not only visited of the gods (for so they still judged us to be), but the great and chief God was now become their God, their king and patron, and themselves were become the only happy and blessed people in the world.

These things being so freely offered, our General thought not meet to reject or refuse the same, both for that he would not give them any cause of mistrust or disliking of him (that being the only place, wherein at this present, we were of necessity enforced to seek relief of many things), and chiefly for that he knew not what good end God had brought this to pass, or what honour and profit it might bring to our country in time to come.

Wherefore, in the name and to the use of her most excellent majesty, he took the sceptre, crown, and dignity of the said country into his hand; wishing nothing more than that it had lain so fitly for her majesty to enjoy, as it was now her proper own, and that the riches and treasures thereof (wherewith in the upland countries it abounds) might with as great conveniency be transported, to the enriching of her kingdom here at home, as it is in plenty to be attained there; and especially that so tractable and loving a people as they showed themselves to be, might have means to have manifested their most willing obedience the more unto her, and by her means, as a mother and nurse of the Church of *Christ*, might by the preaching of the Gospel, be brought to the right knowledge and obedience of the true and everliving God.[7]

The annals of pioneer colonialism are full of such misunderstandings—some more deliberate than others. The sequence of events is usually something like this: settlers arrive to take possession of the 'ceded' land; the alarmed natives protest about the exploitation of themselves and their territory; the settlers make a show of strength to enforce the original 'treaty'; this leads to war of a shorter or longer duration; the final outcome is that the original inhabitants are dispossessed of their homelands and condemned to a life of servitude. Fortunately for the Miwok this did not happen to them; Drake's 'colonisation' of California was never followed up. Perhaps it was unfortunate for England that this was so. Had Elizabeth

*The word 'Hyóh' may be an English rendering of 'hiopa' a Miwok word which does, indeed, mean 'chief'. Equally it may just be an exclamation, possibly even the salutation 'How', beloved of early movie directors.

made good her 'rights' to this territory she would soon have had access to that private source of bullion which she always hoped her adventurers would discover. Some hundred and fifty miles inland from Drake's anchorage lies Coloma and that was where the gold rush began in 1848.

After this impressive ceremony the Indians mingled with their visitors. Some attached themselves to members of Drake's company who took their fancy and offered gestures of private devotion or friendship. When the friends of the favoured Englishmen dragged them away to the tents the Indians became very agitated. It may be (though there is no proof and the documents certainly—and understandably—make no mention of it) that all this adulation went to the heads of some of Drake's men. According to Spanish accounts there were over eighty men aboard the *Golden Hind* as it cruised along the coast of New Spain. When it reached the Moluccas its complement had been reduced to little more than seventy. Death may explain this reduction in numbers but to have lost about an eighth of his crew through natural shipboard hazards in the space of six months would have caused considerable alarm to Drake and would surely have been recorded in one of the accounts of the voyage. Desertions, on the other hand, would almost certainly be hushed up.

On any ship there were always disgruntled men who might prefer the anonymous risks of an unknown shore to the continued hardships of the voyage. We know that John Doughty was kept under close observation and never allowed ashore and the reason for this must have been the fear that he might desert, perhaps taking other men with him. The only knowledge we have of a possible desertion from the expedition is the strange, adventurous story of Peter Corder.

When Drake's ships were battling with the elements near the western end of Magellan's Strait the admiral put Corder and seven companions (William Pitcher, Richard Joyner, a Dutchman called Artyur, Richard Burnish, John Cottle, Pascoe Goddy and one other) into a pinnace without food and told them to remain with the fleet. This was obviously a punishment and it occurred at a time when many men, including the vice-admiral, wished to turn back. The pinnace lost the other ships during the night, and we may well conjecture how accidental this was. The eight men re-entered the Straits and found their way back to the Atlantic coast. Subsisting on fish, crustacea and penguin meat which they had obtained and salted down, they sailed northwards and gained the Plate estuary in safety. Here, four men were captured by Indians and the others were badly wounded. Two of the survivors succumbed to their injuries, leaving only Corder and Pitcher. Unable by themselves to handle the pinnace, they lost it in a storm, spent a month on the shore living on crabs and eels and almost died of thirst. At last they managed to construct a raft and continued their journey. When they next made land they found a stream at which Pitcher so over-indulged himself with fresh water that he died. Corder next fell in with a cannibal tribe who accepted him as one of themselves. In return for food and shelter he was able to teach them improved fighting methods and it was with reluctance that they eventually let him go. Corder at last reached the port of Bahía and surrendered himself to the Portuguese authorities. For some years he served on board coastal ships and in 1586 he made the trans-atlantic crossing. Off the Azores Corder's ship was captured by an English vessel and thus it was that the weary traveller regained his homeland.[8] Some authorities have dismissed the whole story as a colourful fiction and certainly Samuel Purchas, the man who wrote Corder's story, was not noted for objective historical writing. Yet the author would scarcely have used Corder's notes (which he probably obtained from Hakluyt) if the man had already been exposed as a fraud, and there were many survivors of Drake's expedition who could have so exposed him.*

Whether or not Corder's adventure is true, it indicates the sort of thing that *could* happen on a long voyage. Drake's mariners were members of a diminishing band. Disease, accident, loss and desertion were the enemies which were decimating their ranks. Those who were left were the guardians of messages and possessions entrusted to them by dead friends and ship-mates to pass on to widows and orphans at home.

Now that the friendship of the Miwok had been aroused their curiosity began to be a nuisance. They came to the camp every day and hung about while the men were trying to work. Sometimes they came without food, so that Drake felt obliged to feed them from his own supplies. There were fish and sea lions in abundance and the expedition was able to lay in a good store of salted protein. The Indians also resorted to their visitors with their aches, pains, injuries and diseases, assuming that the god-men who had such marvellous things as enormous boats, fire-sticks, metal knives, would be able to cure all ills. Drake and his men gave what help they could with ointments, bandages and simples. Whether these remedies did any good is doubtful but the natives seemed very grateful. All in all the stay on the California coast was a pleasant interlude between the stormy passage from New Spain and the unknown hazards of the Pacific crossing. All the work on the *Golden Hind* was completed and Drake once more had a fully sea-worthy craft. The gold and silver, the wine, cloth, porcelain, money, jewels and food were stowed carefully so as to make the best use of every available inch of space, for Drake had resolved to abandon the Spanish prize.

July was now well advanced and the sailing season for the Moluccas had begun. But before departing Drake decided to explore the hinterland of his bay. As soon as the *Golden Hind* was refloated and the shore camp broken up, he left a strong guard aboard the ship and set off across the coastal plain with the gentlemen and most of the crew. The people inland were

---

* It is significant that Juan Griego told Sarmiento de Gamboa that Drake had lost three pinnaces and their crews, two in the Atlantic and one around the south of the continent. None of these losses is reported in the English narrative, (cf. Wagner, p. 388).

to all outward appearances identical to those at the coast but their food came mainly from hunting deer and ground squirrels of which there was an abundance.

Somewhere, at some prominent point, probably a hilltop, Drake had a large stake driven firmly into the ground and nailed to it a brass plate which was already prepared. It was engraved with the date of Drake's arrival and announced his claim to the land in the name of Queen Elizabeth. By way of authentication he inset a sixpenny piece into the plate. The plaque which was displayed to the critical gaze of the world's historians in 1936 answers the description exactly. Its roughly engraved description reads:

BE IT KNOWN UNTO ALL MEN BY THESE PRESENTS

JUNE 17 1579
BY THE GRACE OF GOD AND IN THE NAME OF HER MAJESTY QUEEN ELIZABETH OF ENGLAND AND HER SUCCESSORS FOREVER I TAKE POSSESSION OF THIS KINGDOM WHOSE KING AND PEOPLE FREELY RESIGN THEIR RIGHT AND TITLE IN THE WHOLE LAND UNTO HER MAJESTY'S KEEPING NOW NAMED BY ME AND TO BE KNOWN UNTO ALL MEN AS NOVA ALBION

FRANCIS DRAKE

Where the sixpence might have been there is only a jagged hole.

The brass plaque discovered at Point San Quentin

Such 'convenient' discoveries always arouse academic scepticism and there is no doubt that Drake's plaque would not be difficult to forge. *The World Encompassed* provides all the information needed. A piece of late sixteenth- or early seventeenth-century brass could be obtained and the inscription made by anyone familiar with Elizabethan orthography and engraving techniques. The 1936 discovery has been examined by experts who have declared that it could be genuine. If the 'discovery' was a hoax, no one has ever claimed responsibility for it. In the absence of other evidence the Point St Quentin plaque must be deemed innocent until proved guilty. As to how it found its way to the place where Mr Shinn picked it up, that must remain forever a mystery. Did the Indians revere the monument as a totem until the post rotted and fell down? Did some brave prise the sixpence loose and wear it as a charm? Or did some later Spaniard who could not read the writing but could recognise money when he saw it pick up the plate and carry it about with him until he could detach the silver piece? Here we leave history for conjecture.

The name 'Nova Albion' (John Drake later stated that his cousin had called the country 'New England') was, doubtless, suggested to Drake by the Spaniards' naming of Mexico 'Nova Hispania'. It is totally in keeping with his almost fanatical sense of rivalry with Spain.* The formal claiming of Nova Albion was nothing more than a gesture on Drake's part, like the setting up of a stone on the southern tip of the Elizabethides and the abortive attempt to mark the western end of Magellan's Strait. He had no plans to return and found a colony and he must have guessed that it would be some years before any Englishmen returned to this spot even if the north-west passage was discovered. Drake was demonstrating a point that the undisputed mastery of Spain and Portugal in the world's undiscovered regions was at an end. Only with tongue firmly in cheek can Nova Albion be claimed as England's first overseas colony (that distinction must remain with Newfoundland annexed by Gilbert in 1583).

The signs of the strangers' imminent departure were now obvious to the Miwoc, who became extremely distressed at the prospect. Whether they thought of the white men as gods or not they had been thrilled to have these strange, powerful beings in their midst and they did not want them to go. There is something very sad about Drake's leave taking of these naive and gentle people.

> ...seeing they could not still enjoy our presence, they (supposing us to be gods indeed) thought in their duties to entreat us that, being absent, we would yet be mindful of them, and making signs of their desires

---

* It may be, as *The World Encompassed* affirms, that the terrain of white cliffs and sand dunes reminded him of parts of England's south coast but such a description seems unnecessarily fanciful.

that in time to come we would see them again, they stole upon us a sacrifice, and set it on fire before we were aware, burning therein a chain and a bunch of feathers. We laboured by all means possible to withhold or withdraw them, but could not prevail, till at last we fell to prayers and singing of Psalms, whereby they were allured immediately to forget their folly, and leave their sacrifice unconsumed, suffering the fire to go out; and imitating us in all our actions, they fell a-lifting of their eyes and hands to heaven, as they saw us do.

The 23 of July they took a sorrowful farewell of us, but being loath to leave us, they presently ran to the top of the hills to keep us in their sight as long as they could, making fires before and behind, and on each side of them, burning therein (as is to be supposed) sacrifices at our departure.[9]

A few hours later the *Golden Hind* reached the Farallones Islands, off San Francisco and may have stopped there to take advantage of the swarming colonies of sea lions and birds observable from the ship.[10] On 26 July Drake put the coast of America behind him and headed for the open ocean. All options except one were now closed to him. He was committed to the circumnavigation of the globe.

CHAPTER ELEVEN

'Wondrous glad of his coming'

27 JULY 1579—9 JANUARY 1580

How good were Drake's charts? If we could answer that question we should be better able to assess his acomplishment during the next stage of the voyage. The expedition was at sea for sixty-six days without sight of land. Is this what Drake expected? The old geographers believed that Asia was much closer to America, and, therefore, to Europe, than was, in fact, the case. For example Drake's Ortelius map showed $87\frac{1}{2}°$ of longitude between Guatulco and Ternate, in the Moluccas. In fact the distance between the two points is $139\frac{1}{2}°$. Thus the Ortelius map carried an error of $52°$. Translated into statute miles that is over three and a half thousand miles.[1] Drake also had Colchero's charts and he was relying on them almost completely for this leg of the voyage. Charts published in Spain at a slightly later date give the difference between Guatulco and Ternate as $114\frac{1}{2}°$. Unfortunately, we cannot assume that these charts accurately reflect the state of knowledge in Spain about the north Pacific. Political propaganda once more waves its distorting wand. The Treaty of Tordesillas had divided Spanish and Portuguese interests by a line running 370 leagues to the west of the Azores. When projected round the 'back' of the world this line passed through the islands of South-East Asia. This was of no consequence in 1494 but as Portugal extended her power eastwards via Africa and India and Spain's captains crossed the Pacific in the opposite direction the exact demarcation of their respective spheres of influence gained a new importance. That importance increased when it was realised that this corner of the world was the home of many wealthy and sophisticated peoples trading in spices, gems, silk, porcelain and other luxury goods commanding high prices in Europe. Portugal and Spain, therefore, both tried to claim as large a section of this area as possible. For the map makers this involved deliberately distorting distances. Spanish maps, therefore, showed the Philippines and the Spice Islands (the Moluccas) as close as possible to the western coast of Spanish America. Experienced Pacific navigators like Colchero may have known full well that the real distance from Guatulco to Ternate was further than the $114\frac{1}{2}$ degrees of longitude on the official maps. Their own private charts may have borne a much closer relationship to the truth.

However accurate the information at his disposal, Drake faced a daunting challenge as he set out from the American coast. Ahead of him lay the longest stretch of open water the *Golden Hind* would encounter on the whole voyage. With over forty tons of bullion and other dead weight booty aboard, and as much food and equipment as she could carry, her speed was much reduced. On the other hand, Drake could comfort himself with the knowledge that Spanish merchant vessels laden with Peruvian silver often made this journey. And what lay in wait for them on the other side of the ocean? Islands whose treacherous natives had murdered Magellan; lands swarming with Portuguese and Spanish colonists. Drake would not have been human if he had not speculated about the hazards ahead. He would not have been Drake if he had not swept aside these speculations and applied himself to the task in hand.

He steered a south-westerly course before the obliging trade winds, seeking the latitudes ($8°–12°$N) followed by the Spanish China fleets. He reached $1\frac{1}{2}°$N somewhere to the west of Christmas Island. From there the combined effects of wind and the north equatorial current carried the *Golden Hind* slightly north of west.[2] If the lookouts saw no sign of land for sixty-six days it seems they must have passed between the Marshall and Gilbert Islands and sailed on until, on 30 September, they sighted some of the Carolines.

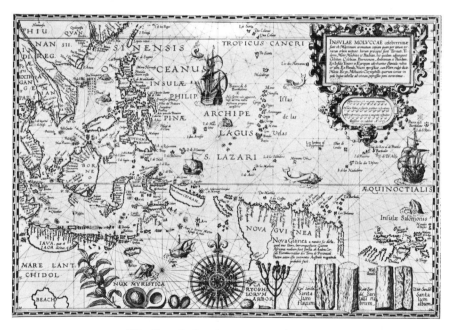

The East Indies from a map of c. *1594*

Apart from the uncertainty of where and when they would strike land, the crossing was probably a pleasant one. The weather was warm and they had a following wind which made the work aboard ship so much easier. A careful check had to be kept on the consumption of food and water, and spare sails were draped about the deck to collect any rain or dew. Drake knew that Magellan had taken three and a half months to cross the Pacific but that had been from the coast of South America. From Colchero he had learned that the crossing from Acapulco to the Moluccas could be accomplished in under three months. Apart from marking off the calendar and watching for land he had no other effective way of checking the ship's progress. He was travelling on an east-west axis which meant that calculations of distance involved calculations of longitude. There was no accurate method of determining longitude. The sixteenth century did not boast chronometers which were sufficiently precise to allow of calculations based on the difference between noon at a fixed point and the declination of the sun at the same moment. There were rough and ready astronomical methods of fixing longitude but they were complex and Drake had certainly not mastered them:

> . . . the First Point of Aries was used as a datum point. Astronomically the half-meridian passing through it served just as the meridian of Greenwich does today for terrestrial longitude. By observing the position and time of transit of planets and stars at the equinoxes, their declination and right ascension, their angular distance measured in time from the First Point of Aries can be recorded in an almanac or plotted on a star map. This makes it possible to find longitude by the occultations of the planets by the moon's disc, that is by observations made when the declination and right ascension of the moon and a planet are identical.[3]

How Drake must have wished, as the empty ocean stretched before him day after day, that he had Thomas Doughty beside him on the poop deck with all his astronomical charts, almanacs and mathematical paraphernalia.

When Magellan's expedition had passed this way, his crew, in the last extremities of hunger and exhaustion, were forced to fight off an attack by the aggressive and thieving natives of the Marianas, which were thereafter called *los Ladrones*, 'the Islands of Thieves'. Drake and his men were, therefore, very wary as they drew near a group of islands in about 8°N on 30 September. Soon a fleet of canoes was seen approaching the ship. The sailors watched as the Polynesian craft approached and they took a great technical interest in the sleek, burnished canoes with their ingenious outriggers which gave them both speed and stability.

The natives were obviously quite accustomed to large European ships for as they drew near they held up fish, fruit, sweet potatoes and coconuts which they had come to barter. The travellers were glad enough to have fresh food and a brisk trade was soon in progress, articles passing back and forth between the ship and the boats. But before long the sailors realised that the commerce was only in one direction; the knives, cloth, beads and other articles which the Polynesians took were not being paid for. They seemed

more intent on quarrelling among themselves over their spoils than in providing food for the white men. The mariners were not slow to shout out
their complaints. In response the natives merely held out their hands for
more goods. When they realised that the market was closed they produced
stones from the bottom of their boats and hurled them at the ship. Drake
had a ready answer. One of the demi-culverins was loaded and fired over the
canoes. The explosion and the fountain of water which spouted up where
the shot fell had the desired effect. With howls of fear the Polynesians
deserted their craft and, as the *Golden Hind* got under way once more,
all that could be seen of them was a crowd of dark heads bobbing on the
water between the boats.

But the people were not to be so easily shaken off. From every island
they came, sometimes professing friendship, sometimes openly aggressive.
To the Englishmen, to whom Drake had probably recounted Magellan's
experiences, the Polynesians seemed a singularly villainous crew, completely
naked, their pierced ear lobes stretched into grotesque shapes by heavy metal
ornaments, their teeth blackened from chewing betel nuts.* At length, in-
timidated by the Polynesians' aggressive importunity, Drake fired several
rounds of arquebus shot directly into a group of canoes killing about twenty
men.† If it was an over-reaction it was an understandable one in the
circumstances.

Not until 3 October did the voyagers shake off their unwanted following.
The behaviour of the natives convinced Drake and his companions that they
had encountered *los Ladrones* but this is very unlikely. Guam, the most
southerly of the Marianas, is in 13°28′N whereas the written accounts place
Drake's 'Islands of Thieves' in about eight or nine degrees. Almost certainly
these islands belonged to the Caroline chain. The travellers would probably
have had a similar reception whatever Polynesian group they had called
at, as some modern voyagers know well.

On the 16th they reached the Philippines and spent five days very
cautiously inspecting them before venturing to anchor on the coast of
Mindanao. Whether they were looking for hostile natives or Spaniards the
accounts do not say—both, perhaps. Anyway, they encountered neither
and were quite unmolested while they took supplies of fresh water and
firewood.

These first Englishmen in the Orient were entering a world in conflict.
The East Indies was the meeting point and the clashing point of cultures.
Confucian Chinese, Arab Muslims, Indian Hindus and Buddhists and

* This custom, universally practised in the orient, stains not only the teeth but the saliva
so that addicts often have discoloured lips, gums and chins, something singularly unpre-
possessing to western eyes. Betel chewers sometimes deliberately blacken their teeth with
betel leaves.

† This seems the most likely explanation of John Drake's statement 'they killed twenty
because a hundred canoes full came out against them' (Nuttall, p. 32).

The port of Malacca, Portuguese headquarters in the East Indies

finally European Christians had all come here, travelling on the pathways of maritime commerce, drawn by the sandalwood of Sumba, the pepper and cloves of Ternate, the nutmegs and mace of Celebes. When the Portuguese and Spaniards arrived in the mid-sixteenth century they found that the most powerful political units in the islands were the small Muslim sultanates established over the preceding century. Some they conquered with ease, some with difficulty, some they could not conquer at all. Even where they imposed their colonial rule they could not eradicate the faith and culture of Islam. Nowhere is this better illustrated than in the Philippines. Between 1565 and 1571 Spanish conquerors overran Luzon, Cebu and most of the northern islands where they came into contact with a largely pagan population. But Sulu and Mindanao were under the rule of the *Moros*, the Muslims, and in those islands the power of Spain was firmly rejected.

Leaving Mindanao, Drake steered a southerly course. He was looking for the fabled Spice Islands, the Moluccas, where he hoped to trade for food and open up commercial relations for his country. The distance from Mindanao to the northern tip of the Moluccas is less than 250 miles but the *Golden Hind* wandered for thirteen days among tiny islands and shoals. Drake's charts were totally inadequate to the task of guiding him through this maze and for the first time since leaving England his navigational skills proved unequal to the task.

At some time during those thirteen days the *Golden Hind* encountered a Portuguese trading ship somewhere between Celebes and Mindanao. Drake was in two minds whether to challenge the vessel or not. He had little room for more booty but her larder would be worth raiding, and he might be able to obtain valuable navigational assistance. On the other hand he had

170

no desire to stir up the Portuguese garrisons by an act of aggression. In the event, the Portuguese captain took the initiative. Observing a ship which was obviously off course, he sent a boat to offer assistance. Drake sent his men below and when the boat drew near he waved it away with angry gestures. Dismissing this strange behaviour as the ingratitude of a proud Spaniard (for the ship could not be of any other nationality), the Portuguese captain pursued his way. Drake decided to follow, perhaps hoping that the other ship would lead him to the Moluccas. The pursuit lasted through the night and by morning Drake had decided on a change of tactics. The culverin were loaded and the gunners ordered to stand ready with their linstocks. He broke the English flag at the masthead and with pennants streaming bravely he brought the *Golden Hind* to within hailing distance.

'Captain Don Francisco de Paragon, Englishman and Lutheran,[4] orders you to strike your sails and surrender, and if you do not do so at once he will make you do so by force.'

The Portuguese captain hurled back a defiant answer and prepared to fight. Here was no timid Spaniard with an unarmed merchant ship. This captain commanded a galleon which had come from Goa or perhaps even round the Cape from Lisbon. She was equipped to deal with Persian Gulf pirates and recalcitrant client sultans. Even as the captain spoke the ship's cannons were being loaded and primed, his men were taking up battle stations. The *Golden Hind* loosed off her culverin, then swung away before the other ship had time to reply. And that was the end of the battle. Drake decided he had more to lose than gain by pressing his point. He increased the distance between him and the enemy and sailed away to the south-east. The Portuguese, for their part, made no attempt to follow.[5]

Next day off the island of Siau, the Englishmen picked up two men fishing in a canoe and persuaded them to guide them to the Moluccas. It was on 3 November that they at last came within sight of their goal. They also came within sight of another Portuguese vessel. It was a boat from Tidore come out to welcome what its oarsman thought was a supply ship from Malacca. He was brought aboard the *Golden Hind* but not until he confronted Drake on the poop deck did he realise, with a shock, his mistake. The English admiral was courteous, gave his visitor refreshment, assured him he had nothing to fear and then plied him with questions. Where was the nearest Portuguese fort? How many men and ships did the colonists possess? Which was the best route from here to Malacca? Who were the local rulers and how friendly were they?

What Drake learned from his conversation and his experiences over the next few days was that for some half a century the Portuguese had been operating in these waters.* In order to tap the incomparable wealth of these few tiny islands (some spices were worth more, ounce for ounce, than gold) they had established a commercial base on Tidore, built a fort and garri-

* They actually established their fort at Tidore in 1521.

Gathering peppers

soned it with troops. They had been able to do this because the sultans of Tidore and Ternate were bitter rivals. Under the pretence of promising support to the former they hoped to bring the entire Moluccas zone firmly within their commercial empire.[6] From Tidore, the Portuguese had overrun neighbouring Ternate and established a fort there also. But their supply lines were too extended: they could never quite manage the complete sub-

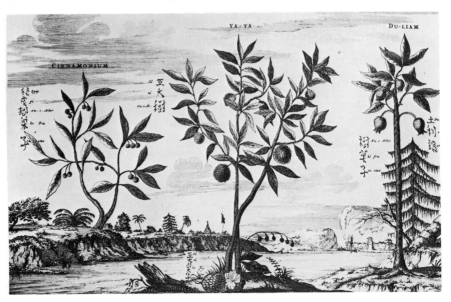

East Indian spices

jection of Ternate. In 1575 they were thrown out of the island for good and their fort became the Sultan's residence. In 1579 the Sultan of Ternate was the extremely astute Baab with whom the Portuguese had an uneasy four-year-old truce. Baab controlled not only Ternate but also Moli and Makian, the other principle clove-bearing islands in the Moluccas chain. He was inordinately wealthy and *ipso facto* powerful.

Drake was affability itself, even when the Portuguese told him that he had been born and bred in the Moluccas and that as he knew nothing of charts or navigation he could not help Drake to plot his homeward route. Drake told the man that, unfortunately, for reasons of security, he must regard himself a temporary prisoner of the English. While they were still talking one of the gentlemen approached and drew the admiral's attention to two boats, bearing down on the *Golden Hind* from the direction of Ternate. They were *caracoas,* the large, armed war canoes of this region. They were (and still are) an impressive sight, high and pointed at prow and stern, propelled by up to a hundred sweat-glistering oarsmen. The boats drew alongside the *Golden Hind* and the Sultan's representatives came solemnly aboard. Using the captured Portuguese as interpreter, Drake conveyed the information that he was an English 'Lutheran' and, as such, a friend to neither Portugal nor Spain. This news was relayed to the Sultan ashore and the ambassadors very quickly returned with a warm invitation to come into the harbour. Drake was assured that he would find on Ternate all he desired and that the Sultan would be 'wondrous glad of his coming'.[7]

Baab was, indeed, delighted to receive the Englishmen. They represented exactly what he most needed, a powerful ally who would help him, once and for all, to get rid of the Portuguese. The next morning Drake sent messengers ashore carrying a velvet cloak as a gift for the ruler. His Majesty responded with a lavish welcome which, to men not familiar with oriental opulence and hospitality, was impressive indeed.

The manner of his coming, as it was princely, so truly it seemed to us very strange and marvellous: serving at the present not so much to set out his own royal and kingly state (which was great), as to do honour to her highness to whom we belonged; wherein how willingly he employed himself, the sequel will make manifest.

First, therefore, before his coming, did he send off 3 great and large Canoes, in each whereof were certain of the greatest personages that were about him, attired all of them in white Lawn, or cloth of Calicut, having over their heads, from one end of the Canoe to the other, a covering of thin and fine mats, borne up by a frame made of reeds, under which every man sat in order according to his dignity; the hoary heads of many of them, set forth the greater reverence due to their persons, and manifestly showed that the king used the advice of a grave and prudent Council in his affairs. Besides these were diverse others, young and comely men, a great number attired in white, as were the other, but with manifest differences: having their places also under the same covering, but in inferior order, as their calling required.

Ternate

The rest of the men were soldiers, who stood in comely order round about on both sides; on the outside of whom, again did sit the rowers in certain galleries, which being 3 on each side all along the Canoe, did lie off from the side thereof, some 3 or 4 yards, one being orderly built lower than the other: in every of which galleries was an equal number of banks, whereon did sit the rowers, about the number of four score in one Canoe. In the forepart of each Canoe, sat two men, the one holding a tabret, the other a piece of brass, whereon they both at once stroke; and observing a due time and reasonable space between each stroke, by the sound thereof directed the rowers to keep their stroke with their oars: as, on the contrary, the rowers ending their stroke with a song, gave warning to the others to strike again; and so continued they their way with marvellous swiftness. Neither were their Canoes naked or unfurnished of warlike munition, they had each of them at least one small cast piece, of about a yard in length, mounted upon a stock, which was set upright; besides every man except the rowers, had his sword, dagger, and target, and some of them some other weapons, as lances, callivers, bows, arrows, and many darts.

These Canoes coming near our ship in order, rowed round about us one after another; and the men as they passed by us, did us a kind of homage with great solemnity, the greatest personages beginning first, with reverend countenance and behaviour, to bow their bodies even to the ground; which done, they put our own messenger aboard us again, and signified to us that their king (who himself was coming) had sent them before him to conduct our ship into a better road, desiring a hauser to be given them forth, that they might employ their service as their king commanded, in towing our ship therewith to the place assigned.

The king himself was not far behind, but he also with 6 grave and ancient fathers in his Canoe approaching, did at once, together with them, yield us a reverend kind of obeisance, in far more humble manner than was to be expected; he was of a tall stature, very corpulent and well set together, of a very princely and gracious countenance.[8]

Drake responded with as lavish a display as he could manage. The ship was dressed overall. The cannons fired a salute. There was a fanfare of trumpets and drums. More presents were conveyed to the Sultan. After the brasher noises had died down, Drake set his own musicians to fill the morning air with sweet sounds. This so delighted the cultured Baab that he asked for the players to be put into the ship's boat and sent across to his own canoe. Taking a line aboard he towed the musicians into harbour just as his *caracoas* were towing the *Golden Hind*. It was, Drake may have reflected, for all the world like a royal pageant on the Thames.

In the harbour Sultan Baab bade his guest goodbye, promising to supply him with food. He was as good as his word. That night and again next morning, the local tradesmen resorted in droves to the *Golden Hind* bearing rice, sugar-cane, chickens, coconuts and plantains. The Englishmen were also introduced to another food staple of Indonesia—sago. This starch, which comes from the pith of sago palms and then undergoes an elaborate process of manufacture, intrigued the visitors. They concluded that it tasted 'in the mouth like sour curds, but melts away like sugar'[9] and were intrigued by the fact that once made into a cake it would 'keep good at least 10 years'.[10]

The traders also offered Drake cloves and, since the price demanded was very low, he took aboard six tons. In doing so he seriously jeopardised his friendship with the Sultan. Baab controlled the clove trade firmly. The bulk of his revenue was derived from a ten per cent export duty and only licensed traders were allowed to sell cloves. The palace was, understandably, vigilant in its efforts to stamp out illicit commerce. Baab registered a strong protest and Drake had to soothe him with more presents before 'normal diplomatic relations' could be re-established.[11]

Drake and several of his gentlemen were received in audience by the Sultan.[12] They were escorted into a large, open-sided house next to the castle. At one end stood the throne covered with a canopy, and all around were hangings of richly-coloured cloth. This was the royal audience chamber, the place where the Sultan met his people to administer justice and receive petitions. All the leading men of the state were present, richly dressed and ranged strictly according to rank. In typical oriental fashion the visitors were kept waiting for half an hour in the hot, crowded, stuffy room.

Drake and his men presented to the Sultan of Ternate

The king at last coming from the castle, with 8 or 10 more grave Senators following him, had a very rich canopy (adorned in the midst with embossings of gold) borne over him, and was guarded with 12 lances, the points turned downward: our men (accompanied with *Moro* the king's brother) arose to meet him, and he very graciously did welcome and entertain them. He was for person, such as we have before described him, of low voice, temperate in speech, of kingly demeanour, and a Moor by nation. His attire was after the fashion of the rest of his country, but far more sumptuous, as his condition and state required: from the waist to the ground was all cloth of gold, and that very rich; his legs bare, but on his feet a pair of shoes of goat skin, dyed red; in the attire of his head, were finely wreathed in diverse rings of plated gold, of an inch or an inch and a half in breadth, which made a fair and princely show, somewhat resembling a crown in form; about his neck he had a chain of perfect gold, the links very great and one fold double; on his left hand was a diamond, an emerald, a ruby, and a turkey [turquoise], 4 very fair and perfect jewels; on his right hand, in one ring, a big and perfect turkey; and in another ring many diamonds of a smaller size, very artificially set and couched together.

As thus he sat in his chair of state, at his right side there stood a page with a very costly fan (richly embroidered and beset with Sapphires) breathing and gathering the air to refresh the king, the place being very hot, both by reason of the sun, and the assembly of so great a multitude.[13]

Baab was quite prepared to allow Drake to revictual his ship and carry away a cargo of cloves but in return he wanted definite assurances of an alliance with England which would bring men and ships to his land and help him overthrow the Portuguese. Drake promised that he would send a major expedition to Ternate within two years and pledged his word as a gentleman to that effect. There is no reason to doubt that he was completely sincere. To scores of adventurous captains and generals at home trade with the Orient and Cathay was a vivid dream. Now that he had established contact with the richest of the Moluccas' rulers Drake had no doubt that he could find volunteers ready to go there and cement relations which would be to the mutual advantage of both sides. A bargain was eventually sealed between the two men by a further exchange of gifts, Drake presenting Baab with a jewelled ring, a coat of mail and a helmet.[14]

This agreement made a profound impression on both sides. Fifty years later Baab's son referred to it in a letter to King James I. Queen Elizabeth clearly regarded it as one of the most significant achievements of Drake's voyage. Soon after his return she presented him with a silver cup engraved upon which was a picture representing Drake's reception by the Sultan of Ternate. If this is so it is difficult to understand Drake's unease. This was his greatest opportunity to show himself as an ambassador for the English Queen (which was how he frequently represented himself to strangers) yet he did not seem to relish it. Despite the fact that his ship needed cleaning and repairing again, he was anxious to be away from Ternate and, indeed, he left after only five days. Had the disagreement with Baab unnerved him? Did he mistrust the Sultan? Was he apprehensive of being discovered by the Portuguese if he stayed too long?

The Portuguese commander at Tidore did, indeed, soon learn of the Englishmen's arrival. Thinking the newcomers were Spaniards he sent two men to Ternate offering the facilities of his port and suggesting it was more seemly for Christians to consort with brother Christians than with Moors.

They were stunned by Drake's characteristic response:

> 'Señores, tell the commander that I kiss his hands many times and I thank him very much for the honour he does me, but I am no Spaniard but an Englishman, a Lutheran of a different persuasion, and that these are Moors who for our money will give us what is necessary.' The two Portuguese . . . asked him where he was going and what he was looking for. He answered that he came to discover the world by order of his Queen. On being asked how he had traversed such a long road in such a small ship he said he had ten other galleons which he had sent on discovery to different parts and he was now going to join them in a certain place.[15]

All that nonsense about 'ten other galleons' and his imminent rendezvous with them, was it just typical Drake bravado or was it a warning to the Portuguese not to meddle with him? Surely we are beginning to see another side of Francis Drake. The flamboyant self-confidence is now repressed; the cautious, responsible commander is to the fore. He had a heavily-laden, perhaps over-laden, ship, a ship decidedly the worse for wear after a voyage half way round the world. He had a depleted crew numbering a little over sixty men. He was in a totally unfamiliar place where Portuguese and Spanish armed ships were frequent visitors. And he had no idea how to get home. Yet getting home—with his ship, crew and cargo all safe was now his sole preoccupation.

That is undoubtedly why he did not accept the Chinaman's offer. The young gentleman in question presented himself with his suite aboard the *Golden Hind* and told Drake that he was a member of a Chinese imperial family (the Shen Tsung) living in exile. Through interpreters the two men exchanged information about their respective countries. The visitor then urged Drake to let him pilot the *Golden Hind* to China where, he insisted, the emperor would give him a warm welcome. Cathay was still largely a closed world. After persistent attempts to open up trade, the Portuguese had been permitted to set up a permanent base at Macao but this was little more than a commercial toe-hold. Generations of Englishmen had dreamed of establishing direct contact with Peking. Now that Drake had this prize within his grasp it is at first sight astonishing that he should have turned it down. The fact that he did so can only underline his growing concern about the safe return of the voyage. He was half a world away from home and his crew was diminishing at an alarming rate. If he added several months to the voyage by visiting the Emperor of Cathay, he might find himself without enough men to sail the ship long before he reached home waters. It was the sort of risk a dedicated explorer would probably have taken. Drake did not take it. The inference is obvious.

The *Golden Hind* lumbered out of Ternate on 9 November, riding low in the water under her weight of booty, legitimate cargo, food and supplies.

Drake ran south-westwards looking for a suitable beach upon which to careen his ship and prepare her fully for the homeward voyage. This brought him to a tiny, wooded island somewhere off the east coast of Celebes. Careful reconnaissance indicated that it was deserted and that it had a suitable sheltered, shelving beach. The entire complement landed, pitched tents, built huts, erected a stockade and positioned the cannons around it at intervals. Then came the laborious task of completely unloading the ship. The smith and the carpenter set up their workshops. The ropes and tackles were run out. The *Golden Hind* was pulled over onto her side and everyone fell to the assorted tasks of scraping, tarring, caulking and mending. Every two or three days a boatload of men had to row to a nearby island for water.

It was not only the ship that needed attention; many of the men were sick or weak. The weather was hot and humid, and every job required an enormous effort. Drake did not press the men. Work was done in the morning. When the sun reached its zenith the sailors were allowed to rest or seek the coolness of the trees. Twenty-six days Drake assigned to repairs and recuperation on Crab Island.

The place was given this name because of the large robber crabs which thronged the shore. These remarkable creatures, between one and two feet long, are, in fact, something between crabs and lobsters and have some remarkable characteristics. When in danger they are remarkably quick and efficient at digging into the sand. They have even been known to climb up tree trunks. But they were no match for Drake's men, who found them very good eating. The travellers were also fascinated by the myriads of fireflies which appeared at dusk and by the large bats which frequented the island.

When it came to reloading Drake had to make some hard decisions. His valuable cargo had to be got home safely. He had to carry as much food and water as possible. Yet to overload the ship before attempting the long haul through the Indian and Atlantic oceans could be courting disaster. Anything unnecessary would have to be jettisoned. Some of the cannons were left behind on Crab Island as, doubtless, were any superfluous barrels of pitch, extra spars, and, perhaps, a tree trunk Drake had cut down in Magellan's Strait as proof of his visit.

These were not the only items left on Crab Island. For Maria, the negress, and the two negroes brought from Spanish America the end of the journey had come. Maria was blatantly pregnant and her continued presence could only be a nuisance. The two able-bodied negroes Drake was probably loth to lose but he could not leave the woman alone and so all three of them were set ashore.[16] They were provided with rice, seeds and the means to make fire. Were they also left a boat or canoe with which to reach that nearby island which was their only water supply? The records do not say that they were. Why were they deserted here in this totally strange, lonely place? A more pertinent question might be, why were they brought away from America? 'To rescue them from Spanish tyranny' is, doubtless, the answer Drake would have given. Was that so much worse than the tyranny of sun, fear, boredom and the loneliness of the empty island?

On 12 December the *Golden Hind* weighed anchor and made her way confidently westwards. Four days later her way was blocked by the bulk of Celebes. Drake knew that he should veer north to find his way into the Celebes Sea but the north-east monsoon was blowing strongly and this was not possible. He had no alternative but to run south and seek a way around the southern end of the island. It was a hazardous passage. There were shoals and reefs everywhere. Throughout every watch constant soundings had to be taken. There had to be frequent course changes in order to find and keep to the deeper channels. Progress was painfully slow. There were days when the ship beat backwards and forwards over the same stretch of sea without finding a way through the encircling reefs. To the mariners it seemed as though they were just as trapped as they would have been if great iron bars had been let down from heaven to hem them in.

At last, at the beginning of January, they escaped. The mainland trended to the westward, the waving coral, for so long clearly visible, slipped deeper into the green depths, and the *Golden Hind* was able to hoist all sails to a following wind. Now the men could really feel that they were on the way home. The *Golden Hind* sailed into the new year with every prospect of seeing England well before its end. Saturday 9 January passed as uneventfully as its predecessor. As the brief equatorial twilight faded Drake said evening prayers and everyone except the duty watch settled to sleep. Slumber had scarcely settled upon them when the tearing, grinding sound every mariner fears was heard. The ship shuddered and was still. The *Golden Hind* had run aground.

The Golden Hind *on the reef*

CHAPTER TWELVE

'Return again ye sons of men'

10 JANUARY — 26 SEPTEMBER 1580

The listing deck was alive with rushing, slipping men. Confused commands rang out over the hiss of the breakers. When some order had been restored Drake took stock of the situation. The *Golden Hind* had drifted, broadside on, on to a steep-sided reef, more like an underwater cliff. She had struck on the port side and the wind coming strong from the other quarter made it impossible to fend or float her off. She was held fast. Drake immediately sent men below to see whether the ship was holed. She was not, thanks, undoubtedly, to her double sheathing. There was no imminent danger of foundering but there were other dangers, very real and very terrifying. Shifting winds might batter the ship against the coral or tear away her masts and spars. The *Golden Hind* might be stranded permanently on the reef, compelling the crew to abandon her and entrust themselves to the mercy of whatever natives inhabited the nearer islands.

With the total ruin of his enterprise confronting him face to face Drake showed the highest qualities of seamanship and leadership. The first task was to stop panic among the crew. He knew the danger they were in; most of them did not. Therefore, they must be kept in ignorance, reassured and given jobs to keep them occupied. He called them all together on the main deck and in the dim light of the ship's lamps he explained that the ship had struck a reef but was not leaking and that he was taking measures to refloat her. First of all, however, they must commend themselves to Almighty God, the Lord of the deep. Everyone knelt and Drake led the crew in brief prayers which as well as beseeching aid in their predicament also touched on the joys of heaven so that, whichever way things fell out, everyone would be prepared.

When calm had been restored, Drake turned to the practical task of trying to get his ship off the reef ('that we might not seem to tempt God, by leaving any second means unattempted which he afforded', as Fletcher piously explained[1]). He personally went into the ship's boat with a sounding party. The object was to probe the bottom on the starboard side of the ship to find some rock or obstruction which would afford lodgement for an anchor. With such a purchase it might be possible to haul the *Golden Hind* off into deeper water. For an hour or more the boat patrolled to and fro while those on the ship strained their ears to hear how Drake and his companions were faring. At no point near the ship could a sounding be taken. Every time the lead was thrown the whole line ran out behind it and the weight never touched bottom.

Drake climbed back aboard and before the men had time to react to the disheartening news he was issuing fresh orders. The ship was to be lightened. Eight guns were trundled overboard. The hatches were removed. Drake and the gentlemen checked off items of cargo and food which could be jettisoned. To and fro went the sailors carrying boxes, sacks, barrels. Three tons of cloves, a quantity of cassava and fresh vegetables—all splashed into the sea. None of the precious gold and silver was thrown away. This may be a comment on human cupidity even in the face of disaster but a more likely explanation is that the heavy bullion was stored in the ballast. In the darkness it was far easier to remove from the hold those items closest to the surface.

All this sacrifice made no difference. The ship did not budge. As dawnlight crept across the water the travellers could for the first time see the extent of the problem. Over the port side the coral gleamed creamy white not seven feet below the surface. The *Golden Hind*'s laden draught was thirteen feet. To the mariners there seemed to be little doubt about her fate—or theirs.

> As touching the ship . . . lying there confined already upon the hard and pinching rocks, did tell us plain, that she continually expected her speedy dispatch, as soon as the sea and winds should come, to be the severe executioners of that heavy judgement, by the appointment of the eternal judge already given upon her, who had committed her there to Adamantine bonds in a most narrow prison, against their coming for that purpose: so that if we would stay with her, we must peril with her; or if any, by any yet unperceivable means, should chance to be delivered, his escape must needs be a perpetual misery, it being far better to have perished together, than with the loss and absence of his friends to live in a strange land: whether a solitary life (the better choice) among wild beasts, as a bird on the mountains without all comfort, or among the barbarous people of the heathen, in intolerable bondage both of body and mind.[2]

As the sun rose another attempt was made to find an anchor hold. It was unsuccessful. Short of throwing out the rest of the cargo there was nothing more that could be done.

Despair settled over the ship; despair and mutual recrimination. Men muttered that their leader cared more about gold and silver than he did about them. He would rather drown with his precious treasure than throw it overboard to gain their salvation. Others assured their comrades in whispers that this plight was a divine judgement for the murder at St

Julian's Bay. At no time was the presence of Thomas Doughty's un-exorcised shade more palpable.

Once more Drake called the crew together. They would, he said, commend themselves to God again. Francis Fletcher would preach to them to explain to them the ways of God and assure them of their certain hope of everlasting life. Then he would administer the sacrament so that all present would face their destiny united in Christian brotherhood.

Fletcher did, indeed, preach but not the sermon Drake was hoping to hear. For months the pastor had been troubled in his conscience. He knew Doughty's execution had been wrong. He knew he had been wrong in condoning it. He knew he had been shirking his spiritual responsibility by failing to confront Drake with his grave sin. Now, standing as he was on the brink of eternity, he knew he must discharge his conscience. He called upon all present to repent of and seek forgiveness for all their trespasses and he stated that the worst trespass for which they all stood in need of God's mercy was the condemnation of Mr Doughty.

Drake listened in silence, his undoubted anger overlaid by the more urgent anxieties crowding his mind. Yet, as he knelt to receive the bread and wine, he may well have momentarily forgotten his present troubles and recalled vividly an earlier Communion when he and another man had, side by side, received the elements weeping.

The service over, there was little for the men to do except, as Fletcher had urged, trust to God. They watched the tide come in and hoped it might float them free but the *Golden Hind* was too far up on the reef. Then, in the middle of the afternoon their prayers were answered. The stiff wind which had held the ship fast against the unyielding coral suddenly dropped. The *Golden Hind* heeled over to starboard. For a moment it seemed she would heel right over. Then, with another grinding, crunching sound her hull slipped down the submerged coral summit. Drake's ship was once again riding free in deep water.

They were safe and they lost no time in giving thanks to God. Then, Drake had another matter to attend to. His authority had been challenged and that was something he could not tolerate. Parson Fletcher's criticisms over the Doughty affair and the connection of that affair with the recent disaster had undermined the admiral's standing with the men. The preacher had said aloud what many of them had been thinking ever since that bizarre day at St Julian's Bay, nineteen months before. Furthermore, he had said it with divine authority. How could Drake possibly overcome the damaging effects of Fletcher's denunciation? The answer of the deeply-offended Drake was so extreme that some historians have regarded it as a jest. There may have been an element of buffoonery about it, designed to amuse the crew and win them over to his side. But Drake was extremely sensitive of any personal affront and far too zealous a Protestant to take holy things lightly. He was therefore in deadly earnest when he summoned the crew together for a ceremony the like of which they had never seen before.

First, he caused a length of chain to be stapled to the fore-hatch. Then Fletcher was brought forth and the chain fixed around his leg with a padlock. The crew now stood around in a circle and Drake seated himself cross-legged on a chest with a pair of slippers in his hand. He told the assembled company that the chaplain had so far abused his sacred office in rousing the men against their lawfully appointed leader that only one sentence was appropriate.

'Francis Fletcher.' he proclaimed, 'I do here excommunicate thee out of the Church of God, and from all the benefits and graces thereof, and I denounce thee to the devil and all his angels.'

Drake then told Fletcher that if he attempted to come beyond the foremast into the body of the ship he would be hanged. Finally, to hammer the point home, he caused to be tied to the chaplain's arm a prepared placard which read, FRANCES fLETCHER (note the verbal joke obtained by making the 'f' small) Ye FALSEST KNAVE THAT LIVETH.[3] How long Fletcher lay on the forecastle, an object of derision to the crew, we do not know. He must have been 're-instated' in the Church before long, but probably only after making an abject submission to the admiral.

The *Golden Hind* continued to thread her way delicately through the islands and reefs between Celebes and the Moluccas. Prevailing winds prevented her making any headway whatsoever around either the northern or southern end of Celebes.[4] About 20 January a west-south-west gale blew up. Abandoning his plans to reach the Celebes Sea or Flores Sea he allowed the *Golden Hind* to drift eastwards. However inaccurate his charts were, they must have shown Java, Timor and the major islands of the Sunda group. Drake now hoped to ride out the storm or find a sheltered anchorage and then return westwards via this chain of islands, thus gaining the Indian Ocean far to the south of the usual trade route.

As the storm abated, on 4 February, the *Golden Hind* lay well to the north-east of Timor. Drake was able to anchor off a small island (perhaps Damar) for water and wood, and then, at last, pursue a westerly course through open water. On the 6th, he saw two canoes approaching the ship from one of the nearer islands. Soon they were alongside and their smiling occupants were holding up items for trade. Remembering their earlier experiences, Drake and his men were cautious but the people seemed to be honest and, since he was once again in need of food, the admiral allowed them to guide him to their island, 'Barateve', and very glad he was of his decision. Both island and people proved to be extremely pleasant. Indeed as one sailor recorded, 'since the time that we first set out of our own country of England, we happened upon no place (Ternate only excepted) wherein we found more comforts and better means of refreshing.'[5]

Drake's company were neither the first nor the last white men to find the hospitality and cheerfulness of these attractive people totally disarming.

Portuguese ships had been trading in these waters since 1520 and they owned a base on nearby Solor. The men wore simple loin cloths and had turbans round their heads; the women dressed in sarongs and decorated themselves with a multitude of armlets and necklaces of gold, silver and bone. All the inhabitants of 'Barateve' did their utmost to make the Englishmen welcome. The guests were plied with fish, the meat of various animals and birds, lemons, cucumbers, coconuts and sago. Many of the dishes were spiced with pepper, ginger and nutmeg, a treat which only the wealthy could afford in England. Here, too, the visitors sampled the betel nut so beloved of orientals. On this well-found island there were also, apparently, mines from which the people extracted gold, copper, silver and sulphur.

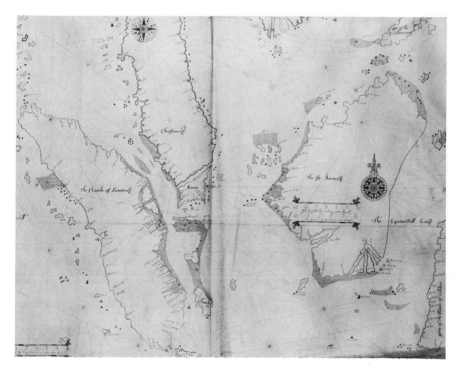

Sumatra and Borneo from an English atlas of the 1580s

Drake re-stocked the *Golden Hind*'s larder at this earthly paradise and then made ready to sail. Most of the men would gladly have stayed longer but Drake was anxious to be away while he still had a favourable wind. The sailors therefore hurriedly concluded their bargains for coloured cloth, knives, bracelets and other souvenirs and climbed back aboard. On 10 February Drake weighed anchor and set course for Java. He sailed through the Ombai Strait north of Timor and thence into the open sea south of the

Sunda Islands. A month's travelling brought him to the southern coast of Java and he then went close inshore looking for a haven. On 10 March a suitable harbour presented itself (perhaps Tjilatjap) and the *Golden Hind* anchored at a safe distance from the land. The next day a boatload of armed men cautiously approached the shore. They were well received by the local people who showed them where to find water. Drake sent the boat back later in the day and his men successfully bartered for food. At sunset Drake thought it safe to enter the sheltered channel between the town and a nearby island. It was to be the *Golden Hind*'s last stay in a foreign harbour.

Java, once the centre of the mighty Hindu empire of Majapahit, had, like most of Indonesia, fallen to the Muslim invaders of the fourteenth and fifteenth centuries. Then it became the battle ground of rival Muslim sultanates. At the time of Drake's visit the greater part of eastern and central Java was under the rule of a great king-general called Senapati. His state of Mataram had conquered all rivals except the western sultanate of Bantam. Senapati ruled his wide domain through a number of emirs or rajahs as they were called in Java where the Hindu sub-culture remained strong.

The next morning Drake sent gifts ashore for the local ruler—silk, linen and woollen cloth. After a few hours his emissaries returned with rice, coconuts, chickens, mangoes and bananas. They also brought welcome news of the most cordial reception they had received from the rajah, of the impressive palace and temples of heavily carved stone and the colourfully dressed people in their sarongs and turbans of bright silk.

On 13 March Drake and the gentlemen dressed in their finest clothes and were rowed ashore to pay an official visit to the rajah. Drake provided himself with a guard of honour comprising his drummer, trumpeter, musicians and a detachment of helmeted pikemen. He was determined to make an impressive show on what (he profoundly hoped) would be the last occasion that he would stand before a foreign prince as ambassador of the Queen of England.

And the rajah was impressed. Like the Sultan of Ternate, he was enchanted by the sound of English viols and tabors. The pikemen put on a display of drill which equally intrigued their hosts. The visitors partook of sumptuous refreshments. By means of signs they sought names for some of the things they could see: coconut—'calapa'; turban—'totopps'; rice—'braas'; silk—'sabuck'.

So began what became an almost exhausting round of mutual entertainments. The rajah was invited aboard the *Golden Hind*. He was feasted, shown over the ship and entertained with music and dancing. The rajahs of the neighbouring districts came to see the strangers. They, too, had to be entertained. They offered hospitality in return. Nor was it only the gentlemen who were involved in this social intercourse. The crew went ashore and mixed freely with the handsome Javanese men and women. They admired the superb workmanship on swords and daggers, the beautiful batik patterns on cloth. They bought many items to take home as souvenirs. They were intrigued by their hosts' way of life—their communal long

A Javanese man

houses, their techniques of hunting, fishing, preparing food. Indeed throughout the whole of their lengthy voyage they had never got to know any people as well as they did the Javanese. One sailor was able to remember in detail his stay on this lovely island some years later:

> The people are of goodly stature, and warlike, well provided of swords and targets, with daggers, all being of their own work, and most artificially done, both in tempering their metal, as also in the form, whereof we bought reasonable store.
>
> They have an house in every village for their common assembly: every day they meet twice, men, women, and children bringing with them such victuals as they think good, some fruits, some rice boiled, some hens roasted, some sago, having a table made three foot from the

ground, whereon they set their meat, that every person sitting at the table may eat, on rejoicing in the company of another.

They boil their rice in an earthen pot, made in form of a sugar loaf, being full of holes, as our pots which we water our gardens withal, and it is open at the great end, wherein they put their rice dry, without any moisture. In the mean time they have ready another great earthen pot, set fast in a furnace, boiling full of water, whereinto they put their pot with rice, by such measure, that they swelling become soft at the first, and by their swelling stopping the holes of the pot, admit no more water to enter, but the more they are boiled, the harder and more firm substance they become; so that in the end they are a firm and good bread, of the which with oil, butter, sugar, and other spices, they make divers sorts of meats very pleasant of taste and nourishing to nature.[6]

All this pressing hospitality, pleasant though it was, delayed the expedition's preparations, The *Golden Hind*'s hull yet again needed cleaning after her to-ing and fro-ing in the Molucca and Banda seas. And there was, of course, the usual task of packing and salting food to keep it in reasonable condition for the next stage of the journey. Yet, the work was gradually being accomplished and Drake adjudged that he could safely wait a few more days before departing. Then something happened to shock him out of his relaxed complacency.

Some Javanese had come aboard and were laughing and chattering with the English sailors in a mixture of words and signs. There was nothing at all remarkable about this; parties of local people came to the ship daily. But one of the men was not joining in the laughter. He was very curious about the *Golden Hind*. He examined her guns. Surreptitiously he tried to count her crew. This aroused the suspicions of one of the sailors who noticed, on closer examination, that the man's skin was not as dark as that of his fellows.

A Malabar craft used by Portuguese merchants

188

He challenged the 'native' and the man tried to escape. He was immediately captured and marched off to the admiral. Drake soon discovered that the man was a Portuguese spy, who had been sent with a colleague to see if the *Golden Hind* could be captured. Almost immediately news arrived of three European ships approaching along the coast. Drake knew that the time for departure had come.

On 26 March the *Golden Hind* pointed her prow at the Indian Ocean and raised her sails. The normal Portuguese *carreira da India* took the merchant vessels from Malacca to Goa where they picked up the monsoon winds to waft them across to Africa. But Drake was anxious to keep away from Portuguese commercial centres. He had no alternative but to attempt the direct crossing to the Cape of Good Hope which Elcano had made in 1521-2 after the death of his leader, Magellan. It meant another long ocean crossing. It also meant reaching the Cape sometime in May or June, the worst time of the year. But Drake had no choice. Helped by the southeast trade winds he achieved the Indian Ocean crossing in fifty-six days. It was very good time; Elcano (starting from the Moluccas) had taken one hundred and thirty-six days. The *Golden Hind* found the coast of Africa on 21 May.

Rather surprisingly, it took the travellers three and a half weeks to round the Cape. Storms are not the reason, for all the accounts insist that the *Golden Hind* had remarkably good weather while doubling Buena Esperanza. The most likely explanation is that Drake spent some time vainly searching for fresh water. Having no pinnace he would be forced to take the ship close to the coast for this purpose. Probably the continuing, strong on-shore wind rendered this hazardous. At last, he gave up the search and made course for the Cape. He rounded it on 18 June.[7] So easy was their journey round the Cape of Good Hope that the sailors were inclined to ascribe the stories of violent storms in this region to Portuguese propaganda:

> ... we ran hard aboard the Cape, finding the report of the Portugals to be most false, who affirm that it is the most dangerous Cape of the world, never without intolerable storms and present danger to travellers, which come near the same.
>
> This Cape is a most stately thing, and the fairest Cape we saw in the whole circumference of the earth ...[8]

The *Golden Hind*'s complement was now down to fifty-nine and one more would die before the vessel reached home. 'Home', that was the idea now possessing every mind. With luck each man would be beside his own hearth in three months or so. But the voyage and its attendant dangers were far from being over. Thirst was now the worst enemy. An attempt to land for water to the west of the Cape was frustrated by wind and weather, so Drake set a course for Guinea, hoping to make a landfall there before the situation became desperate. The water was severely rationed and

Drake would probably have lost more men had a fortuitous rain storm not eased the situation slightly. Some of the crew kept alive by sheer will-power. Having survived so many dangers and hardships, they were determined not to submit during the last stage of the voyage. On 22 July the coast of Sierra Leone hove into view. There were just over eight pints of stale water left in the cask.

Drake anchored, replenished the water supplies, and allowed the men ashore to refresh themselves and forage for fresh food. There, many of the mariners saw elephants for the first time in their lives. But by this time they were all sated with marvels, and wanted only to get home to recount their adventures to their families and friends. Within two days they had resumed their journey.

Standing well out to the north-west to avoid the northerly coastal winds (and perhaps to keep clear of the Hispano-Portuguese shipping lanes), Drake went on, navigating comfortably now by the Pole Star, until he reached 50°N. Then he turned for Devon with a following wind. The worries of the voyage were almost over but other worries lay ahead. The admiral could not share with his men the uncomplicated relief and delight as the familiar landmarks—the Scillies, Wolf Rock, Lizard—came into view. On Monday 26 September the *Golden Hind* drew steadily into Plymouth Sound on the flood. The first countryman Drake saw was a fisherman also entering the harbour. The vital question the circumnavigator asked, leaning over the ship's rail, was, 'Is the Queen still alive?'

CHAPTER THIRTEEN

'His doings cannot but prosper'

AFTERWARDS

The *Golden Hind* dropped anchor but her sails remained loosely furled. There was no uncovering of hatches preparatory to landing cargo. There was no excited bustle of sheets being made fast, of equipment being locked away, of sea chests being packed, such as would normally have marked a journey's end. Drake's men were kept aboard and his ship was ready to slip out of port as quickly and quietly as she had entered.

The admiral sent a message ashore to his wife. Mary, sensible woman that she was, went straight to the mayor. Together they were rowed across to the *Golden Hind*. The crew looked on enviously as their leader was reunited with his spouse. Then they waited anxiously while Drake and his visitors discussed the situation in the admiral's cabin. The mayor told Drake that he, like all the port authorities along the coast, had been ordered to keep a watch for the *Golden Hind*'s return. The instructions came from Drake's friends on the Council and their advice was scarcely reassuring. The situation at court was delicate. Drake should therefore send up word of his arrival secretly and lie low until he received further instructions. In any case, the mayor added, it would be unwise for the ship's complement to go ashore as there was contagion in the town. Drake broke the news to his disappointed crew, wrote letters to the Queen, Hatton, Walsingham and Leicester, and sent a messenger off post-haste on the London road. Then he settled to several days of anxious waiting as unnerving as any period he had spent throughout the last thirty-four months.

The political waters which Drake now exchanged for the world's oceans were strewn with many perilous rocks. Craggiest and most unyielding of these hazards was Don Bernardino de Mendoza who had arrived as Spanish ambassador to England in March 1578. He had been sent by an impoverished king who did not want war, to ease relations with an impoverished queen who equally did not want war. He was a strange choice for such a role—arrogant, brusque and highly accomplished in the arts of espionage.[1] It was the misfortune of both Elizabeth and Philip that men like Mendoza and Drake represented much more closely than they did themselves the prevailing mood in their respective countries.

When Mendoza took up his post, Don John of Austria was still triumphant in the Netherlands. Elizabeth poured money into the open hands of

Calvinist mercenaries but the Catholic hero defeated them in the field, while the faction-fighting of the Dutch burghers sapped the Protestant cause from within. The Catholic, pro-Spanish Guise party was in the ascendant in France. Elizabeth and her government were in despair. As a last resort the Queen raised again the possibility of her marriage. The suitor was Francis, Duke of Alençon, younger brother of Henry III of France. He was the current champion of the French Huguenots, and the Prince of Orange was also hopeful of his assistance. Courtship began in earnest between the 45-year-old queen and the the pock-marked duke. It was Elizabeth's last and most serious foray into the marriage mart. It had the blessing of Burghley and those councillors who favoured peace at any price and still hoped for a legitimate heir. It was opposed by the younger, radical members of the Council, and abhorred by the majority of Englishmen.

In October 1578 the major political reason for the marriage was removed. Don John of Austria died. The States General of the Netherlands asked Alençon to become their protector and the immediate prospect of invasion across the Narrow Seas subsided. But Philip II sent Alexander Farnese, Duke of Parma to be his new governor in the Netherlands and this most able of all Spanish statesmen-generals began the reassertion of Habsburg authority and the consolidation of power which would ultimately make the prospect of Spanish conquest of England a terrifying reality. The courtship continued, growing in intensity as Alençon's proxy became more ardent and the opponents of the liaison more alarmed. The affair came to a head in October 1579 with angry, tearful scenes between Elizabeth and her councillors. But for all that Elizabeth stormed, she knew that she could not persist against her closest advisers and the majority of her subjects. The Alençon marriage was locked away in the bulging chest containing Elizabeth's other broken 'romances' and the Queen resigned herself to a continuance of political instability.

That instability was made worse by enthusiasts on both sides. Pope Gregory XIII was determined to bring England back within the Roman fold. Having failed to stir King Philip to decisive action and having lost his great champion, Don John, he was obliged to use renegade English Catholics and other men of lower status. A stream of seminary priests flowed into England from the English College in Douai. From 1580 they were joined by Jesuits trained in Rome. In 1579 and 1580 small detachments of troops were sent with papal blessing to foment Catholic rebellion in Ireland.

Philip II tried to keep his hands clean but he did allow some of these soldiers to be trained and recruited in Spain. More worrying to the English government was his claim to the Portuguese crown. The aged Cardinal Henry was dying and Philip, in order to ensure his succession, began preparing an army and a fleet in 1579. The prospect of the two most powerful colonial powers being united was worrying enough but what was Philip planning to do with his invasion force after Portugal had been pacified?

The remaining irritant in Anglo-Spanish relations was Francis Drake. In June 1579 John Wynter had returned bearing the first news of the expedition. It was not encouraging; for all Wynter knew, the *Golden Hind* had foundered in the terrible storms around Cape Horn. At first Elizabeth received Wynter graciously and questioned him closely about Drake and his other vessels. So did the other backers of the voyage. If there was little prospect of the admiral's safe return they wanted to know what Wynter had brought back to help defray the costs of the expedition. The answer was the bulk of the cargo removed from Nuño da Silva's ship, consisting mainly of cloth, tools and implements.

But there was another claimant to these goods. Antonio de Castilla, the Portuguese ambassador, demanded restitution of this 'pirate plunder' on behalf of the lawful owners. The *Elizabeth*'s cargo was impounded at Bristol while claims and counterclaims were lodged in the Court of Admiralty and while, more important, the Queen and Council decided whether or not it was good policy to yield to Portuguese demands. If the expedition's backers hoped for support from Wynter they soon discovered that he was a broken reed. Before their lordships of the Admiralty he protested

> ...the taking of which ship...was utterly contrary to my good will which I could not let nor gainsay, for that I had no authority there, but such as pleased the said Drake, to give and take away from me at his will and pleasure, and being in great fear of my life if I should have contraried him or gone about to practise to withstand him in any part of this his doing, he would have punished me by death, for that his word and threatening many times tended thereunto by open speeches as by example of a gentleman whom he executed afterward. And for that I was there with the said Drake where no Justice would be heard, was inforced to content my self with silence, And now that I am come to a place of Justice I do here [manifest] and declare of certain goods put into the said ship by the said Drake wherein I was by the said Drake appoint-ment and by his commandment, but how or where he had the said goods I know not. Notwithstanding I do here notify unto this court and you the Judge thereof, that I did never give my consent or allowance any way to the taking of any ship or goods unlawfully...[2]

Wynter dutifully accounted for every item he had brought home and for those items which had been used or disposed of during the journey.

It remained only for the government to decide whether or not to appease the Portuguese and, thereby, dub both Wynter and Drake 'pirates'. After a year of delay and vacillation Castilla received a commission signed by the Queen authorising full restitution of all goods 'piratically taken on the seas by Francis Drake and his accomplices',[3] and Wynter was left to languish in prison. Such a decision on the part of Elizabeth boded ill for Drake on his return.

But would he return? It had been the previous August that the alarming despatches from the Spanish Americas had begun to reach Madrid. Officials at the Escorial sifted the information relating to Drake's depredations and soon it became apparent that the corsair had made off with a record haul in bullion, cash and jewels belonging to King Philip and his subjects. The king relayed the information to Mendoza with instructions that no action was to be taken until Drake's return. By now English merchants in Spain had got hold of the news and transmitted it home. In London it was, of course, well received. Mendoza grumbled that the backers of the expedition were 'beside themselves with joy'. Officially, however, the attitude of the Queen and Council was that Master Drake had gone on a voyage of exploration. If he had plundered Spanish shipping he had acted entirely on his own initiative.

Every ship from the Main brought more letters from anxious or self-justifying officials. At last, most of Drake's exploits were known up to the time when he left Guatulco. Then silence. Every few months a strong rumour would go round the City that the *Golden Hind* had anchored secretly in some small west-coast port, or that Drake had unloaded his treasure secretly in France, or that he was sailing bravely into the Thames estuary, all flags flying. Every one proved false. Perhaps it was only after Elizabeth had abandoned hope that she agreed to throw Wynter to the wolves. It was at least a friendly gesture towards Portugal (and that must mean towards Spain). If the expedition gave her nothing else it could at least be used for diplomatic advantage.

In June 1580 the goods from the *Elizabeth* were released into Antonio de Castilla's keeping. In July Spanish troops overran Portugal. During the summer Parma, by force and diplomacy, detached one Netherlands region after another from the Protestant alliance. Early in September news came to court of the reinforcements which had reached the Irish rebels from Spain. For England the political scene had seldom looked more overcast. In the southern ports men were mustered and ships made ready to guard the Channel.

On 29 September Sir Christopher Hatton received in his chambers at court news that a man had arrived with a secret message. He was astounded when he recognised the messenger. It was John Brewer, a servant who had sailed on the *Golden Hind* as Francis Drake's trumpeter.

In response to his eager questions, Hatton learned that Drake had docked at Plymouth three days previously, sent Brewer to announce his return and then withdrawn from the harbour to anchor close by St Nicholas Island in the Sound. There he and his men were waiting to know whether it was safe to let their arrival be generally known. Brewer handed his master letters written by Drake to Hatton and the other major shareholders. Doubtless they expatiated on the amount of treasure the *Golden Hind* had brought home. Perhaps Drake even intimated that he had provided his backers with a return on investment of 4,700 per cent.

The news was conveyed to the Queen and she sent orders that Drake was to come to court immediately. Drake had had plenty of time to prepare himself for the summons. The finest treasures from his haul had been selected and were waiting in his cabin. As soon as the Queen's message arrived the corsair set out on the road for London at the head of a train of pack horses well guarded by armed men.

Long before Drake arrived at Richmond, news of his gilded return had spread far and wide. The realm was abuzz with rumours of his exploits and treasure. Mendoza was trying, without success, to gain an audience with the Queen. Instead he had to content himself with writing letters demanding full restitution. Elizabeth, as was her wont, would make no decision until she was forced to do so. First she wanted to see Drake herself and learn from his own lips what he had brought back from the distant corners of the globe.

She received him in private as she had done at the inception of this whole adventure. For six hours, the shrewd stateswoman sat captivated by the tales of the rough Devonian captain. She was even more enthralled by the cascade of jewels, coins, gold crosses, and silver bars he poured at her feet. Drake also presented her Majesty with his diary of the journey; that volume in which he had noted down all the important events of the expedition and which contained the painstaking drawings made by him and his cousin.[4]

Mendoza might have been refused access to the Queen but members of the Council could not escape him. He put his point of view to Burghley and other conservatives. He stressed the justice of his demand for restitution and threatened reprisals against the English trading community in Spain if it was not met. The Lord Treasurer and some of his colleagues did not need persuading; they knew that the Queen was morally bound to restore the property taken from King Philip and his subjects. They knew Elizabeth had already conceded the principle in the case of John Wynter. And they firmly believed that to give open support to Drake's flagrant piracy would be to strain the Spanish king's patience to breaking point. They urged these considerations on the Queen when she summoned them to discuss what should be done about Drake's treasure. It was a long meeting; the Queen was torn between her desire for peace and her equally strong desire for cash. But none of Drake's backers was present at the meeting and at last Burghley had his way. Or did he? Elizabeth authorized an order for all the treasure to be stored in the Tower and catalogued as a preliminary to being handed over to Mendoza. When she did this she knew that the order would have to be taken to the absent councillors for their signatures, and that would give Hatton, Leicester and Walsingham their chance to raise objections. They did, of course, object. They went to see the Queen and, as a result, she countermanded her instructions. Instead, orders were sent to Edmund Tremayne, Plymouth magistrate, to see all the treasure stowed safely in Saltash Castle. First, however, Drake was permitted to retain £10,000 for his trouble and £8,000 for the crew. He was also to be allowed free access to the treasure (doubtless for the purpose of removing any more that he wanted).

Drake had no difficulty whatsoever in reaching a most amicable relationship with Tremayne who was, probably, an old friend. The magistrate wrote to tell Walsingham how Her Majesty's, deliberately vague, instructions had been interpreted.

> To give you some understanding how I in particular proceeded with Mr Drake, I have at no time entered into the account to know more of the very value of the treasure than he made me acquainted with. And to say truth, I persuaded him to impart to me no more than need, for I saw him commanded in Her Majesty's behalf that he should reveal the certainty to no man living. I have only taken notice of so much as he has revealed and the same I have seen to be weighed, registered and packed ... And to observe Her Majesty's command for the secret delivery on leaving of the ten thousand pounds to remain in his hands, we agreed that he should take it to himself out of the portion that was landed secretly and to remove the same out of the place before my son Henry and I should come to the weighing and registering of that which was left; and so it was done and no creature living by me made privy to it but himself and myself no privier to it than as you perceive by this.[5]

Total secrecy, consignments of treasure landed privily, ostentatious turning of blind eyes—it all adds up to one conclusion: all the interested parties from the Queen down were in collusion to salt away a large part of the treasure so that only a fraction of it would ever be officially registered. Early in November Elizabeth ordered this official fraction to be brought up to London and lodged in the Tower. If it became necessary to offer restitution to her brother monarch there were five tons of silver locked up safely in London. All concerned would be prepared to swear that there was no more. Meanwhile her treasury would benefit from the greater part of Drake's haul.

It is largely for this reason that it is impossible to calculate the total value of the loot Drake brought back to England. Spanish merchants who had been robbed of registered gold and silver submitted claims amounting to some £332,000. Beyond that there was all the unregistered bullion, the jewels and the legitimate cargo of cloves. If the shareholders were paid back at the rate of £47 for every pound invested they must have received between them a sum not far short of £200,000. The Queen probably

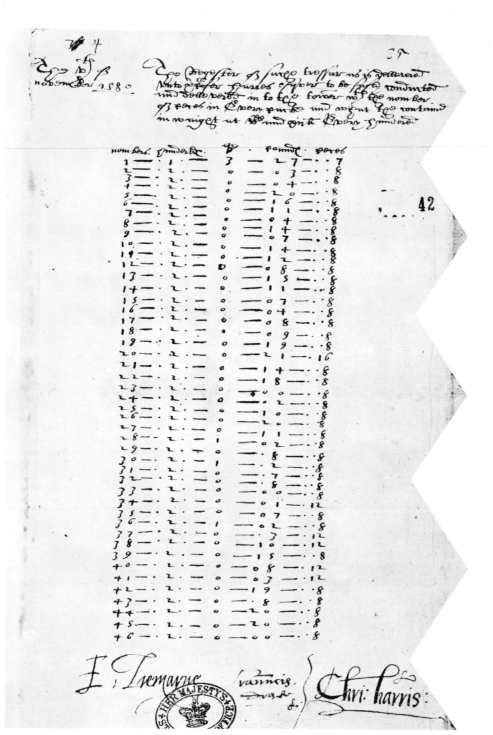

The last page of the inventory of Drake's treasure, signed by Drake himself

197

received £160,000 (enough to meet government expenses for almost a year) besides the 'trinkets' Drake presented to her—for instance a crown set with large emeralds and a diamond-encrusted frog, in honour of Alençon whom Elizabeth nicknamed her *grenouille*. The grand total can scarcely have amounted to less than half a million of sixteenth-century money. The computation of this in modern terms is fraught with difficulty but if we reckon it at £25,000,000 we shall probably not be far wrong.[6]

No wonder Drake was a hero with his own men, with the Queen, with his backers and with the people at large. Wherever he went people flocked to gaze upon him. Ballads and pamphlets poured from the presses extolling his virtues and his exploits. His achievements would have attracted admiration at any time but in 1580 England needed a hero. The psychological moment was right for Drake. Isolated, threatened by the coalescing Catholic forces of the continent, impoverished, her Protestant identity balanced on the slender life of a middle-aged woman, the realm needed something to celebrate and Drake provided that something not simply because of what he had achieved but because of the new hope he opened up for the future. He had shown that English mariners could challenge the seagoing power of Spain and Portugal, and plunder the wealth of the colonies. He had shown that English explorers could open up new markets and new fields of endeavour. Mendoza's reports were frequently laced with sour comments about the circumnavigator's popularity: 'Drake has returned to Court, where he passes much time with the Queen, by whom he is highly favoured and told how great is the service he had rendered her;' 'The Queen shows extraordinary favour to Drake and never fails to speak to him when she goes out in public [i.e. into her public audience chamber], conversing with him a long time;' 'The Queen often has him in her cabinet, often indeed walking with him in the garden.'[7] Elizabeth always admired manliness and valour. Drake who was forceful and imaginative in word as well as deed had the power to enthrall and amuse her to an extent that aroused considerable jealousy among her stay-at-home courtiers. For this reason alone she would have found it difficult to sacrifice him on the altar of Anglo-Spanish amity.

Nor would the people have stood for it. 'The people generally applauded his wonderful long adventures and rich prizes . . . his name and fame became admirable in all places, the people swarming daily in the streets to behold him, vowing hatred to all that misliked him.'[8] Tremayne's enthusiasm was typical of that of many who admired Drake. He was anxious, he said,

> to recompense all men that have been in this case dealers with him, as I dare take an oath he will rather diminish his own portion than leave any of them unsatisfied. And for his mariners and followers, I have been an eye witness, and have heard with mine ears upon the shutting up of these matters, such certain show of good will as I cannot yet see that

Buckland Abbey

many of them will leave his company wheresoever. His whole course of his voyage hath showed him to be of great valour, but my hap has been to see some particularities, and namely in this discharge of his company as doth assure me that he is a man of great government and that by the rules of God and his Book. So as proceeding upon such a foundation, his doings cannot but prosper.[9]

Prosper Drake certainly did. Despite his lavish offerings to the Queen, he gave expensive gifts to many members of the Council and prominent personalities at court. He could now afford for himself all the clothes, plate and fashionable gee-jaws of the sophisticated gentleman he had always aspired to be. One of the first objectives he set himself was the acquisition of a substantial estate. And he knew exactly which one he wanted. Sir Richard Grenville hated the upstart Drake and was bitterly jealous because Drake had been allowed to make the expedition he had been refused in 1574. Drake, for his part, resented the arrogance of Grenville and the influence he wielded in South Devon. Now the Grenvilles had, at the dissolution of the monasteries, acquired the impressive Cistercian Abbey at Buckland, not far from Plymouth, and Sir Richard had converted the church and conventual buildings into a fine house. It was this that Drake wanted. He knew that Grenville would never sell to him so he appointed two agents to act for him, with instructions to keep secret the identity of their principal. Grenville was not interested in selling his fine new house but the staggering offer of £3,400 was too tempting. Buckland Abbey passed to Francis Drake in 1581. Grenville was furious when he learned how he had been tricked. The rivalry between the two men reached feud proportions and was continued by their descendants for over a century and a half.

Admiration for Drake was widespread; it was certainly not universal. There were many who had cause to regret that he had ever returned safely from his epic voyage. Burghley and the Earl of Sussex ostentatiously rejected the gifts Drake offered them. They were appalled at the havoc Drake's exploits had wrought in the delicately balanced machinery of foreign relations. At such a time, they believed, it was senseless to provoke Philip of Spain by needless acts of hostility. They, therefore, regarded Elizabeth's attitude towards Drake and his treasure as supremely irresponsible. The London merchant community, with its strong Spanish interests, was also inflamed by Drake's piracy.

And ever in the background, fuming and plotting, was Bernardino de Mendoza. The Queen still refused to grant him a private audience; at least in his official capacity as ambassador. She could not, she said, consent to receive the representative of a monarch who sent soldiers into her realm to help rebels. Coming from a queen who had for years been giving aid to rebellious Spanish subjects in the Netherlands, this snub was to Mendoza little short of outrageous. He constantly stirred the merchants to make representations and he urged his master to extract revenge by confiscating the goods of English subjects in Spain. But Philip would not. With the pacification of the Netherlands and Portugal on his hands he did not wish to involve himself in more foreign trouble. Maintenance of healthy and stable mercantile relations was in the best interests of Spain. Above all, Philip had little personal cause to seek revenge on England. His personal losses in Drake's escapades had been small. The foundering of a single ship of the Indies treasure fleet would have cost him far more than the royal bullion Drake had lifted from the *Cacafuego*.

Elizabeth, persuaded by Walsingham, Leicester and Hatton, believed she could call Philip's bluff but she did not know. The closing weeks of 1580 were, therefore, very tense. Elizabeth sent two Council secretaries to Mendoza with a haughty message complaining of his criticism of the reception she had given Drake. She had closely examined her captain's conduct, she said, and found him innocent of any damage to Spanish property. Mendoza probably knew the 'English Jezebel' well enough not to be totally overwhelmed by this affrontery. In his reply he pointed out that as well as robbing his Most Catholic Majesty and his Most Catholic Majesty's subjects, Drake had destroyed Spanish shipping and wounded Spaniards in battle. While these high-handed exchanges were taking place Hatton and his colleagues were trying another approach: they offered the

Spanish ambassador 50,000 crowns to drop his open hostility to Francis Drake. Neither outrage nor bribery could shift Mendoza from his ground. On the other hand, nothing Mendoza did could shift Philip from his determined non-belligerence.

This attitude was made easier for him by another subterfuge of the interested councillors. They went to Philip behind Mendoza's back through a Spanish agent, Pedro de Zubiaure. They suggested that the matter of the confiscated treasure be removed from the diplomatic arena to that of civil law. Let the Spanish merchants present a case against Drake in the courts. If it appeared that they had suffered loss they would, doubtless, gain redress. Despite the frenzied protests of Mendoza who knew all about the delays and technical quibbles which could effectively prevent justice being done in the halls of justice, Philip agreed to this course of action. There then followed months of legal wrangling, evidence and counter-evidence, assertion and denial. Whether King Philip's subjects ever received any satisfaction is not at all clear. If they did it was only a fraction of the value of what they had lost. The bulk of Drake's captured treasure was already in a number of very English hands.[10]

By January 1581 Elizabeth and the Council knew that their bluff had been successful. Most of the expedition's spoils had been spirited away by the Queen and her fellow-conspirators. It was in January that Elizabeth let it be known that she intended to visit the *Golden Hind* and that on that occasion she would confer a knighthood on Francis Drake.

Drake's ship had been brought round from Plymouth to the Thames in November and anchored at Deptford. Crowds immediately flocked to gaze on the weatherbeaten hulk that had braved and survived all the great oceans. It soon became obvious that the *Golden Hind* was a national monument. The government decided to build a special covered dry dock for it where for generations to come the public could see this historic vessel.[11] But first the *Golden Hind* had to be prepared for the royal visit. She was taken across to Greenwich, hauled out of the water, and lodged in the nearby arsenal. Then painters and carpenters swarmed all over her, removing signs of the damage endured during the voyage and decking her out as though she were a pageant ship rather than a vessel which had battered her way round the world.

During those winter days the possibility of the Alençon marriage (which had never been officially discarded) was revived in earnest. It is doubtful whether the Queen's heart was really in the negotiations, but as a political weapon it was useful. The anti-Spanish faction now urged it as a means of forging a Protestant alliance against Philip's augmented power. It would demonstrate that England ranged herself clearly alongside the Netherlands in their struggle for independence. It would draw the nation closer to France and create a firm counter-balance to the Habsburg dominions. For that very reason other councillors, of course, opposed it. The last thing they wanted was to provoke Philip by an alliance with Alençon against Parma.

Meanwhile Francis Drake was busy making his preparations for what would be the greatest day in his life. The *Golden Hind* was hung with sumptuous drapes, banners were raised bearing the royal arms in gold on silk damask, a kitchen set up and cooks hired to produce what was to be the best banquet money could buy. Chests of silver plate were carried aboard, trestles set up. Casks of wine were ordered, musicians and entertainers hired. Drake, Mary his wife, and the servants all had special clothes

Miniature of Drake by Nicholas Hilliard

for the occasion. The great hero was in his element, ordering about an army of craftsmen and artisans, making sure that everything was absolutely right, putting everything in readiness for the day when everyone, the Queen, her ladies, her scoffing courtiers and the greatest men in the land would be coming here to see his ship and to honour him.

On 4 April Queen Elizabeth, her retinue, and a host of special guests filed aboard the *Golden Hind* over a special bridge that had been built across to the ship from the surrounding gallery. As the Queen set foot upon the deck one of her purple and gold garters detached itself, perhaps not accidentally, and slipped to the floor. The French ambassador Monsieur de Marchaumont swiftly stooped to retrieve it. As Elizabeth replaced it she promised him, with a laugh, that he should have it later as a trophy for Alençon. Then Captain Drake received her, showed her over the ship, and the festivities began. It was, says Mendoza, a banquet such as had not been seen since the days of Henry VIII. He was reporting from hearsay, for he was the only member of the diplomatic corps who was not invited.

Drake swaggered proudly among the crowd with his Queen at his side, resting her hand on his. He gave his royal mistress more presents and received gifts in exchange, including a miniature portrait of the Queen by Hilliard, a personal memento of the kind she granted to few. He listened solemnly to speeches and poems in his honour. One Latin poem by a scholar of Winchester College was fixed to the mainmast. For the unlearned a translation was provided:

> DRAKE, on the Herculean columns these words write,
> Thou farther wentst than any mortal wight.
> Though Hercules for travel did excell,
> From him and others thou didst bear the bell.
>
> Brave DRAKE, that round about the world didst sail,
> And viewedst all the Poles, when men shall fail
> Thee to commend, the stars will do't the Sun
> Will not forget how with him thou didst run.
>
> THAT SHIP whose good success did make thy name
> to be resounded by the trump of Fame:
> Merits to be beset with Stars divine,
> Instead of waves, and in the Sky to shine.[12]

Everything passed off very smoothly with the exception of one incident. An enormous crowd had inevitably gathered to watch the festivities from a distance. Despite the efforts of royal guards to hold back the press, a hundred or more eager onlookers forced their way on to the bridge by which the guests had arrived. It had not been built for such a stress. Its boards creaked, its supporting timbers groaned and then it collapsed, pitching its shrieking burden into the well beneath. No one, we are told, was seriously hurt, which probably means, if we interpret aright the parlance of a callous age, that nothing worse than broken arms and legs were sustained.

When the feasting was over and the trestles cleared, Elizabeth, seated in Drake's great chair, summoned her admiral to kneel before her.

'Master Drake, the King of Spain has asked for your head, and we have a weapon here with which to remove it.'

She took a gilded sword from one of her gentlemen. Then she held it out to the man standing at her side.

'We shall ask Monsieur de Marchaumont to be the headsman.'

Somewhat taken aback, the French ambassador performed the dubbing ceremony. Then everyone cheered and threw their caps in the air. It was all very chivalric, very good-humoured and very pleasant. Yet behind it there lay an extremely serious political message. The Queen of England had involved her ally of France in the knighting of her corsair. It was a magnificent gesture of defiance to Philip of Spain. Not only was the great pirate publicly honoured as a hero, but also France and the Netherlands' rebels were symbolically united with England to resist the power of Spain by sea and land.

For Drake it was the summit of his career. Wealth and fame were his in full measure. To support his new dignity he received from the Queen landed estates and a grant of arms. The latter, soon to be proudly featured in

Drake's coat of arms

coloured plaster over the fireplace in one of Buckland Abbey's principal rooms, emblazoned his achievements in comprehensive symbolism. In heraldic terms the arms are: 'Sable, a fess wavy between two stars argent.

Crest: a ship under reef, drawn round a terrestrial globe with a cable by a hand issuing from clouds all proper. Motto: *Sic Parvis Magna*.' The fess wavy represents the sea; the twin stars are the north and south poles and the crest represents *Golden Hind* drawn round the world by God (a legend across the clouds reading *Auxilio Divino*, 'with divine aid'). The motto pronounced to the world that Drake had arrived: 'Greatness from small beginnings,' it read.

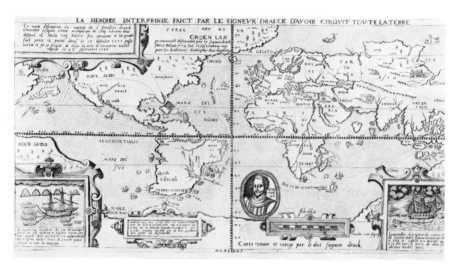

Map by van Sype showing Drake's journey

He was, justly, recognised as the greatest navigator and the greatest maritime authority of the age. Prints and ballads about him filled the bookshops. Foreign princes begged his portrait. Captains, geographers and would-be adventurers sought his acquaintance. The city of Plymouth elected him as mayor.

Yet all was by no means *couleur de rose*. Drake, like all great men, attracted powerful enemies. Nor were they only to be found among the ranks of Mendoza and his friends who had good reason to hate the corsair. There were those who could not stomach Drake's swaggering braggadocio. He flaunted his opinions around the court and told anyone who would listen that the power of Spain was nothing. He was, himself, prepared to finance further expeditions aimed at breaking once and for all Spanish maritime dominance. Many people were impressed by this talk. Walsingham, the Queen, Leicester, even cautious Burghley joined with the great expert in a scheme to capture the Azores in the name of Don Antonio, the Portuguese pretender. This base, it was suggested, would be used to disrupt the flow of American treasure and thus completely undermine Philip's power. The scheme eventually foundered because of disagreements between the principals.

Others did not respond so positively. At one supper party at Sussex's house, the Earl of Arundel grew weary of Drake's boasting about his Pacific exploits.

'It strikes me as no great thing for an armed vessel to capture a treasure ship with only eight unarmed men aboard,' he drawled.

Drake flushed angrily.

'Give me a good English ship and I'll take on all the King of Spain's armed galleons!'

'Single-handed?' The retort was loaded with elegant scorn. 'I cannot imagine King Philip trembling in his shoes at such a boast as that.'[13]

The laugh was on Drake, but many of his adversaries were not laughing. They were raking up every discreditable incident from the voyage in order to smear the too-bright image of the popular hero. The story of Maria was repeated with relish as were the accounts of Drake's deliberate destruction of Spanish ships and the injuries inflicted on Spanish subjects. Some of these accusations Drake took very seriously. He had little option; in Tudor times a man could be convicted in court on perjured or hearsay evidence. In Plymouth he had Edmund Tremayne interrogate every member of his crew who was still available (there were forty-nine of them) on three counts:

> Whether Mr Drake and his company had taken from . . . King of Spain and his subjects in gold and silver to the value of one million and a half or not.
>
> Secondly, Whether they have in their voyage taken any ships or vessels of the said King or his subjects and after sunken them with their men or mariners or not.
>
> Thirdly Whether they had at any time in any fight killed any of the said King's subjects or had cut off their hands or arms or otherwise with any cruelty mangled any of them.[14]

The answers were all negative, as one might expect: no ship had been deliberately sunk (a lie: a ship had been burned at Arica and of the vessels cast adrift some must have foundered); the quantity of gold and silver taken was 'a very small sum in respect of that that is reported' (technically true if Drake was really being charged with having stolen a round million or more); no Spaniard had been slain or deliberately injured, save for one man 'hurt in the face, which our General caused to be sent for, and lodged him in his own ship, set him at his own table, and would not suffer him to depart before he was recovered'[15] (if it was true that no Spaniard suffered death or serious injury it was more by luck than judgement that it was so).

Accusations of political crimes were of paramount importance to Drake. Of more interest to historians has been the major moral indictment against him: the execution of Thomas Doughty. It was also of overmastering importance to the dead man's brother who had travelled right round the world boiling for revenge. He wasted no time pursuing his objective.

He was kept aboard the *Golden Hind* until it reached London's river in November 1580. Then, like the rest of the crew, he was released. Drake must have known the young man's mood and his determination. He may have tried to reason with him for, although it is difficult to see the great admiral pleading with anyone, yet he could ill afford, at that time when his fortunes were so delicately balanced, to have his name dragged through the law courts on a charge of murder.

John Doughty had probably had a legal training like his brother and he knew the correct procedures. The case was in certain essential respects rather peculiar and if Doughty had not made a study of the courts and their functions he might well have never got his suit presented at all. First of all he went to Queen's Bench, the supreme judiciary with oversight over other common law courts. There he was granted leave to bring a private suit of murder in the court of the Constable and Marshal. This ancient court of chivalry was the only one competent to consider the case because, 'If a subject of the King be killed by another of his subjects out of England in any foreign country, the wife or he that is heir of the dead may have an appeal for this murder or homicide before the Constable and Marshal'.[16]

By the time that Doughty had got this far the period of uncertainty was over: Drake was the toast of the town and the Queen's acknowledged darling. Undaunted, the young man continued with his mission of vengeance against the hero of all England. The court of the Marshal and Constable had almost fallen into obsolescence. Most areas of its jurisdiction had been taken over by the common law courts. The Marshal's court remained in existence to give judgement almost exclusively on heraldic issues; it was not competent to judge Doughty's case. For that the Earl Marshal and Lord High Constable had to sit together. Unfortunately for Doughty, while England still had an Earl Marshal, the office of Constable had ceased to be a permanent creation in 1521. It was a title only granted *pro tempore* for such state occasions as coronations. It was, of course, fully within the competence of the sovereign to create a Constable so that the court could convene to decide the issue. Charles I did so under conditions which were basically not dissimilar.[17] Doubtless the Queen was petitioned to take the necessary action. She did not do so. The national and international repercussions of allowing the hero of the hour to stand trial on such a grave charge would have been catastrophic. Thus the suit of John Doughty versus Francis Drake failed on a technicality.

But not before Drake had taken counter-measures of his own. The facts about Doughty's eventual downfall are obscure but what happened was something along these lines: Doughty, as well as proceeding openly in the courts, loudly and openly voiced his complaints about Drake whenever he had a chance. He talked wildly of assassinating Drake if he could obtain no legal satisfaction. This brought him to the attention of Mendoza and the agent Zubiaure and some kind of plot was set afoot in which Doughty was involved with the Spanish interests. Drake, endeavouring to calm his adversary, spoke with Doughty's uncle and received from him a letter in which the young malcontent avowed, 'When the Queen did knight Drake she did then knight the arrantest knave, the vilest villain, the falsest thief and the cruellest murderer that ever was born.' Drake's patience gave way. He had Doughty confined in the Marshalsea pending a suit for libel.

Worse charges soon came to light. Doughty's indiscretions with Zubiaure aroused suspicion. Another spy involved called Masor was examined in the Tower. On the rack he confessed that King Philip had offered money for the arrest or death of Francis Drake and that Doughty had been approached with a proposition. Nothing more positive could be proved against the would-be avenger and probably Drake had no interest in bringing him to trial in any case. So John Doughty languished in the fever-ridden Marshalsea for month after month. In October 1583 he appealed to the Council. Let them either charge him in court or set him at liberty. In the margin of this appeal a bureaucratic hand scrawled four words. They were the last words in the long, tragic saga of Thomas and John Doughty: 'Not to be released'.[18]

In that same month of October 1583 another letter was written, or rather was dictated, in another capital city.

> King Philip, etc. to Doctor Gomez de Santillan, of our Council of the Indies, Our President of the Board of Trade of Seville. Nuño da Silva, Portuguese pilot, came to this our Court where he spent several days and has been duly examined, as seemed expedient. He is returning to Seville with our licence, but he is first to go and see his family. You are to issue an order that, as he was seized by force by the Corsair Francis Drake, Englishman, who passed into the South Sea, he is not to be arrested or to be annoyed or molested in any way by the jailor of the prison in Seville or by any other person. On his arrival then, you are to employ him in our service, according to the order that we shall send to you, to carry a certain despatch that is to be delivered to him, which is being written and will be sent you shortly.
>
> You are to keep us informed, through our Council in the Indies, of what is done in this matter.[19]

Poor da Silva had endured much suffering before thus gaining his release. On being deserted at Guatulco in April 1579 he was arrested and closely examined by the authorities. It is obvious from the tone of his sworn declaration that the pilot was very bitter at his treatment by the Englishmen. He had co-operated fully with his captors, had even drawn close to them in comradeship during their shared hardships. In return they had cast him away without recompense to fend for himself on a hostile shore. He offered to tell the Spaniards how to fortify the Straits of Magellan against more of Drake's kind and reported that Drake had gone off in search of the Straits of Anian. In his opinion no such straits existed: 'This Englishman is searching for it simply by way of bragging or boasting of his ability'.[20]

It was immediately obvious to the Spaniards that in the pilot they had a most valuable prisoner, one who knew all about Drake and his intentions, one who could give details of all the corsair's crimes along the coast of Spanish America. After a month he was sent under escort to the Viceroy in Mexico. There he made another long written statement giving all the information he could about the journey of the *Golden Hind*. Other reports were now coming in to the Viceroy and some of them did not reflect well on da Silva. It was suggested that he was in league with the pirates and had taken part in their heretical worship.

For examination on this latter charge he was handed over to the Inquisition. He was subjected to torture but would only confess that he had participated in 'Lutheran' ceremonies under duress. The interrogators were not convinced so Nuño da Silva remained confined in the Inquisition prison for three years. At length, as usually happened, he was prepared to confess anything. One day in 1582 the pilot was taken out in a penitent's gown to make public abjuration at an *auto da fé*. After penance he was sentenced to 'perpetual exile from the Indies' and despatched to Spain on the treasure fleet later that year. He was imprisoned at Seville and would have remained there indefinitely if the King had not heard about him. Philip was intrigued at the prospect of meeting someone who had known the corsair so intimately and been present on his plundering expedition. Thus it was that the dishevelled prisoner was smartened up and presented before his sovereign at the Escorial. He obviously made a good impression on Philip who decided that da Silva had suffered enough and wrote that letter on 7 October ordering the man's release. And so, after five years, the little man who had done so much to make the voyage of circumnavigation possible returned in peace to his own home.[21]

In classroom 'history' bored pupils are frequently asked to assess the 'results' of great events. If one were to enumerate what would pass for the tangible results of Francis Drake's encompassing of the world, the list would not be very impressive. Spain was not impoverished by the corsair's depredations in 1578-9. No English adventurers followed Drake through the Straits of Magellan to plunder the silver of Peru. The voyage had its importance as one of the irritants which inflamed Anglo-Spanish enmity and led to the confrontation of 1588, but it was only one of many such irritants. Drake's accomplishment did not usher in a new age of exploration and mercantile expansion. Indeed, the only expeditions planned as an immediate consequence of the 1577–1580 voyage ended in dismal failure. The Azores project, as we have seen, never got under way. The Fenton venture of 1581 did, at least, set sail. This was a fleet of four ships led by Edward Fenton to travel eastwards to the Moluccas and take up the trading opportunities pioneered by Drake. The leadership of the expedition was divided from the start and in the Atlantic the fleet split up, John Drake taking his *Francis* off along the coast of South America in a harebrained attempt to repeat his cousin's exploits. He only succeeded in getting himself and his men captured by the Spaniards, while Fenton took the other ships back home.

Any attempt to enumerate the consequences of Drake's great voyage misses the point because it fails to grasp the enormous inspirational value of the enterprise. It was one of those very rare events which sets the heart of a nation beating faster. It happened at the right time when Englishmen needed a 'boost'. Drake provided that boost in no uncertain terms. From every point of view his accomplishment was breathtaking. His was no surreptitious poaching on Spanish and Portuguese preserves; he marched boldly through their thickets, bagging whatever trophies came his way. The value of his haul was staggering. He challenged and surpassed the most celebrated feat of navigation which had, until then, ever been recorded.

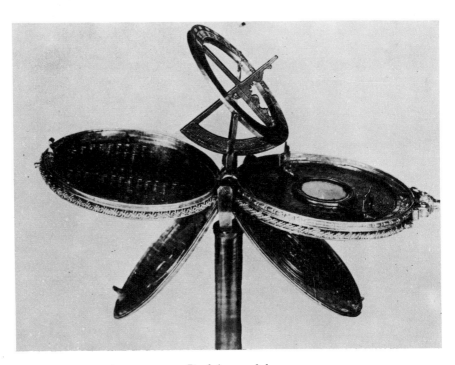

Drake's astrolabe

Though the Magellan-Elcano voyage must still rank higher for sheer courage in facing the unknown hazards of totally uncharted oceans, it almost ended in complete disaster: the ship that limped into Seville at the end of a 36½-month voyage carried eighteen men out of the expedition's original complement of 234 and Magellan himself was among those lost. The *Golden Hind* returned in relatively good order. Fifty-nine men reached England under Drake's command and, though we do not know how many came home in the *Elizabeth*, we shall not be far wrong if we estimate the survivors of the voyage as about half of the original complement of 164, a good score for such a long journey in Tudor times. Magellan's voyage was widely regarded as a brave venture which could not be repeated and very few attempts had ever been made to emulate it. Drake's voyage proved that the seas were wide open to bold and well-prepared expeditions. It opened up real practical possibilities for commerce and colonisation.

And it opened them up to Englishmen. It gave Albion a future stake in the wider world. There were many adventurous young men and seasoned mariners chafing at the bit, longing to make discoveries, establish settlements, open up new areas of trade. Now someone had shown them that nothing was impossible. Francis Drake's circumnavigation of the globe was the first major accomplishment by an Englishman on a world stage. It was the first great English adventure. As the years and centuries unfurled, his nation established a pre-eminent place in the annals of exploration and heroic endeavour. The story glows with the names of Raleigh, Cook, Livingstone, Scott and a host of others. But Drake was the first, the pioneer of pioneers.

He became a legend. As the hero of ballads, mythology and even serious works of history and biography, his virtues were magnified, his vices often denied. He became a symbol of all that Englishmen liked to think was best in the national character—a sense of adventure, courage and determination in the face of daunting odds, natural leadership and a healthy contempt for foreigners. Popular imagination would not even let him die; like King Arthur he was believed to be only slumbering, awaiting the beat of his famous drum summoning him once more to his country's aid.

Legends are colourful, yet it does not follow that truth is, by contrast, drab. To discover the truth of the real Francis Drake is no easy matter. His life was so full of achievements and excitements that it is possible to lose sight of the man among all his accomplishments. But for one thousand and forty-six days Drake stood alone, pitting his skill and judgement against the elements; imposing his will on his followers; employing his cunning and ruthlessness against his enemies. It is as we study those one thousand and forty-six days that we discover the man at the heart of the myth. And having discovered him we can each make up our own mind about him.

APPENDIX

There has always been some confusion about the movements of Drake's ships during the storms of September and October 1578. Several earlier writers, e.g. J. S. Corbett, *Drake and the Tudor Navy*, I, pp. 266 ff., stated that the tempest blew from the north-east, driving the expedition hundreds of miles south-westwards into the Pacific. There are three pieces of evidence for this: (i) The relation of the voyage made by Nuño da Silva for the Viceroy of New Spain in May 1579. The relevant passage is as follows:

> Being out of the strait on the other side, upon the sixth of September . . . they held their course Northwest . . . and the third day they had a Northeast wind, that by force drew them West south west, which course they held for the space of ten or twelve days with few sails up: and because the wind began to be very great, they took in all their sails, and lay driving till the last of September.
>
> The 24. day of the same month having lost the sight of one of their ships, which was about an hundred ton, then again they hoisted sail because the wind came better, holding their course Northeast for the space of seven days, and at the end of the said seven days, they had the sight of certain islands, which they made towards for to anchor by them, but the weather would not permit them: and being there, the wind fell Northeast: whereupon they sailed West Southwest. (Vaux, pp. 257–8)

The sheer impossibility of those last few words suggests that we must view the whole passage with some caution. We then find other inconsistencies: were the ships driven south-west until 'the last of September' or until 'The 24. day of the same'? If they were driven by violent winds for fifteen or twenty-one days and nights away from the land how can they possibly have regained the coast in seven days steady sailing?

(ii) *The Famous Voyage of Sir Francis Drake into the South Sea and thence about the whole Globe of the Earth.* This was printed by Hakluyt, *The Principall Navigations, Voiages, and Discoveries of the English Nation made by Sea or over land to the most remote and farthest distant quarters of the earth, etc*, III, pp. 730–742 (cf. also Vaux, pp. 227–253). It stated:

> The seventh day, we were driven by a great storm from the entering into the South Sea two hundred leagues and odd in longitude, and one degree to the Southward of the strait: in which height, and so many leagues to the Westward, the fifteenth day of September, fell out the eclipse of the Moon . . . (Vaux, p. 237)

Corbett says of this author, 'He seems . . . to have been a soldier who took little interest in navigation or seamanship. Whenever he attempts to be detailed on.

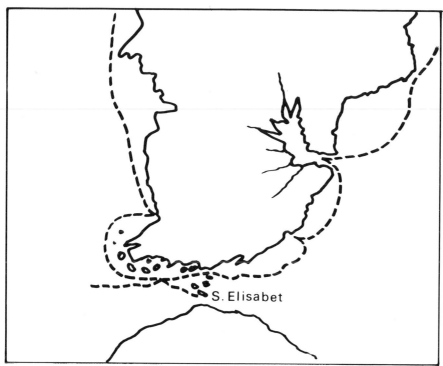

S. Elisabet

Drake's travels in the waters to the south of South America: (above) *according to Nicola van Sype;* (below) *according to Jodocus Hondius.*

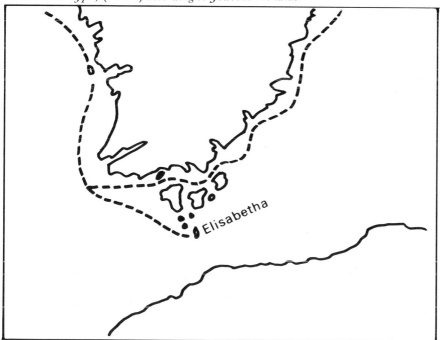

Elisabetha

these points he is almost invariably wrong' (*Drake and the Tudor Navy*, I, pp. 426–7). This is not, of course, to say that the author *was* wrong about Drake having been driven 600 miles out into the south-east Pacific but it does lay him open to challenge based on other evidence.

(iii) Nicola van Sype's map. This was engraved from a French original which claimed to have been corrected by Drake himself. It was the first map made showing the circumnavigation.

The evidence against this interpretation seems to me overwhelming: (i) Nuño da Silva's log. This was discovered by Miss Nuttall in Seville in 1909 and is the earliest surviving document relating to the journey. The relevant entries are as follows:

September

6th   This day we sailed out of the strait into the self-same South Sea

7th   The wind came from the prow, we going south-east with a strong northwest wind

      All this month we went along in this manner.

28th   On this, the 28th day, we lost *Maragota* [the *Marigold*]

October

1st   On the first day of this month we set sail in a north-easterly direction

2nd   On the same course

3rd   The prow to the North

4th   On the same course

5th   The same

6th   The same

7th   Made land in 51 degrees and came to anchor for one hour in 40 fathoms of water (Nuttall, pp. 284–5)

There is immediacy and truth about these brief, factual entries. (ii) Francis Fletcher's narrative. Fletcher is very short on nautical detail but one factor emerges very clearly from the dramatic account of the storm from which I have already quoted at length: as the ships were driven before the wind the mariners' worst fear was of running on the rocks. Had they been flying before a north-easter they would have been forced immediately and totally away from all land. (iii) Jodocus Hondius' map. This was drawn soon after Cavendish's circumnavigation of 1586–8 and shows both English voyages. It knows nothing of any foray to the south-west. Hondius was in England between 1583 and 1588 and made maps of Drake's West Indian voyage among others. He had opportunities to check his facts and he probably knew of the van Sype map. For craftsmanship and accuracy there is no comparison between the two maps. Hondius' is superior in every way. It was prepared to accompany the Dutch account of the voyage and may well have been based on Fletcher's journal as well as other verbatim reports.

The French map was, admittedly, earlier and claimed to have been vetted by Drake himself. Unfortunately, that does not prove that it *was* vetted by Drake; such assertions were often made by unscrupulous publishers in order to improve sales. Even if we could be sure that it was approved by Drake that would not in itself be proof conclusive of its accuracy. How would the public hero react on being shown a map which accredited him with more than he had in fact achieved?

He might well have decided to say nothing. After all, no one could prove that he had sailed south westwards towards the supposed *Terra Australis*. Or he might have pointed out the error to the printers who, in their turn, decided not to go to the expense of cutting a new plate.

However it may have come about, there were within a few years of 1580 two maps in existence which provided contradictory information about this stage of the voyage. This means that, at a very early stage, contradictory accounts were circulating. This makes the earliest record of all, the pilot's log, very important and Nuño da Silva says the ships were driven to the south-east. But why did he apparently alter the facts when forced to tell his story to the Spanish authorities? Possibly there is nothing more profound at the root of the mystery than a piece of indifferent scribal transcription. Da Silva made a verbal statement in Portuguese. It was written down, then translated into Spanish. There was plenty of scope for errors over dates and details of wind directions especially if the scribe was a man totally ignorant of nautical matters.

Another possibility is that Nuño da Silva deliberately falsified his story. Why? He was a captive Portuguese giving evidence on navigational matters to the Spaniards who were the colonial rivals of his own people. Why give them the benefit of the latest discoveries if it could be avoided? The significance of the Englishmen's storm-tossed wandering was the realisation that in the region of the Elizabethides the Atlantic and Pacific Oceans met. Magellan's Strait was not the only passage connecting the Spanish and Portuguese spheres of influence (as defined by the Treaty of Tordesillas). Any true Portuguese would want to keep that information out of Spanish hands as long as possible.

I have left the most obvious piece of evidence until last. The prevailing winds in this quarter and the ones which give rise to the notorious storms 'around the Horn' are westerlies and north-westerlies. John Wynter, in his report to the navy office which was clearly based on his log, stated that the wind 'was continually betwixt the W.S.W. and the N. from the 20th of June to the 20th of August, and continued there betwixt the N.W. and the W. from the 20th of August till the 11th of November, and changed not till we came into 40 degrees' (E. G. R. Taylor in *Mariner's Mirror*, XVI, p. 151). Wynter left the west coast and retreated well inside Magellan's Strait about 10 October so he is scarcely a reliable witness on prevailing weather conditions after that date but there is no reason to doubt his evidence for the period with which we are concerned. Wynter's report was written immediately on his return to England some nine months after the great storm. It is, therefore, another very early account and, taken with Nuño da Silva's log must be considered to have overwhelming significance.

NOTES

Chapter 1

1. Spanish Calendar II. 410. The 'prince' was James the future king of Scotland and England.
2. W.S.W. Vaux, *The World Encompassed by Sir Francis Drake*, p. 7.
3. *The Book of the Sea Carte* was one of the first printed rutters but handwritten manuals had existed for decades, perhaps centuries, before Drake's time. These carefully preserved collections of vital information about tides, landmarks, compass bearings and soundings were the early mariners' bibles.

Chapter 2

1. Quoted in J. E. Neale, *Queen Elizabeth*, p. 235.
2. Ibid., p. 237.
3. There were eighteen regular members of the Council. With the exception of those mentioned only Sir Henry Sidney was below the age of fifty and the average age was fifty-five. Cf. M. B. Pulman, *The Elizabethan Privy Coucil in the Fifteen Seventies*, p. 45.
4. J. Dee, *The Elements of Geometrie*, 1570.
5. B. W. Beckingsale, *Burghley: Tudor Statesman*, p. 141.
6. E. G. R. Taylor, 'The Missing Draft Project', *Geographical Journal*, 1930.
7. W. S. W. Vaux, *The World Encompassed by Sir Francis Drake*, p. 216.
8. Ibid., p. 215–6.
9. Only a badly burned draft of Drake's charter has survived. An attempted reconstruction of the vital passage, with the missing words in italics, runs as follows:

> . . . *shall enter the Strait of Magell*anas *lying in 52 degrees of* the pole, and, *having passed therefrom into* the South Sea then *he is to sail so* far to the northwards as *xxx degrees seeking* along the said coast af-*orenamed like* as of the other to find out *places meet* to have traffic for the vent*ing of commodities* of these her Majesty's realms. Wher-*eas at present* they are not under the obedience of *any Christian* prince, so is there great hope of *gold, silver,* spices, drugs, cochineal, and *divers other* special commodities, such as may *enrich her* Highness' dominions, and also *put* shipping a-work greatly. And *having* gotten up as afore said in the xxx *degrees* in the South Sea (if it shall be thought *meet* by the afore named Francis Drake to pro*ceed so* far), then he is to return by the same way homewards as he went out. Which voyaging by God's favour is to be performed in xiii months, all though he should spend v months in tarrying upon the coasts, to get knowledge of the princes and countries there.

This version is by E. G. R. Taylor, 'More Light on Drake', *Mariner's Mirror,*

XVI, p. 135. Unfortunately, the very secrecy surrounding the real objectives of the venture almost wrought its undoing. John Wynter and Thomas Doughty, those next in seniority to Drake, were fired with enthusiasm for a voyage of exploration and discovery. They did not share his hatred of Spain nor were they a party to his piratical intentions. As their journey unfolded and their leader was gradually revealed as little more than a corsair, unbreachable rifts appeared in the command of the enterprise.

10. E. G. R. Taylor, *The Original Writings and Correspondence of the two Richard Hakluyts*, I, p. 115.

Chapter 3

1. Almost his last words before he went down with a fatal attack of dysentery on the 'Mosquito Gulf' in 1596 bear this out: 'God hath many things in store for us and I know many means to do Her Majesty good service and to make us rich, for we must have gold before we see England.' G. M. Thomson, *Sir Francis Drake*, p. 314.

2. This account was written in 1579, which makes Drake thirty-six give or take two years at the outset of the voyage. This ties in fairly accurately with the deductions of most historians and biographers, the consensus of whose opinions is that Francis was born between 1540 and 1542.

3. Z. Nuttall, *New Light on Drake*, pp. 301–2.

4. Report of Jaspar de Vargas, 14 April 1579, quoted by Z. Nuttall, *New Light on Drake*, pp. 239–40.

5. G. M. Thomson, *Sir Francis Drake*, p. 78.

6. I. A. Wright (ed.), *Documents Concerning English Voyages to the Spanish Main 1569–1580*, p. 52.

7. Ibid., p. 69.

8. Any reader familiar with the attitudes of colonial administrators of all places and periods will recognise common themes in the many reports sent to Madrid—the consciousness of sitting on a 'native' powder keg, the urgent and largely unheeded demands for help from home, the fear of foreign interference. Here, for example, is an appeal from the municipal council of Panama, dated 24 February 1573:

> . . . This league between the English and the negroes is very detrimental to this kingdom, because, being so thoroughly acquainted with the region and so expert in the bush, the negroes will show them methods and means to accomplish any evil design they may wish to carry out and execute. These startling developments have agitated and alarmed this kingdom. It is indeed most lamentable that the English and negroes should have combined against us, *for the blacks are numerous.*
>
> Therefore, in this city and in Nombre de Dios we are keeping very careful watch, and a guard is posted every night as against these dangers and to forestall the numerous evils which may ensue therefrom.
>
> Humbly we entreat your majesty to deign to send here prompt relief and defence, the best form for which we believe would be two galleys to patrol this coast, *as we have many times previously asked your majesty to*

provide, for if the sea is safe we shall be safe on land...[my emphases]
I. A. Wright, op. cit., p. 50.

9. Letter of Gonzalo Nuñez de la Cerda, from Panama, 22 September 1574.
I. A. Wright, op. cit., p. 93.

10. Letter from the city authorities of Panama to King Philip, 15 April 1577.
I. A. Wright, op. cit., pp. 111–13.

11. Z. Nuttall, op. cit., p. 8.

12. Cf. D. W. Waters, *The Art of Navigation in England in Elizabethan and Early Stuart Times*, p. 536.

13. *Harleian MSS* 167. E. G. R. Taylor, 'The Dawn of Modern Navigation', *Journal of the Institute of Navigation*, Vol. I.

14. Born in 1541, Devereux was almost exactly the same age as Drake. Cf. *D.N.B.*

15. Parson Fletcher in N. M. Penzer's *The World Encompassed*, p. 125.

16. The full complement according to Fletcher, Cooke and the author of *The Famous Voyage* was '164 able men'. There may in addition have been a few supernumeraries—boys, servants, musicians, etc.—who did not fall into this category. Scrutiny of all the records yields the following ninety-five names:

> *Gentleman Adventurers:* Nicholas Anthony, Gregory Cary, — Caube, — Charles, John Chester, Edward Cliffe, John Cooke, John Doughty, Thomas Doughty, John Drake (Francis' cousin), Thomas Drake (Francis' youngest brother), Lawrence Elyot, Francis Fletcher (chaplain), George Ffortescu, William Hawkins, Thomas Hord, William Markham, John Saracold, John Thomas, Leonard Vicarye, Emanuel Wattkyns, Robert Winterhey, John Wynter.
>
> *Seamen and others:* Luke Adden, — Artyur, John Audley, John Blacoler, Thomas Blacollers, John Brewar, Thomas Brewar, Edward Bright, Richard Burnish, Richard Cadwell, Peter Corder, Richard Clarke, John Cottle, William Cowke, John Cowrttes, Thomas Crane, Thomas Cuttill, Renold Danielles, John Deane, Diego (Drake's Cimarron servant), Denne Fforster, Thomas Ffloud and Thomas Flud (possibly the same man), John Fowler, John Fry, John Gallaway, Laucelot Garget, George (a musician), Pascoe Goddy, Bartelmyeus Gotsalk, Richard Graye, John Grepe, Thomas Grige, Christopher Hals, Thomas Haylston, Christopher Hayman, William Haynes, Thomas Hogges, William Horsewill, John Huse, Povll Jemes, Richard Joyner, John Kidde, Roger Kingesoud, Jhan Laus, William Lege, John Mariner, Thomas Markes, John Martyn, Thomas Martyn, Thomas Meckes, Jeames Milles, Richard Minivy, Thomas Moon, Necolas Mour, Great Nele (a Dane), Little Nele (a Fleming), — Oliver, William Pitcher, Roger Player, Robert Pollmane, Grygorye Raymente, Richard Rowles, William Shelle, Willan Smyth, Thomas Sothern, John Marten Stewerd, — Thomas, Christefor Waspe, John Watterton, Simon Woodd, Edward Worrall, Richard Writ.

17. Z. Nuttall, op. cit., p. 303.

18. Z. Nuttall, op. cit., p. 301.

19. Ibid.

20. No accurate details of the *Pelican's* dimensions have survived and scholars computing from known facts—e.g. tonnage, contemporary shipbuilding tech-

niques, the dimension of the dock built at Deptford to house it—have arrived at different estimates. F. C. Prideaux Naish ('The Mystery of the Tonnage and Dimensions of the Pelican—Golden Hind', *Mariner's Mirror*, XXXIV, pp. 42–5) in 1948 computed the dimensions as: overall length 89 ft, beam $18\frac{1}{2}$ ft, draught fully laden 13 ft. On the other hand the replica, laid down at Appledore in 1971, was constructed, after careful research, to the following measurements: overall length 102 ft, beam 20 ft, mean draught 9 ft (this figure agrees well with Mr Naish's, since the replica's laden draught would be about 13 ft).

21. Z. Nuttall, op. cit., pp. 302–3.

Chapter 4

1. The outcome of the Moroccan situation, though it has no bearing on Drake's voyage, is interesting and not without significance for the history of Europe. Later in this year, 1578, the 21-year-old Portuguese King Sebastian personally led an expedition into Morocco to aid ex-Sultan Muhammad. On 4 August the combined forces of the allies were defeated by 'Abdul-Malik at Wadi al-Makhazin. The engagement came to be known in Moroccan annals as the Battle of the Three Kings for the three rulers who took part in it were all killed. Sebastian had no heir and it was as a direct result of his death that Portugal was united to Spain and thus the world's two great overseas empires came under the control of one man, Philip II, England's arch enemy.

2. N. M. Penzer (ed.) *The World Encompassed and Analogous Contemporary documents*, p. 88. There is a strong temptation to regard the story of the lions prowling along the shore as a traveller's tale but lions had not, in the sixteenth century, become totally extinct north of the Sahara so Fletcher's yarn is possible. Why lions should be seen wandering about on a sandy beach is, however, inexplicable.

3. N. M. Penzer, op. cit., p. 3.

4. N. M. Penzer, op. cit., p. 4.

5. In *The World Encompassed* Drake's nephew claimed that his uncle took a pinnace load of men ashore and trekked several miles inland in search of Fry but Francis Fletcher's notes, on which the nephew based his reconstruction, made no mention of any such attempt. Indeed, Fletcher stated bluntly, 'we departed, without any notice what was become of our man' (N. M. Penzer, op. cit., p. 90). This claim of the younger Drake must, therefore, be regarded as one example among many of his desire to show his uncle in the best possible light.

6. *Lansdowne MSS*, 100, No. 2 reprinted by E. G. R. Taylor, 'More Light on Drake: 1577–80' in *Mariner's Mirror*, XVI, p. 148.

7. N. M. Penzer, op. cit., p. 90.

8. Z. Nuttall, *New Light on Drake*, p. 25.

9. N. M. Penzer, op. cit., p. 92.

10. The wine was referred to in Nuno da Silva's first deposition to the Inquisition in May 1579, cf. Nuttall, op. cit., p. 245. The other items come from an inventory drawn up by John Wynter. At a later stage of the voyage most of

the *Mary*'s cargo was lodged in the *Elizabeth*. When Wynter and his ship returned to England he had to give account of the goods confiscated from the Portuguese shipowners, cf. Nuttall, pp. 388–9 and see pp. 193–4.

11. *The Hawkins Voyages*, Hakluyt Society, Ser. I, Vol. 57.
12. One of the many minor problems concerning a reconstruction of the voyage concerns dates. At several points Nuño da Silva's log disagrees with the account of Fletcher, Wynter and other English sources. For instance da Silva gives 19 January as the day when his ship was captured by the English pirates. Since the Portuguese was recording events as they happened it would seem on the face of it that his is the most reliable account. But Thomas Wynter also kept a log throughout the voyage and we must assume that Fletcher's journal was based on notes made on the journey. Where these and other independent accounts agree we must accept their evidence. It has been suggested that the Portuguese was using the Gregorian calendar which differed from the Julian calendar by ten days, but it was not until 1582 that the pope authorised the use of the new calendar.

Chapter 5

1. W. S. W. Vaux, *The World Encompassed by Sir Francis Drake*, p. 29.
2. W. S. W. Vaux, op. cit., pp. 38–9.
3. N. M. Penzer, *The World Encompassed and Analogous Contemporary Documents*, p. 121.
4. E. G. R. Taylor, 'More Light on Drake', *Mariner's Mirror*, XVI, pp. 148–9.
5. Fletcher gave a very long description of these people and their customs (Penzer, op. cit., pp. 111 ff.). Unfortunately many of his details are so blatantly untrue that they bring into question the reliability of his entire narrative. He speaks, for instance, of women who lightly roast their young children in order to impart to their skin a protective quality against the cold, and of nursing mothers who fling their pendulous breasts over their shoulders to nurture the infants carried on their backs.
6. N. M. Penzer, op. cit., p. 111.
7. N. M. Penzer, op. cit., p. 114.

Chapter 6

1. This is, obviously, my own interpretation of the disputed Doughty affair, having read all the relevant documents. All the accounts of the trial and the events leading up to it were written by those who were biased for or against Drake so that it is difficult to sift truth from prejudice. Fletcher was anti. *The World Encompassed* was pro. The account written by John Cooke was decidedly on the side of Doughty. These are the main sources. On the charges which actually brought Doughty to his death there is considerable confusion, which may well reflect a very real confusion experienced by those present at the trial. Of the hostility between the two men there is no doubt. Nor is there any doubt that that hostility arose from two tragic and fundamental misunderstandings about the voyage. Drake and Doughty were not in accord over its objectives, nor were they agreed upon the authority Doughty possessed. Granted this clash it is immaterial whether or not Drake engineer-

ed evidence against his colleague. The continuance of the expedition was at stake and Drake put the expedition above everything. For other points of view cf. J. S. Corbett, *Drake and the Tudor Navy*, I, p. 250 ff.; W. S. W. Vaux, op. cit., pp. xviii; H. R. Wagner, *Sir Francis Drake's Voyage Around the World*, p. 62 ff.

2. H. R. Wagner, op. cit., p. 66.

Chapter 7

1. W. S. W. Vaux, *The World Encompassed by Sir Francis Drake*, p. 211.
2. Drake's meaning here has been misunderstood by some writers. His actual words as reported by John Cooke were: 'I must have gentlemen to haul and draw with the mariner, and the mariner with the gentleman. What, let us show ourselves all to be of a company, and let us not give occasion to the enemy to rejoice at our decay and overthrow. I would know him that would refuse to set his hand to a rope, but I know there is not any such here; and as gentlemen are very necessary for government's sake in the voyage, so have I shipped them for that . . .' (cf. Vaux, op. cit., p. 213). A superficial reading of these words suggests that Drake was downgrading the gentlemen to the ranks. The passage as a whole makes it quite clear that he was trying to establish a camaraderie, a sense of purpose which would override not abolish class distinctions.
3. This point has been much discussed by historians interested in the legality of Doughty's trial. We know that full judicial rights were sometimes granted to leaders of expeditions. Such provisions were, for instance, written into the commission for Grenville's abortive 1574 voyage. However, for all Drake's flaunting of pieces of paper before the crew no one appears to have been allowed to scrutinise his commission. Thomas Doughty was convinced that Drake had no right to proceed against him by martial law. In 1581, when John Doughty accused Drake in the courts of murder no commission was produced, which would have been the quickest way of disposing of the charge. (cf. W. Senior, 'Drake at the suit of John Doughty', *Mariner's Mirror*, VII, pp. 291–7).
4. Drake's nephew stated quite definitely that renaming took place at this time. However Fletcher's account cites no specific date; it vaguely refers to the name having been changed by the end of October. John Wynter, on the other hand, seems to have been unaware of the new name. Right up until the time when he became separated from Drake he referred to the flagship as the *Pelican* in his log. As late as April 1579 Nuño da Silva could call Drake's ship 'the *Pelican* or *Golden Hind*'.
5. Wynter's log, reproduced by E. G. R. Taylor, *Mariner's Mirror*, XVI, p. 150.
6. W. S. W. Vaux, op. cit., p. 280.
7. E. G. R. Taylor in *Mariner's Mirror*, XVI, p. 150.
8. H. R. Wagner, *Sir Francis Drake's Voyage Around the World*, pp. 438–41 and E. G. R. Taylor, op. cit., pp. 134–43 suggest that Wynter's statement and his possession of Magellan's *Voyage* prove that circumnavigation was always the object of the voyage. This misunderstands the whole nature of commercial/exploratory voyages in the sixteenth century. Success was

measured in terms of financial return. Drake might make many discoveries and come home laden with new geographical information but if he was not also laden with something more substantial he would have some hard explaining to do to his backers. Wynter knew this perfectly well but he believed that the venture's profit should be achieved by honest trade if at all possible. Thus his interest in the Moluccas and his possession of Magellan's book. For Drake, trade with the Spice Islands was only one of the options open to him. If he could 'make' his voyage as a result of preying on Spanish treasure ships he would not bother to travel further. We may be sure that if he could have found a short, northerly route home after his successful ventures along the coast of Spanish America he would have taken it.

9. John Drake gave this piece of information to the Inquisition at his examination in 1584. Apparently Wynter was still in prison when John left England again in June 1582. The young man insisted that Wynter would have been hanged but for his cousin's intervention (cf. W. S. W. Vaux, op. cit., p. 27).

Chapter 8

1. At this point Fletcher has a fanciful story of at least two thousand Indians parading on the shore, some performing a war dance around their prostrate captives while at the same time hacking off pieces of their flesh to eat. No other account of the voyage records this graphic incident which must, therefore, be catalogued as another of the chaplain's traveller's tales. But it is with some regret that we now part company with Francis Fletcher. The first part of his narrative closes with the affray at Mocha Island. He promises us a continuation in Part II. If this was written, as seems likely, it has long been lost although it was a principal source for *The World Encompassed*.

2. Nuño da Silva's *Second Relation*, Z. Nuttall, *New Light on Drake*, p. 261.

3. The Spaniards took from his body a polemical work in English which contained many notes and scriptural quotations in Minivy's hand. It was burned by the local magistrate. Cf. Z. Nuttall, op. cit., p. 45n.

4. This paragraph is an attempt to reconcile conflicting accounts of this stage of the journey. John Drake (cf. Z. Nuttall, op. cit., p. 45) said that the pinnace was constructed aboard the *Capitana* but Nuño da Silva's log, although stressing the constant fear the Englishmen were under from natives and Spaniards, asserts that the pinnace was built ashore. Major weight must be given to the pilot's log being the earlier account but Drake could hardly have been completely mistaken. In justification of my interpretation I would claim that Francis Drake was looking for a harbour where he could spend long enough to build a pinnace and overhaul his own ship. Having found such a place it would be galling in the extreme to be able to make no use of it. If at all possible he would have used the beach for building the pinnace and careening the *Golden Hind*. However, he made a cautious start and did all the preliminary work on the pinnace on the *Capitana*'s empty deck. By that time he had spied out the land and decided that no major attack was likely and that a calculated risk was justifiable. To have done anything else would have meant taking an unconscionable time over the pinnace and leaving essential work undone on the *Golden Hind*'s bottom.

5. Reckoning of the amount of silver found on Corso's ship vary. I have relied on the report later made by Nicolas Jorje (cf. Z. Nuttall, op. cit., p. 135).
6. John Drake later claimed that the firing of the Peruvian ship had been carried out without the admiral's orders and this was doubtless a story that Drake spread. He tried to avoid flagrant destruction of civilian property just as he refrained from killing Spaniards for he was always conscious of the reports and complaints about him which would inevitably reach London. Doubtless when he had cooled down Drake regretted the burning of the ship and decided to disclaim responsibility. With Mr Wagner, I find it impossible to swallow such a disclaimer (cf. H. R. Wagner, *Sir Francis Drake's Voyage Around the World*, p. 107, Z. Nuttall, op. cit., p. 46).
7. Narrative of Pedro Sarmiento de Gamboa in H. R. Wagner, op. cit., p. 387.

Chapter 9

1. The exact dating of events for this section of the voyage is very difficult. Nuño da Silva's log is unreliable for he gives the date of the *Golden Hind's* arrival at Lima as 15 February, which we know from Spanish documents to be wrong. From then until 1 March when Drake took the *Cacafuego* reports are either vague or contradictory. However, the outline of events is clear.
2. Letters of Benito Díaz Bravo, in H. R. Wagner, *Sir Francis Drake's Voyage Around the World*, p. 356.
3. Ibid.
4. Ibid.
5. Ibid.
6. According to San Juan, the *Nuestra Señora* was unarmed which, in his submission, accounted for her easy capture. If so, this makes nonsense of her nickname *Cacafuego*, recorded by Nuño da Silva and English accounts. It also renders quite unnecessary the ruse Drake employed to capture her. It is possible that San Juan lied to the royal authorities in order to excuse the fact that he surrendered without a struggle. But this is unlikely as the facts were easily verifiable. It is more likely that Drake had been given the wrong information about the *Nuestra Señora* either in genuine error or in an attempt dissuade him from assaying her capture.
7. It was Mrs Nuttall who first suggested the possibility that San Juan was of English extraction *(New Light on Drake*, p. 155). This view was supported by the discovery of an early English version of the captain's deposition (British Museum, Cotton MSS., *Otho*, E, VIII) where his name is given as St John of Ampton. 'Ampton' or 'Hampton' was commonly used for the name of the seaport (cf. E. G. R. Taylor, 'More Light on Drake' in *Mariner's Mirror*, XVI, p. 144).
8. Z. Nuttall, op. cit., p. 207.
9. Testimony of San Juan de Anton, Z. Nuttall, op. cit., p. 161.
10. H. R. Wagner, op. cit., p. 366n.
11. Z. Nuttall, op. cit., pp. 16–17.
12. H. R. Wagner, op. cit., p. 377.
13. H. R. Wagner, op. cit., p. 127.

14. One can find many excuses for Drake's heartless desertion of the pilot. Da Silva was, after all, a navigational expert and a Portuguese. Drake was, perhaps, about to discover the Straits of Anian which he certainly would not want England's maritime rivals to know about. On the other hand if Drake were to go home by way of the Moluccas he would be sailing into Portuguese colonial waters and Da Silva's patriotism might well display itself to the detriment of the voyage. When all that has been said it remains true that the pilot deserved better of the man whose expedition he had saved.

Chapter 10

1. The exact route followed by the expedition between April and July has never been exactly clear. An account published by Hakluyt under the title 'The course which Sir Francis Drake held from the haven of Guatulco . . . to the Northwest of California, as far as fourty-three degrees . . . etc.' is vague on details (cf. W. S. W. Vaux, *The World Encompassed by Sir Francis Drake*, pp. 219 ff.). John Cooke's declarations (cf. Z. Nuttall, *New Light on Drake*, pp. 18 ff.) are aggravatingly scanty. *The World Encompassed* tells much more but, unfortunately, is extremely suspect. As well as exaggerating for effect the achievements of the voyage and the experiences of the crew, it seems likely that the accounts on which this work is based deliberately falsified the evidence for propaganda purposes (see below, p. 234 and notes). Wagner (*Sir Francis Drake's Voyage Around the World*, pp. 135 ff.) carefully summarised all the evidence and put forward a reasoned itinerary, taking into account all the details of winds and currents. It is his account that I have largely followed.

2. Some early accounts and maps claimed that Drake reached a point much farther north—about 48 degrees. It seems that this was a deliberate distortion on the part of Drake's apologists in order to assert that he had reached farther up the coast than the Spaniard Rodriguez Cabrillo who had already travelled along the fringe of California as far as 43 degrees.

3. Something must be said here of the incredible account in *The World Encompassed* about the appalling weather experienced on this leg of the voyage. The relevant passage reads as follows:

> in the night following we found such alteration of heat, into extreme and nipping cold, that our men in general did grievously complain thereof, some of them feeling their healths much impaired thereby; neither was it that this chanced in the night alone, but the day following carried with it not only the marks, but the stings and force of the night going before, to the great admiration of us all; for besides that the pinching and biting air was nothing altered, the very ropes off our ship were stiff, and the rain which fell was an unnatural congealed and frozen substance, so that we seemed rather to be in the frozen Zone than any way so near unto the sun, or these hotter climates.
>
> Neither did this happen for the time only, or by some sudden accident, but rather seems indeed to proceed from some ordinary cause, against the which the heat of the sun prevails not; for it came to that extremity in sailing but 2 deg. farther to the Northward in our course, that though

seamen lack not good stomachs, yet it seemed a question to many amongst us, whether their hands should feed their mouths, or rather keep themselves within their coverts from the pinching cold that did benumb them. Neither could we impute it to the tenderness of our bodies, though we came lately from the extremity of heat, by reason whereof we might be more sensible of the present cold: insomuch as the dead and senseless creatures were as well affected with it as ourselves: our meat, as soon as it was removed from the fire, would presently in a manner be frozen up, and our ropes and tackling in few days were grown to that stiffness, that what 3 men afore were able with them to perform, now 6 men, with their best strength and uttermost endeavour, were hardly able to accomplish: whereby a sudden and great discouragement seized upon the minds of our men, and they were possessed with a great mislike and doubting of any good to be done that way; yet would not our General be discouraged, but as well by comfortable speeches, of the divine providence, and of God's loving care over his children, out of the Scriptures, as also by other good and profitable persuasions, adding thereto his own cheerful example, he so stirred them up to put on a good courage, and to quit themselves like men, to endure some short extremity to have the speedier comfort, and a little trouble to obtain the greater glory, that every man was throughly armed with willingness and resolved to see the uttermost, if it were possible, of what good was to be done that way. (Vaux, pp. 113–115)

We are thus asked to believe that at midsummer in 1579 the coast of sunny California was experiencing sub-Arctic conditions and that these conditions persisted for several weeks. A cold snap we might be able to accept but anything more stretches the credulity too far. John Drake's statements before the Inquisition at Santa Fé in 1584, though brief, give a different picture of this stretch of the voyage. In his first declaration he said, 'On their voyage they met with great storms. All the sky was dark and full of mist'. (Nuttall, p. 31). In his second declaration all he had to say about the conditions on the Californian coast was: 'the climate is temperate, more cold than hot. To all appearance it is a very good country.' (Ibid., p. 51.).

It is difficult to believe that we are dealing here with one of Francis Fletcher's usual exaggerations, particularly as the account in *The World Encompassed* contains other obvious inaccuracies. For instance it says that the Pacific coast of North America inclines steadily north-westwards and almost certainly links up with the coast of Asia. This is totally wrong about the direction of the coastline and, since Drake's expedition never came within a thousand miles of Alaska, the conjecture about its proximity to the Asian mainland was without foundation. *The World Encompassed* concluded that the Straits of Anian was a myth, an opinion which was not shared by three generations of English adventurers and geographers for whom the discovery of the north-west passage was the principal spur to exploration.

Here, it seems to me, we are at the heart of the matter. The writer of the account on which *The World Encompassed* was based was surely taking a leaf from the Spaniards' book. They falsified their maps of South America. They spread stories about the impossibility of getting back through the Straits of

Magellan from west to east. They did all this to protect their interests. England had a major interest in the discovery of the Straits of Anian. With an easy route to the Pacific not only the oriental trade, but also the Americas would be open to her. This might lead to colonisation and direct competition with Spain. What more natural than that English mariners who had sailed in the north Pacific should spread the story that weather conditions there were atrocious and that, in any case, the Straits of Anian did not exist?

4. H. R. Wagner discussed the evidence at length in Chapter VIII of *Sir Francis Drake's Voyage Around the World*. He strongly canvassed a stay by Drake in Trinidad Bay, largely on the grounds that two hundred years later the natives of this place were found to possess old steel knives. His final conclusion was

> ... Drake anchored in Trinidad Bay, and other evidence has been brought forward to indicate that he remained there long enough to find out something about the Indians. He also probably stayed long enough in Bodega Bay to get acquainted with the Pomo Indians and witness some of the ceremonies. The truth probably is that Drake stopped at two or three different places on the coast and the writer of the original narrative or the compilers who worked on it embodied in one description those of all the Indians he met. (p. 169)

This conclusion only illustrates the difficulty of reaching any clearcut decision with the paucity of evidence at our disposal. We would probably be better advised to follow R. F. Henzer who, at the end of his detailed study *Francis Drake and the California Indians*, concluded,

> For nearly a century, historians, geographers, and anthropologists have attempted to solve the problem of locating Francis Drake's anchorage in California, but the opinion of no one investigator has been universally accepted. Indeed, it seems likely that the problem will forever remain insoluble in detail, although it may well be reduced to the possibility that one of two bays; either Drake's, or Bodega, was the scene of Drake's stay in California.

5. W. S. W. Vaux, op. cit., p. 121.
6. W. S. W. Vaux, op. cit., p. 122–4.
7. W. S. W. Vaux, op. cit., pp. 128–9.
8. Samuel Purchas, *His Pilgrimes*, 1625–6, XVI, p. 136, ff.
9. W. S. W. Vaux, op. cit., pp. 133–4.
10. But this assertion is regarded as an inaccurate interpolation in *The World Encompassed* by Wagner, op. cit., p. 168.

Chapter 11

1. Calculating a degree of longitude as 69.17 miles at the equator, the exact distance is 3596.84 miles but this must be reduced slightly to allow for difference of latitude. The island of Ternate straddles the equator but Guatulco lay in about $15°$ north.
2. I am following here the account given by John Drake (cf. Z. Nuttall, op.

cit., p. 51). For a fuller discussion of all the possibilities of Drake's route across the Pacific see H. R. Wagner, *Sir Francis Drake's Voyage Around the World*, pp. 170–1.

3. D. W. Waters, *The Art of Navigation in England in Elizabethan and Early Stuart Times*, p. 58.

4. Drake was a Calvanist, but Catholics tended to call all Protestants 'Lutherans', i.e. disciples of the arch-heretic.

5. Report by the Spanish official Francisco de Dueñas quoted by H. R. Wagner, op. cit., p. 173.

6. This 'divide and rule' policy seems to have been almost standard procedure for the Portuguese colonists in their invasion of the Muslim trading states which fringed the Indian Ocean. The chronic state of almost continuous warfare between Muslim sultanates enabled Europeans to break with ease into an ancient trading area which otherwise would have had little difficulty in repelling the interlopers. Many similar instances to the Tidore-Ternate situation could be cited. For example at the other end of the Portuguese eastern empire were the East African coast states of Malindi and Mombasa. Mombasa repelled the Portuguese but her rival Malindi welcomed them. It was, thus, Malindi which became the Portuguese base for the conquest of all the Arab settlements along the coast.

7. W. S. W. Vaux, *The World Encompassed by Sir Francis Drake*, p. 137.

8. W. S. W. Vaux, op. cit., pp. 139–41.

9. W. S. W. Vaux, op. cit., p. 142.

10. Ibid.

11. It is the Spanish writer Bartolome Leonardo de Argensola who tells us this story and enables us to make sense of an apparent inconsistency in the English accounts. *The World Encompassed* waxes euphoric over Drake's sumptuous welcome by Baab, then calmly states that the Sultan refused to come aboard the *Golden Hind* the following day as promised. Drake turned down an invitation to go ashore because he feared treachery at the hands of the Ternate people. *The World Encompassed* could not, of course, admit that its hero had been guilty of what was, at best, an unconscious breach of etiquette and, at worst, a piece of deceitful chicanery. But Argensola in *Conquista de las Malucas*, 1609, p. 107, states the confusion over the cloves and the hostility it provoked. Though obviously hostile to the English, there is no reason to dismiss the story as complete fabrication. According to Argensola, this is how matters were eventually patched up:

Drake, expert in fraud, to whose ingenuity the arts of dissimulation were not new, gathered together his fleet[!] to escape by flight. He then tried to appease the king with some presents which he sent him, and this was not a difficult matter. With this he purchased his good will, and an audience with that astute tyrant. He went ashore at different times to visit him and arranged with him that the King should be a friend and confederate of the Queen and the English nation, and that factories should be founded there very soon. The King agreed to this, and Drake promised him arms and protection for his provinces. Carrying away, among other gifts, a valuable ring, which the King gave him for the Queen, he left the country with a great quantity of cloves. (Quoted in H. R. Wagner, op. cit., p. 179.)

12. Again the English authorities insist that Drake never went ashore but they are contradicted by Argensola. Perhaps the English writers did not want to show Drake abasing himself before an oriental despot. It is difficult to believe that the mighty Baab would have been fobbed off with underlings when he wished to see the Queen's representative in person.

13. W. S. W. Vaux, op. cit., p. 143–4.

14. This account is based on a report located by H. R. Wagner in the royal Spanish archives. It was by Francisco de Dueñas, a Spanish agent sent out by the Governor of the Philippines in 1581 to reconnoitre the situation in the Moluccas. Among other information in this extremely important first-hand report, Dueñas, related all he could discover about the visit of the notorious corsair. (cf. H. R. Wagner, op. cit., pp. 176 ff. *passim*).

15. Dueñas in Wagner, p. 182.

16. The authority for Maria's story the *Short Abstract of the Present Voyage in Handwriting of the Time,* an account by a member of the crew who clearly had a grudge against the admiral and was at pains to record many small instances which showed him in an unfavourable light. Of the negro woman the author says:

> Drake took out of this ship . . . a [proper] negro wench called Maria, which was afterward gotten with child between the captain and his men pirates . . .
> Drake left behind him upon this Island the two negroes which he took at Agwatalca, and likewise the negro wench Maria, she being gotten with child in the ship, and now being very great, was left here on this Island . . . (W. S. W. Vaux, op. cit., pp. 183, 184)

While I have ignored the petty incidents recorded in this narrative as being untrustworthy by themselves, I have included Maria's story because her presence on the *Golden Hind* is supported by other accounts. If she was present it is almost inconceivable that she would not have become pregnant.

Chapter 12

1. W. S. W. Vaux, *The World Encompassed by Sir Francis Drake*, p. 151.

2. Vaux, p. 153. This passage from *The World Encompassed* has the unmistakable flavour of Fletcher's flowery prose.

3. There is probably here a parody of the 'papistical' ceremony of excommunication but the principle of excluding an unrepentant sinner from the life of the Church was by no means rejected by Calvinist churchmen, which is what Drake was. Excommunication was certainly carried out by Anglican clergymen from time to time but I know of no other instance of its being employed by a layman. In Drake's book there was little distinction between minister and layman; every Christian participated in the priesthood of all believers and this probably provided him with sufficient excuse for carrying out his own, somewhat burlesque, service of excommunication. The wearing of a placard announcing the offence was a phenomenon perfectly familiar to Englishmen. Condemned criminals frequently carried such placards when they were placed in the stocks or paraded through the streets of their home

towns. Humiliation was an important part of correction in Tudor times.

4. The English accounts give several references to locations and latitudes but any attempt to use them as a basis for plotting the ship's course is doomed to failure. Latitude calculations were either made or recorded inaccurately; the names of islands were transliterated poorly from the native languages; in many cases such names have, in any case, changed over the intervening centuries.

5. *The Famous Voyage*, Vaux, p. 250.

6. *The Famous Voyage*, Vaux, p. 251.

7. This is the date given in *The Famous Voyage*. *The World Encompassed* ascribes the rounding of the Cape to 15 June.

8. W. S. W. Vaux, op. cit., p. 252.

Chapter 13

1. His embassy lasted six years. During that period relations between the two states deteriorated steadily and Mendoza was eventually sent packing after master-minding the Throckmorton plot which would have brought a Catholic army into England under the leadership of the Duke of Guise.

2. Z. Nuttall, *New Light on Drake*, pp. 387–8.

3. Z. Nuttall, op. cit., p. 385.

4. The disappearance of this diary is, perhaps, the greatest of all the mysteries concerning the circumnavigation. The French ambassador asked for the loan of it on behalf of his master but whether the request was granted we do not know. On the whole it is not very likely that Elizabeth would allow it out of her keeping. It revealed all the secrets of the voyage and was therefore a politically dangerous document. It was an invaluable guide to navigation in hitherto unknown waters and there was therefore no reason why it should be allowed to fall into the hands of rival maritime nations. When Hakluyt was collecting accounts of the voyage a few years later Drake's diary was obviously not available to him. In fact, this incomparably important document seems to have disappeared immediately after being presented to the Queen.

5. *State Papers Domestic, Elizabeth*, Vol. 144, No. 17.

6. For a discussion of Drake's haul cf. H. R. Wagner, *Sir Francis Drake's Voyage Around the World*, pp. 204–5.

7. Spanish Calendar, III, passim.

8. John Stowe, *Annales*, 1631, fol. 807–8.

9. *State Papers Domestic, Elizabeth*, Vol. 144, No. 17.

10. The legal tangle was unravelled, as far as it was capable of so being, by Wagner (op. cit., pp. 202–3). In the interests of presenting a rounded story I now quote his conclusions *in extenso*. After describing the documents presented by the Spaniards in proof of their claim, Wagner continues:
    An abridgement of Mendoza's complaint entitled *An abridgement of the relation and proves made against Sir Francis Drake knighte towchinge his doings in the Sowthe Sea beyond the streighte of Magalanus* exists in the Lansdowne MSS in the British Museum. At the end is a note to the effect

that Drake denied that he had ever had or seen any of the unregistered silver referred to in the complaint, but that he thought that having been hid under the ballast, it had been taken by the mariners on board the ships. The abridgement evidently contains the substance of the documents just referred to as presented by Mendoza, except the register of the *Cacafuego*. Then follows a translated copy of the power of attorney given to Pedro de Zubiaure. At the end of the document in a different handwriting is an answer, in legal terms, in which it is set forth that the relation of the voyage is no real proof, being only the bare assertion of the parties pretending to be damaged; that the copy of the register shows nothing beyond the fact that so much had been put aboard the ship; that none of the witnesses were sworn in the presence of Sir Francis Drake; that the deposition of the witnesses had been taken before the prior and consuls trading into the Indies, who were both parties complaining and judges as well, and that, admitting that the witnesses had been examined before a competent judge, yet being chiefly mariners of the ships claimed to have been robbed, they had charged Sir Francis with taking goods which they themselves had taken, or at least the most part thereof.

A greater piece of pettifoggery could hardly be imagined than this answer to a legitimate complaint. Having succeeded in removing the controversy from the sphere of diplomacy to that of common business, the English were willing to take advantage of any technicality the lawyers could suggest to delay matters, in hopes that the complainants, finally becoming worn out, would accept anything in settlement. Of similar character, although on a somewhat higher plane, was the answer the Queen made to Mendoza, . . . She is reported by Camden to have said that the Spaniards had brought on themselves the evil by their injustice towards the English in hindering their business, against the rights of nations, and that Drake would answer before the law if they could by just indictments and proper testimony convict him of having committed anything against equity. She said that she had sequestrated the riches he had brought back in order to give satisfaction to King Philip, although she had spent more money against the rebels whom the King had raised up against her in England and Ireland than Drake was worth. She could not see why Spain should prevent her subjects from sailing to the Indies and then entered into some abstract declarations on the rights accruing on taking possession of unoccupied territory. As usual, instead of answering Mendoza's charges against Drake she brought forward her own complaints against Spain. Whether any other answer was ever made to Mendoza or not is not known, as no further reference to the affair occurs in his correspondence so far printed. That of the Queen and the one attached to his complaint indicate that neither she nor the Council had any intention of making any restitution. Long before this, she had found out that the soldiers in Ireland who had gone there to assist the Catholics in their struggle with England were Italians sent by the Pope and not by Philip. Camden said that great sums of money were afterwards paid back to Zubiaure, who said he was an attorney for the return of the gold and silver, but that when too late it was discovered that instead of making restitution to private persons the money was spent against the Queen by the Spaniards to maintain the war in Flanders. Antonio de Herrera made a statement so similar, except that he did not say it was a large sum, that it seems likely he took his facts from Camden's book, which had appeared two years before his own. During some complication with France it may have been deemed advisable to placate Philip for the moment by making some settlement; Camden should be a good authority but it may well be doubted that any large sum was restored. (Wagner, pp. 202–203).

11. Sadly, enthusiasm for the ship waned steadily. She was never properly looked after and within less than a century her timbers had rotted beyond repair. In Charles II's reign the *Golden Hind* was broken up. A chair was made out of some of the timber and the King presented it to Oxford University. It is now on display at Buckland Abbey.

12. William Camden, *Annales*, 1625, pp. 426–7.

13. On the subject of Drake's arrogance most early commentators are agreed. The distinguished naval historian Sir William Monson, writing in the early seventeenth century, probably made the most balanced assessment:

> he would speak much and arrogantly, but eloquently, which was a wonder to many that his education could yield him those helps of nature. Indeed he had four properties to further his gift of speaking, viz. his boldness of speech, his understanding in what he spoke, his inclination to speak, and his use in speaking; and though vain-glory is a vice not to be excused, yet he obtained that fame by his actions, that facility in speaking and that wisdom by his experience, that I can say no more, but that we are all the children of Adam. His friends further say, that his haughty and high carriage is somewhat excusable, when it appears not but in his command; for a general ought to be stern to his soldiers, courageous in his person, valiant in fight, generous in giving, patient in suffering, and merciful in pardoning: and if Sir Francis Drake was to be praised for most of these virtues, let him not be blamed or condemned for one vice only. (*Sir William Monson's Naval Tracts*, p. 367.)

14. *State Papers Domestic, Elizabeth*, Vol. 144, No. 17.

15. Ibid.

16. Sir Edward Coke, *Institutes of the Laws of England*, I, Lib. 2, cap. 3, sec. 102.

17. Cf. W. Senior, 'Drake at the Suit of John Doughty', in *Mariner's Mirror*, VII, p. 295. In this article Mr Senior unravels the whole legal tangle of Doughty's suit against Drake.

18. *State Papers Domestic, Elizabeth*, clxiii, 19.

19. Z. Nuttall, op. cit., p. 398.

20. Z. Nuttall, op. cit., p. 252.

21. Fletcher asserted, 'if the Portugal pilot had not been appointed of God to do us good we had perished without remembrance'. Vaux, p. 285. Even Drake is reported to have confessed 'had it not been for the Portuguese . . . he could never have made the journey', W. S. W. Vaux, *The World Encompassed by Sir Francis Drake*, p. 35.

NOTE ON SOURCES AND FURTHER
READING

The most important source manuscript for the circumnavigation voyage, to the best of our knowledge, no longer exists. This is, of course, the log written and illustrated by Drake and his cousin and presented to Queen Elizabeth on their return. It was probably kept under lock and key to prevent it falling into the hands of foreign powers who might have derived useful information from it. An embargo also seems to have been placed on the publication of other accounts of the voyage. This concern for secrecy explains the otherwise puzzling fact that no account of the voyage in English was printed for over a decade despite the enormous interest aroused by the voyage at home and abroad.

Other members of the expedition certainly kept logs and journals. Francis Fletcher, the Chaplain, did and so did John Wynter. Probably the other early accounts to which I shall refer shortly were based upon records kept on shipboard. Fletcher wrote an account of the journey but, unfortunately, only the first part has survived. It is in the British Museum—*Sloane MSS*, No. 61. As well as describing events and discoveries it also contains some delightful, if crude, drawings such as flying fish and penguins and also maps of some of the places visited. It is far from being an objective report. Fletcher's main aim seems to have been to display the wonders of God in creation. In pursuit of this laudable end he did not consider it inappropriate to exaggerate wildly, as when he described the 'giants' of Patagonia. He also took every opportunity of expatiating against 'papists'. Another prejudice which coloured his work was his opposition to Drake over the Doughty affair. If one takes due account of these peccadilloes Fletcher's narrative remains the most informative source and one can only regret that the manuscript as we now have it terminates with the *Golden Hind*'s visit to Mocha Island. Lengthy extracts from this account were published by W. S. W. Vaux in *The World Encompassed by Sir Francis Drake, being his next Voyage to that to Nombre de Dios collated with an unpublished manuscript of Francis Fletcher, chaplain to the expedition*, Hakluyt Society, 1854. It was published in full by N. M. Penzer, *The World Encompassed and Analogous Contemporary Documents concerning Sir Francis Drake's Circumnavigation of the World*, Argonaut Press limited edition, 1926.

Soon after his return in June 1579, John Wynter wrote an account of the journey as far as the Straits of Magellan which was undoubtedly based on his own log. This is to be found in the British Museum as *Lansdowne MSS*. 100, No. 2 and was printed by E. G. R. Taylor in *Mariner's Mirror*, XVI, 1930, pp. 147–151. Wynter's main concern was to clear himself of involvment in Drake's acts of piracy and to justify his desertion of the expedition. It is briefer and more matter-of-fact than Fletcher's narrative and is very useful for verifying dates and other small details.

At this point mention should be made of the other documents relating to the

232

Elizabeth's return and the restitution of the *Mary*'s cargo at the suit of the Portuguese ambassador. They are to be found in *State Papers Domestic, Elizabeth*, Vol. 139, Nos. 1, 5, 24. They are printed by Z. Nuttall, *New Light on Drake*, Hakluyt Society, 1914, pp. 383–392.

An account of the first part of the voyage was also written by John Cooke, one of the mariners who returned with Wynter. It was probably written some years after the events it describes at the request of Richard Hakluyt. Cooke was no friend of the Admiral and much of his account is devoted to Drake's alleged persecution of Doughty. The manuscript is in the British Museum, *Harleian MSS*, No. 540, fol. 93. It has been printed by Vaux, op. cit., pp. 187–218; Penzer, op. cit., pp. 142–167 and H. R. Wagner, *Sir Francis Drake's Voyage Around the World, its aims and achievements*, 1926, pp. 245–262.

In 1589 Richard Hakluyt, a country parson with a passion for geography and travel, became the foremost recorder of Elizabethan overseas expansion when he published, *The Principall Navigations, Voiages and Discoveries of the English Nation made by Sea or over land to the most remote and farthest distant quarters of the earth at any time within the compass of these 1500 years*, a work later expanded into a much longer study. The official embargo on mention of the 1577–80 voyage must have still been in force for it did not appear in Hakluyt's original version. However, at some time within the next ten years some extra pages were bound into the book under the heading *The famous voyage of Sir Francis Drake into the South Sea, and there hence about the whole Globe of the Earth, begun in the year of our Lord 1577*. This was compiled, probably by Hakluyt from contemporary accounts some of which may have been commissioned by the author. Two of these accounts have been traced; that written by John Cooke (referred to above) and an anonymous narrative describing the journey from Mocha Island to the expedition's return. The latter (*Harleian MSS*, No. 280, fol. 23) was printed by Vaux, pp. 178–186, and, in part, by Wagner, pp. 264–273.

When Hakluyt published his much-extended version of *The Principall Navigations* in 1600 he incorporated more material dealing with the circumnavigation voyage. Two fragments used in this edition were by members of the expedition. Edward Cliffe was one of the men who returned with Wynter. He wrote a clear account of the early part of the voyage which, from its use of precise dates and navigational details gives every indication of having been compiled from a shipboard log (Hakluyt, *Principall Navigations*, 1598–1600, III, pp. 748–753). The other fragment was, *The course which Sir Francis Drake held from the haven of Guatulco, in the South Sea, on the east side of Nueva Espanna, to the Northwest of California, as far as fourtie three degrees: and his returne back along the said Coast to thirty eight degrees: where finding a faire and goodly hauen, he landed, and staying there many weekes, and discovering many excellent things in the countrey, and great shewe of rich minerall matter, and being offered the dominion of the countrey by the Lord of the same, hee tooke possession thereof in the behalfe of her Maiestie, and named it Noua Albion.* (Hakluyt, III, pp. 440–442). The best modern edition of Hakluyt's work is that published in twelve volumes by the Hakluyt Society (1903–1905).

The only other accounts of the voyage by an English eye-witness were two documents written under very different circumstances. In 1584 John Drake, during his abortive attempt to repeat his cousin's exploits, was captured at Buenos Aires and examined by the civil authorities. He was subsequently sent to the Inquisition headquarters at Lima and made a second declaration there. These two documents ended up in the *Archivo General de Indias* at Seville (E.2, C.5, L.2–21, 49). They were translated by Lady Eliott-Drake in *The Family and Heirs of Sir Francis Drake*, App. I and II. A version was also printed by Z. Nuttall, *New Light on Drake*, pp. 24–56.

The first full length account of the journey was *The World Encompassed by Sir Francis Drake, Being his next Voyage to that to Nombre de Dios formerly imprinted; Carefully collected out of the Notes of Master Francis Fletcher, Preacher in this imployment, and diuers others his followers in the same; Offered now at last to publique view, both for the honour of the actor, but especially for the stirring up of heroick spirits, to benefit their Countrie, and eternize their names by like noble attempts.* It was published in 1628 over the name of Francis Drake, the circumnavigator's nephew, though the real extent of that man's involvement is by no means clear. What is clear is that the central personality is no longer a real man but a national legend. Though the compiler relied closely on the narratives of Fletcher, Cliffe and the *Famous Voyage*, every reference which shows Drake in a poor light is expunged and every effort made to magnify his achievements. Close comparison between *The World Encompassed* and the earlier source narratives reveals this most clearly. Unfortunately, for many years *The World Encompassed* was widely regarded as the authoritative account of the voyage and a number of biographers placed far too great reliance on it. The latest editions were those published by Vaux and Penzer in works already cited.

The other important documents relating to the expedition are those emanating from Spanish colonial officials. The appearance of English pirates on the Pacific seaboard of South and Central America started a frenzy of official activity. Reports were written, men who had been Drake's prisoners were questioned, claims and accusations against Drake were lodged. The majority of these official pieces of paper ended up in government offices in Mexico, Madrid and Seville. In the early years of this century Mrs Zelia Nuttall performed the monumental task of unearthing most of the documents relating to Drake held in Spanish and Spanish-American archives. These were translated and presented to the world in *New Light on Drake*, the most important single piece of work ever done on the circumnavigation voyage. It was Mrs Nuttall, for instance, who first published Nuño da Silva's log and his various accounts of the voyage given under examination before the Spanish civil and religious authorities. In 1923, H. R. Wagner discovered more documents in the Madrid royal archives, these were letters by Gonzallo Ronquillo de Peñalosa, Governor of the Philippines and Francisco de Dueñas, one of his agents. They related to the *Golden Hind*'s wanderings through Indonesia and threw valuable light on an otherwise sparsely documented phase of the voyage. Wagner quoted these letters extensively in *Sir Francis Drake's Voyage Around the World*.

Wagner's book, published in 1926, is the most complete study of the circumnavigation voyage yet attempted. As well as providing a complete narrative it included a large documentary section in which most of the important sources were printed. It was also copiously illustrated with maps and charts. Mr Wagner essayed a fresh, critical approach to Drake, the man, his achievements and his methods and, though his work was marred by an over sensitiveness to the limitations of earlier workers in the field, he did free the subject from the hero-worship which had hampered other historians.

Since 1926 such new information and fresh insights on the voyage as have emerged have been published almost exclusively in articles and journals. Among the more significant are:

Drake's Plate of Brass, California Historical Society, special publications XIII, 1937, pp. 1–57; XIV, 1938, pp. 1–26.

F. C. P. Naish, 'The Mystery of the Tonnage and Dimensions of the *Pelican/Golden Hind*', *Mariner's Mirror*, XXXIV, 1948, pp. 42–45.

G. Robinson, 'The Evidence about the *Golden Hind*', *Mariner's Mirror*, XXXV, 1949, pp. 56–65.

W. Senior, 'Drake at the Suit of John Doughty', *Mariner's Mirror*, VII, 1921, pp. 291–297.

E. G. R. Taylor, 'The Missing Draft Project', *Geographical Journal*, 1930, pp. 43–8.

E. G. R. Taylor, 'More Light on Drake', *Mariner's Mirror*, XVI, 1930, pp. 134–151.

Biographies and general works on Drake give reasonable coverage of the circumnavigation voyage. The most important are:

K. R. Andrews, *Drake's Voyages*, 1967.

J. S. Corbett, *Drake and the Tudor Navy*, 2 vols, 1898.

G. M. Thomson, *Sir Francis Drake*, 1972.

N. Williams, *Francis Drake*, 1973.

J. A. Williamson, *The Age of Drake*, 1946.

There are a number of excellent books on navigational and naval matters:

C. R. Boxer, *The Portuguese Seaborne Empire*, 1969.

G. Connell-Smith, *Forerunners of Drake*, 1954.

J. H. Parry, *The Age of Reconnaissance*, 1963.

—— *The Discovery of the Sea*, 1975.

—— *The Spanish Seaborne Empire*, 1966.

B. Penrose, *Travel and Discovery in the Renaissance, 1420–1620*, 1952.

D. B. Quinn, *England and the Discovery of America, 1481–1670*, 1974.

A. L. Rowse, *The Expansion of Elizabethan England*, 1955.

E. G. R. Taylor, *Late Tudor—Early Stuart Geography*, 1934.

D. W. Waters, *The Art of Navigation in England in Elizabethan and Early Stuart Times*, 1958. (This excellent book has a monumental bibliography.)

J. A. Williamson, *Hawkins of Plymouth*, 1946.

I. A. Wright, *Documents Concerning English Voyages to the Spanish Main, 1569–1580*, Hakluyt Society, 1932.

On the political background to the voyage, the following are some of the many valuable books available:

B. W. Beckingsale, *Burghley, Tudor Statesman*, 1967.

G. R. Elton, *England Under The Tudors*, 1955.

G. Mattingly, *Renaissance Diplomacy*, 1955.

J. E. Neale, *Queen Elizabeth*, 1934.

P. Pierson, *Philip II of Spain*, 1975.

M. B. Pulman, *The Elizabethan Privy Council in the Fifteen-Seventies*, 1971.

Conyers Read, *Mr Secretary Walsingham and the Policy of Queen Elizabeth*, 3 vols., 1925.

R. B. Wernham, *Before the Armada, The Growth of English Foreign Policy, 1485–1588*, 1966.

INDEX

237